Writing Business Letters in Japanese

日本語ビジネス文書の書き方

Business Japanese Forum

Keisuke Maruyama ● Mami Doi ● Yuko Iguchi ● Kazuko Kuwabara
Masahiro Onuma ● Tatsuya Yasui ● Ryuko Yokosuka

The Japan Times

First edition: January 1999
Second printing: April 2002

Editorial assistance: Shizuko Matsumoto
Layout design: Horinsha, Inc.
Jacket design: Akihiro Kurata

Published by The Japan Times, Ltd.
5-4, Shibaura 4-chome, Minato-ku, Tokyo 108-0023, Japan
Phone: 03-3453-2013
http://bookclub.japantimes.co.jp/

ISBN4-7890-0951-3

Printed in Japan

Foreword
(A Japanese manager's lament . . .)

Recently we've had a trickle of foreigners joining our company. That's not new, but how they perform is. It used to be that our foreign employees were more guests than anything else: they didn't do much work, and they didn't stay long. Their Japanese was up to simple greetings, if we were lucky. Actually, they didn't need Japanese, because their work was almost entirely carried out in English.

But today's foreigners are as productive as our Japanese employees. They do everything in Japanese—section meetings, answering the phone, calling on clients. And since they came to us with business experience in their home countries, they know the basics; I have no problem entrusting them with responsibility. It's not just that they are good workers—they go out with their Japanese colleagues to karaoke after work, too. They've really become an integral part of our company.

They do have a weak point, though: letters. With all their competence in Japanese, when it comes to reading a business letter, it's like they're trudging wearily up Mount Fuji—and they're even more hopeless at writing them. Our office is littered with word processors for them to use, but they don't know what to write. It's odd: they chat away just like a Japanese person, but can't cope with a simple letter. If they really could understand business letters and compose their own, they'd be able to take on even more responsible jobs. I wish they'd buckle down and study reading and writing more.

OK, we've gotten the message, and this textbook is the answer.

Business Japanese Forum

目　次

本書について

1 本書の特徴

本書は、日本語のビジネス文書に慣れていないビジネスマンが、日々の業務に必要な文書をどう書いたらいいか、そして自分が受け取った文書をどう読みどう理解したらよいかを、より効率的に学べるように、次のような特徴を備えています。

特徴1 日本の企業で交わされるビジネス文書をビジネスのプロセスに沿って取り上げています。

本書は、外国人ビジネスマンのための上級用日本語会話教材『Talking Business in Japanese』(ジャパンタイムズ刊)の本文と同様に、アメリカのインテリア・家具製造販売会社が日本の専門商社と販売契約を結ぶというストーリーを追って各課が展開しています。そしてその一連のストーリーの各プロセスでやり取りされる文書を、社外・社内を含めて約100文書取り上げています。日本企業における業務の進め方とそれにともなう文書のやり取りの実際が、各プロセスごとに総合的に理解できます。

特徴2 文書本文は、すべて現役の日本人ビジネスマンが書いています。

本書のすべての文書は、現役の日本人ビジネスマンが執筆しています。特にやさしい語句や表現を使うことはしていません。文書の形式も日本の企業でやり取りされる形そのままです。したがって、真の日本語のビジネス文書のありようを知ることができます。自分で文書を書くときにも、本書の本文を見本にして、適切な表現を使った、適切な形式の文書を簡単に書くことができます。また、各課の説明部分も日本人ビジネスマンが執筆しており、ビジネス現場の生の情報が得られます。

特徴3 主要なビジネス文書の文章構成を分析し、視覚的にわかりやすく示しています。

各課の「フローと文例」のセクションでは、その課の業務プロセスで重要な文書を取り上げ、その文書の文章構成を分析して、視覚的にわかりやすく示してあります。この「フロー」を利用することによって、文書の内容や意図を的確に理解して、日本語のビジネス文書にふさわしい構成を持った文書を、効率よく書くことができます。

2 ストーリー設定と登場人物

1 ストーリー

アメリカのインテリア・家具製造販売会社Ｓ＆Ａ社の日本支社長ハワードＧ.スミスは、東京商事の小川部長を介して、吉田物産と特殊カーペット「デュクロン」の販売契約を結ぼうと交渉します。何回かのやり取りの後、交渉はまとまり、取り引き開始となったのですが、納入品の一部にしみがあることがわかり、Ｓ＆Ａ社はすばやく対処します。

その後、スミスは、吉田物産を紹介してくれたお礼に小川部長を食事に招待します。やがて、Ｓ＆Ａ社は支社昇格一周年の記念パーティーを催します。

2 主な登場人物

◉Ｓ＆Ａ社　ニューヨークに本社を、アトランタその他に工場を持つアメリカのインテリア・家具製造販売会社。東京支店を日本支社に昇格させ、本格的な日本進出をねらっています。

ハワードＧ.スミス

Ｓ＆Ａ社の初代日本支社長。アメリカ人。かなり日本語が使えるのですが、十分ではありません。東京商事の小川部長とアメリカ駐在中から親交を持っており、日本進出の便宜を図ってもらいます。

山本良雄　Ｓ＆Ａ社・営業部長。

◉東京商事　事務機器商社。

小川　正　東京商事・営業部長。アメリカ駐在中にスミスと親交を持っていました。スミスに頼まれて、Ｓ＆Ａ社と吉田物産との仲介をします。

◉吉田物産　インテリア・家具販売の専門商社。

鈴木　弘　吉田物産・営業担当常務。

山田栄三　吉田物産・営業部長。Ｓ＆Ａ社との交渉にあたります。

❸ 本書の構成

1 「ビジネス文書の基本」

文書の基本書式、全文書に共通するあいさつの表現、封書(ふうとう)の宛名(あてな)の書き方など、ビジネス文書を書くための基本事項と、ビジネス文書をやり取りする際の基本的なマナーについてまとめて解説してあります。

本文に入る前に必ず目を通しておいてください。

2 本文（第１課～第20課）

アメリカの家具・インテリア販売会社が、商事会社の仲介を得て、日本の専門商社と販売契約を結ぶというストーリーに沿って、それぞれのビジネス段階でやり取りされる文書を取り上げています。

⑴各課の文書について

各課には３～８例ほどの文書例を収録(しゅうろく)していますが、その中の最初の文書（第一文）は、本書のストーリーに沿っている文書で、その課で扱うビジネス段階で最も中心的な役割を果たすものです。Ｓ＆Ａ社が、東京商事の仲介で吉田商事と特殊カーペット「デュクロン」の販売契約を結ぶまでの交渉を想定(そうてい)し、前ページで紹介した登場人物の設定に基(もと)づいた内容になっています。

それに続く２番目の文書（第二文）は、第一文とは状況や内容は異なりますが、同じ目的・同じ文章構成を持つ文書です。第一文の応用例として掲載(けいさい)しました。

３番目以降に収録した文書は、その課のビジネス段階でやり取りされるその他の文書例です。

⑵文書のページ

①文書の目的

見出し上のボックス内に、その文書が「社外」「社内」のどちらに宛(あ)てて送られるものか、またどのような目的の文書かを示しました。また、「あいさつ文」「照会(しょうかい)文」など、一般的な文書名があるものは、それを〈　　〉内に示しました。

②状況

その文書が使われる状況を説明しています。

③文書本文

日付・宛名から結びのことばまで、実際の文書形式で載(の)せてあります。漢字の使用についても、特にやさしくひらがなに書き換(か)えることはしていません。また、漢字・ひらがな両方の書き方が

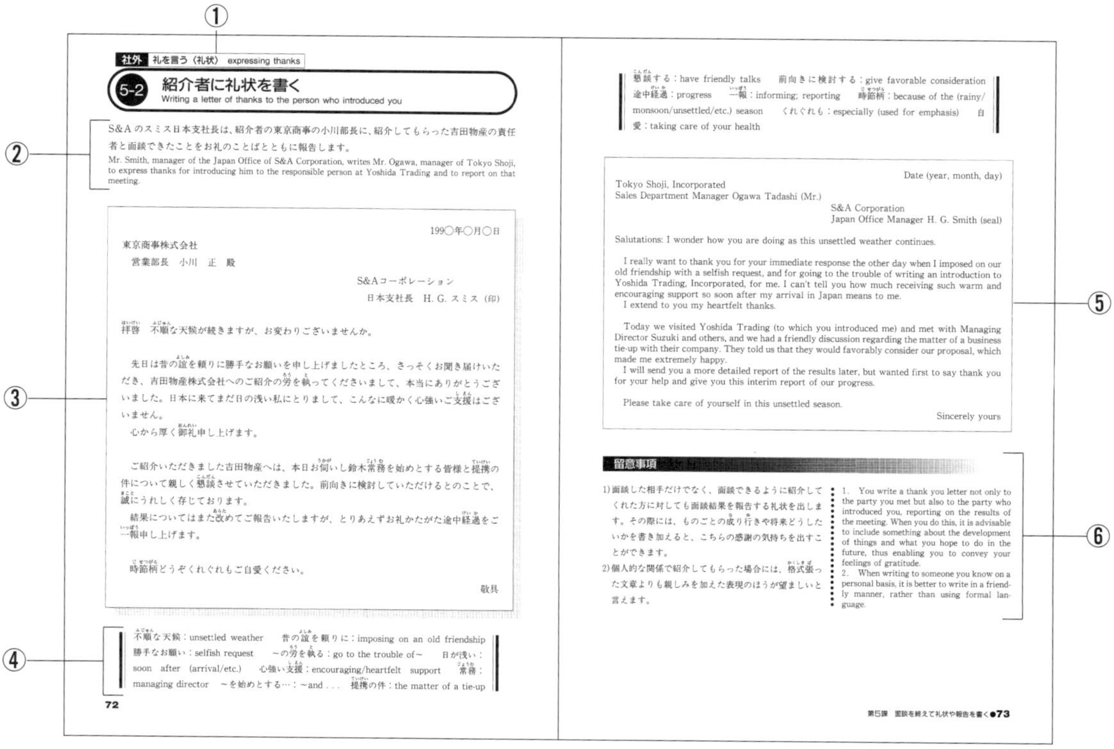

①

社外　礼を言う〈礼状〉 expressing thanks

5-2 紹介者に礼状を書く
Writing a letter of thanks to the person who introduced you

②
S&Aのスミス日本支社長は、紹介者の東京商事の小川部長に、紹介してもらった吉田物産の責任者と面談できたことをお礼のことばとともに報告します。
Mr. Smith, manager of the Japan Office of S&A Corporation, writes Mr. Ogawa, manager of Tokyo Shoji, to express thanks for introducing him to the responsible person at Yoshida Trading and to report on that meeting.

③
199○年○月○日

東京商事株式会社
営業部長　小川　正　殿

S&Aコーポレーション
日本支社長　H. G. スミス（印）

拝啓　不順な天候が続きますが、お変わりございませんか。

先日は昔の誼を頼りに勝手なお願いを申し上げましたところ、さっそくお聞き届けいただき、吉田物産株式会社へのご紹介の労を執ってくださいまして、本当にありがとうございました。日本に来てまだ日の浅い私にとりまして、こんなに暖かく心強いご支援はございません。
心から厚く御礼申し上げます。

ご紹介いただきました吉田物産へは、本日お伺いし鈴木常務を始めとする皆様と提携の件について親しく懇談させていただきました。前向きに検討していただけるとのことで、誠にうれしく存じております。
結果についてはまた改めてご報告いたしますが、とりあえずお礼かたがた途中経過をご一報申し上げます。

時節柄どうぞくれぐれもご自愛ください。

敬具

④
不順な天候：unsettled weather　昔の誼を頼りに：imposing on an old friendship　勝手なお願い：selfish request　～の労を執る：go to the trouble of～　日が浅い：soon after (arrival/etc.)　心強い支援：encouraging/heartfelt support　常務：managing director　～を始めとする…：～and . . .　提携の件：the matter of a tie-up

72

懇談する：have friendly talks　前向きに検討する：give favorable consideration　途中経過：progress　一報：informing; reporting　時節柄：because of the (rainy/monsoon/unsettled/etc.) season　くれぐれも：especially (used for emphasis)　自愛：taking care of your health

⑤
Date (year, month, day)
Tokyo Shoji, Incorporated
Sales Department Manager Ogawa Tadashi (Mr.)
S&A Corporation
Japan Office Manager H. G. Smith (seal)

Salutations: I wonder how you are doing as this unsettled weather continues.

I really want to thank you for your immediate response the other day when I imposed on our old friendship with a selfish request, and for going to the trouble of writing an introduction to Yoshida Trading, Incorporated, for me. I can't tell you how much receiving such warm and encouraging support so soon after my arrival in Japan means to me.
I extend to you my heartfelt thanks.

Today we visited Yoshida Trading (to which you introduced me) and met with Managing Director Suzuki and others, and we had a friendly discussion regarding the matter of a business tie-up with their company. They told us that they would favorably consider our proposal, which made me extremely happy.
I will send you a more detailed report of the results later, but wanted first to say thank you for your help and give you this interim report of our progress.

Please take care of yourself in this unsettled season.

Sincerely yours

⑥
留意事項

1) 面談した相手だけでなく、面談できるように紹介してくれた方に対しても面談結果を報告する礼状を出します。その際には、ものごとの成り行きや将来どうしたいかを書き加えると、こちらの感謝の気持ちを出すことができます。
2) 個人的な関係で紹介してもらった場合には、格式張った文章よりも親しみを加えた表現のほうが望ましいと言えます。

1. You write a thank you letter not only to the party you met but also to the party who introduced you, reporting on the results of the meeting. When you do this, it is advisable to include something about the development of things and what you hope to do in the future, thus enabling you to convey your feelings of gratitude.
2. When writing to someone you know on a personal basis, it is better to write in a friendly manner, rather than using formal language.

第5課　面談を終えて礼状や報告を書く●73

可能で会社や人によってさまざまな表記をすることばについては、あえていろいろな書き方で掲載しています。なお、巻末の資料6に、「ビジネス文書でよく用いられる、複数の書き方がある語句・表現」がまとめてあります。参照してください。

④単語リスト

ビジネス文書に特有の表現や難しい語彙を取り上げ、英訳を付けました。

⑤本文英訳

文書本文の英訳。日本語の意味が反映されるよう、英語として不自然にならない程度に逐語的に訳しています。また、「なお」「つきましては」などのように、文脈に応じてさまざまな訳をあてている語句があります。

⑥留意事項

その文書についての説明、また同様の文書を読んだり書いたりする際に注意すべき点、知っておかなければならない点などを解説しています。

⑶第一文と第二文の「フロー と文例」

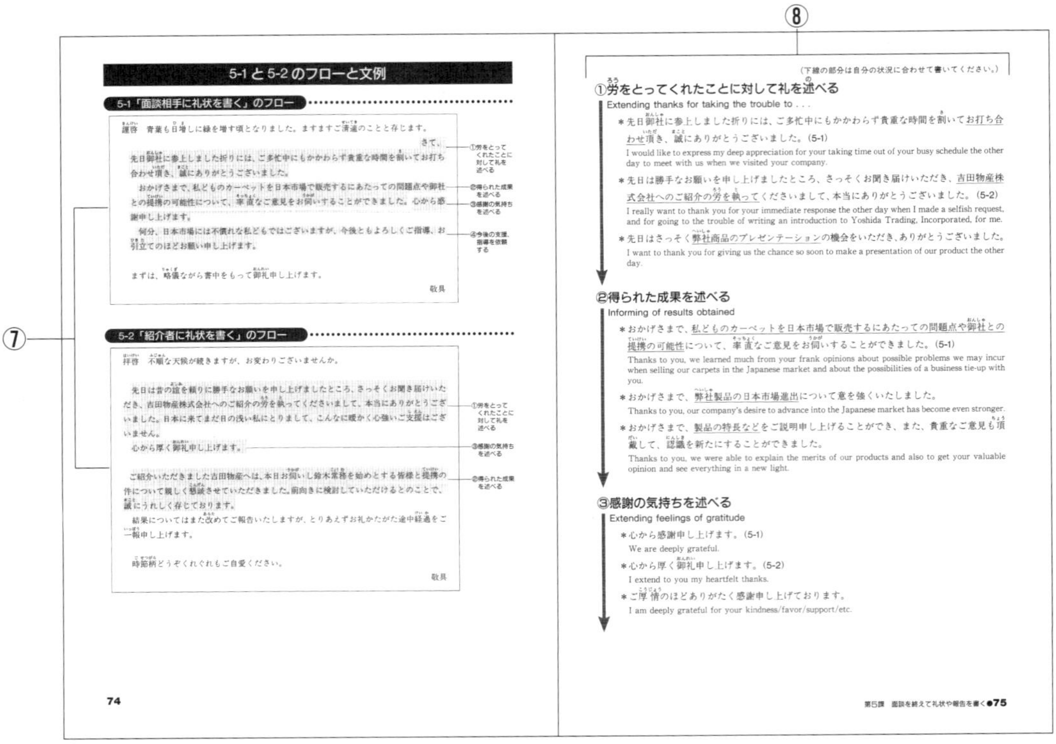

⑦ ⑧

5-1と5-2のフローと文例

5-1「面談相手に礼状を書く」のフロー

謹啓　青葉も日増しに緑を増す頃となりました。ますますご清適のことと存じます。

さて、

先日御社に参上しました折りには、ご多忙中にもかかわらず貴重な時間を割いてお打ち合わせ頂き、誠にありがとうございました。 ——①労をとってくれたことに対して礼を述べる

おかげさまで、私どものカーペットを日本市場で販売するにあたっての問題点や御社との提携の可能性について、率直なご意見をお伺いすることができました。 ——②得られた成果を述べる

心から感謝申し上げます。 ——③感謝の気持ちを述べる

何分、日本市場には不慣れな私どもではございますが、今後ともよろしくご指導、お引立てのほどお願い申し上げます。 ——④今後の支援、指導を依頼する

まずは、略儀ながら書中をもって御礼申し上げます。

敬具

5-2「紹介者に礼状を書く」のフロー

拝啓　不順な天候が続きますが、お変わりございませんか。

先日は昔の誼を頼りに勝手なお願いを申し上げましたところ、さっそくお聞き届けいただき、吉田物産株式会社へのご紹介の労を執ってくださいまして、本当にありがとうございました。日本に来てまだ日の浅い私にとりまして、こんなに暖かく心強いご支援はございません。 ——①労をとってくれたことに対して礼を述べる

心から厚く御礼申し上げます。 ——③感謝の気持ちを述べる

ご紹介いただきました吉田物産へは、本日お伺いし鈴木常務を始めとする皆様と提携の件について親しく懇談させていただきました。前向きに検討していただけるとのことで、誠にうれしく存じております。 ——②得られた成果を述べる

結果についてはまた改めてご報告いたしますが、とりあえずお礼かたがた途中経過をご一報申し上げます。

時節柄どうぞくれぐれもご自愛ください。

敬具

74

（下線の部分は自分の状況に合わせて書いてください。）

①労をとってくれたことに対して礼を述べる

Extending thanks for taking the trouble to . . .

＊先日御社に参上しました折りには、ご多忙中にもかかわらず貴重な時間を割いてお打ち合わせ頂き、誠にありがとうございました。(5-1)

I would like to express my deep appreciation for your taking time out of your busy schedule the other day to meet with us when we visited your company.

＊先日は勝手なお願いを申し上げましたところ、さっそくお聞き届けいただき、吉田物産株式会社へのご紹介の労を執ってくださいまして、本当にありがとうございました。(5-2)

I really want to thank you for your immediate response the other day when I made a selfish request, and for going to the trouble of writing an introduction to Yoshida Trading, Incorporated, for me.

＊先日はさっそく弊社商品のプレゼンテーションの機会をいただき、ありがとうございました。

I want to thank you for giving us the chance so soon to make a presentation of our product the other day.

②得られた成果を述べる

Informing of results obtained

＊おかげさまで、私どものカーペットを日本市場で販売するにあたっての問題点や御社との提携の可能性について、率直なご意見をお伺いすることができました。(5-1)

Thanks to you, we learned much from your frank opinions about possible problems we may incur when selling our carpets in the Japanese market and about the possibilities of a business tie-up with you.

＊おかげさまで、弊社製品の日本市場進出について意を強くいたしました。

Thanks to you, our company's desire to advance into the Japanese market has become even stronger.

＊おかげさまで、製品の特長などをご説明申し上げることができ、また、貴重なご意見も頂戴して、認識を新たにすることができました。

Thanks to you, we were able to explain the merits of our products and also to get your valuable opinion and see everything in a new light.

③感謝の気持ちを述べる

Extending feelings of gratitude

＊心から感謝申し上げます。(5-1)

We are deeply grateful.

＊心から厚く御礼申し上げます。(5-2)

I extend to you my heartfelt thanks.

＊ご厚情のほどありがたく感謝申し上げております。

I am deeply grateful for your kindness/favor/support/etc.

第5課　面談を終えて礼状や報告を書く●75

各課の第二文のあとに、「フローと文例」というセクションを設け、文章構成の分析をしています。

⑦フロー

各課のビジネス段階において中心的な文書である第一文と第二文の文章構成を、「フロー」として図示しました。各課のフローを把握することによって、日本語のビジネス文書をよりスムーズに書いたり読んだりすることができます。

⑧文例

ここでは、「フロー」で示した構成部分ごとに、よく用いられる文例をあげました。具体的にどのような文を使ったらいいか、すぐわかります。状況に応じて書き換えるべき部分は＿＿＿＿で示してあります。＿＿＿＿の部分を書き換えて、あるいはそのままで使ってください。また、「～の書き方」として、その目的をもった文の形をあげました。

なお、本書の文書から抜き出したものは、文末に（　）で文書番号が示してあります。

3 巻　末

(1)「資　料」

ビジネス文書でよく用いられる独特(どくとく)の語句、自分や相手のさまざまな呼び方、授受(じゅじゅ)に関(かか)わる表現、使ってはいけない表現、書き手によってさまざまな漢字・カナ表記をすることばなどを、リストにして載せてあります。実際のビジネス文書を読むときや書くときに参照してください。

(2)「文書のインデックス」

本書で扱った文書を次のような目的別に整理してあります。自分の書きたい文書と同じ用途(ようと)の文書を探すときに便利です。

- **社交を主な目的とする文書**
- **情報のやり取りを主な目的とする文書**
- **相手に行動を促(うなが)す文書**
- **相手の気持ちを聞いたりこちらの気持ちを伝えたりする文書**
- **その他**

(3)「語句さくいん」

本書の語彙(ごい)の総(そう)さくいんです。

How to Use This Book

1 Special Features

This book was written for the businessman who is not familiar with Japanese business correspondence and wants to know both how to read and understand it and how to write the letters that are necessary in everyday business situations. The following special features of this book will assist the reader in learning these skills as efficiently as possible.

1 **The business correspondence regularly exchanged in Japanese companies is presented here according to each stage of the business process.** Just like the advanced Japanese conversation textbook *Talking Business in Japanese* (Japan Times, 1991), this book covers business correspondence topics as they appear in the story of an American furniture and home furnishings manufacturing and marketing company that is negotiating a sales agreement with a Japanese trading company.

By following each step in the development of this business venture, this book covers approximately 100 letters that are used for business communications with someone outside or within the company. In this way, the reader can gain a comprehensive understanding of how business is conducted in a Japanese company and what actual correspondence is involved in each step of the business process.

2 **The basic materials for this book and all of the letters were written by Japanese businesspeople who are currently engaged in business.** No effort has been made to use words or expressions that are particularly easy. The style of the correspondence, as it is actually used within Japanese companies, has been preserved so that readers will encounter real-life examples of Japanese business communications. Likewise, by using the sample letters in this book as a guide, you will be able to choose the appropriate expressions and style of writing needed for your own business correspondence. Furthermore, since the explanatory remarks for each section were also written by a businessperson, you will also gain considerable information and knowledge regarding actual business situations.

3 **The major forms of business correspondence are analyzed and presented in a visually comprehensible manner.** Each chapter contains a section entitled フローと文例 ("Flow and Model Sentences"), which covers the most important types of letters involved in that particular stage of the business process. The structure of each letter is analyzed and presented in a numbered, easy-to-comprehend format. By using the "flow" section of each chapter, you will be able to accurately understand the content and purpose of each letter and efficiently learn to write appropriately structured Japanese business letters.

2 The Story Setting and Characters

1 Story

Howard G. Smith, manager of S&A Corporation's Japan Office, an American furniture and home furnishings manufacturer, is negotiating a sales agreement with Yoshida Trading regarding the company's special carpet Dukelon, through the mediation of Mr. Ogawa, the sales department manager of Tokyo Shoji, Inc. Following a series of negotiations, the interested parties reached an agreement and began transacting business, but it was discovered that a portion of the goods scheduled for delivery were stained and S&A Corporation dealt with this problem as quickly as possible.

After this, Mr. Smith invites Mr. Ogawa to dinner to express his appreciation for having been introduced to Yoshida Trading. In due course, S&A Corporation celebrates its one-year anniversary since the establishment of the Japan Office.

2 The Main Characters

◉ **S&A Corporation:** An American furniture and home furnishings manufacturing and marketing company with factories in Atlanta and elsewhere and headquarters in New York. What was formerly the Tokyo branch office has been promoted to the status of the company's Japan Office, which begins to seriously branch out into the Japanese market.

- Howard G. Smith: The first manager of S&A Corporation's Japan Office. He is a United States citizen, and although he is able to use some Japanese, it is not adequate for the job.
- Yamamoto Yoshio: The sales department manager who directs business operations for S&A Corporation.

◉ **Tokyo Shoji, Inc.:** A computer and OA equipment trading company.

- Ogawa Tadashi: The sales department manager of Tokyo Shoji, Inc., has been a friend of Mr. Smith's since the time they both worked in the United States. He has been asked by Mr. Smith to act as the mediator in the negotiations between S&A Corporation and Yoshida Trading.

◉ **Yoshida Trading:** A trading company specializing in interior furniture sales.

- Suzuki Hiroshi: The managing director at Yoshida Trading, responsible for routine business operations.

- Yamada Eizo: The sales department manager at Yoshida Trading, responsible for the negotiations with S&A Corporation.

❸ The Structure of the Book

1 The Basics of Business Letters

The prescribed forms for business letters, the preliminary greetings, which are a part of all letters, the proper way to write the addressee's name on the envelope, and the various items essential to any business correspondence are all explained, along with the basic rules and manners required in Japanese business communications. Please read over this general explanation of Japanese business correspondence before proceeding to the main text.

2 The Main Text (Chapters 1-20)

These chapters cover the various types of business correspondence that are exchanged at different stages in the business negotiations, following along with the story of an American furniture manufacturing company's efforts to conclude a sales agreement with a Japanese trading company through the mediation of a third party.

(1) Introducing the Letters

There are between three and eight sample letters in each chapter, but it is the first letter that deals directly with the stage in the business negotiations being addressed in the story. The content of these letters revolves around the characters introduced in page [19], and their role in the business negotiations story regarding a sales agreement for Dukelon carpet between S&A Corporation and Yoshida Trading Company.

The second letter provides another example letter, which has the same purpose and form but with a different situation and content. The second example is provided as a practical application of the first letter.

The third and following letters in each chapter provide additional examples of correspondence that is relevant to the stage of business being discussed.

(2) Sample Letters

① The Purpose of the Letter

The box above the caption indicates whether the addressee is someone inside or outside the company as well as the purpose of the letter. When the letter follows a general pattern, such as あいさつ文 or 照会文(しょうかい), the Japanese name for that type of letter is indicated in parentheses.

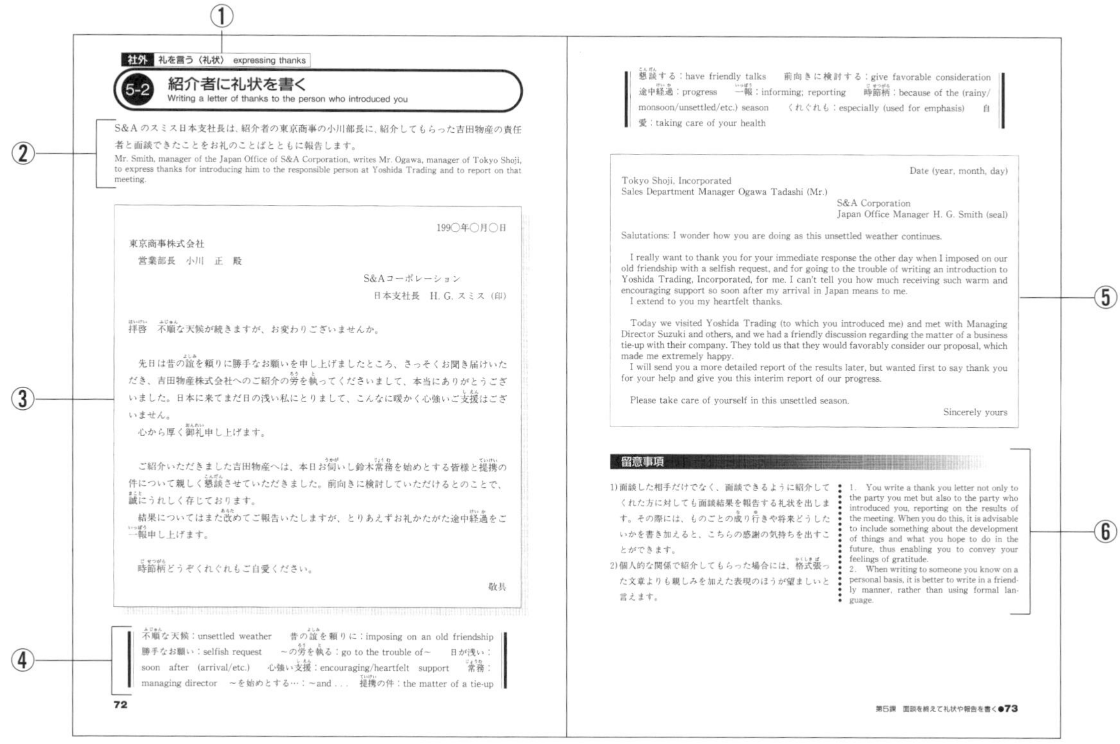

①

社外 礼を言う〈礼状〉 expressing thanks

5-2 紹介者に礼状を書く

Writing a letter of thanks to the person who introduced you

② S&A のスミス日本支社長は、紹介者の東京商事の小川部長に、紹介してもらった吉田物産の責任者と面談できたことをお礼のことばとともに報告します。

Mr. Smith, manager of the Japan Office of S&A Corporation, writes Mr. Ogawa, manager of Tokyo Shoji, to express thanks for introducing him to the responsible person at Yoshida Trading and to report on that meeting.

199○年○月○日

東京商事株式会社
　営業部長　小川　正　殿

S&Aコーポレーション
日本支社長　H. G. スミス（印）

③ 拝啓　不順な天候が続きますが、お変わりございませんか。

先日は昔の誼を頼りに勝手なお願いを申し上げましたところ、さっそくお聞き届けいただき、吉田物産株式会社へのご紹介の労を執ってくださいまして、本当にありがとうございました。日本に来てまだ日の浅い私にとりまして、こんなに暖かく心強いご支援はございません。

心から厚く御礼申し上げます。

ご紹介いただきました吉田物産へは、本日お伺いし鈴木常務を始めとする皆様と提携の件について親しく懇談させていただきました。前向きに検討していただけるとのことで、誠にうれしく存じております。

結果についてはまた改めてご報告いたしますが、とりあえずお礼かたがた途中経過をご一報申し上げます。

時節柄どうぞくれぐれもご自愛ください。

敬具

④ 不順な天候：unsettled weather　昔の誼を頼りに：imposing on an old friendship　勝手なお願い：selfish request　～の労を執る：go to the trouble of～　日が浅い：soon after (arrival/etc.)　心強い支援：encouraging/heartfelt support　常務：managing director　～を始めとする…：～and . . .　提携の件：the matter of a tie-up

72

懇談する：have friendly talks　前向きに検討する：give favorable consideration　途中経過：progress　一報：informing; reporting　時節柄：because of the (rainy/monsoon/unsettled/etc.) season　くれぐれも：especially (used for emphasis)　自愛：taking care of your health

Date (year, month, day)

Tokyo Shoji, Incorporated
Sales Department Manager Ogawa Tadashi (Mr.)

S&A Corporation
Japan Office Manager H. G. Smith (seal)

Salutations: I wonder how you are doing as this unsettled weather continues.

I really want to thank you for your immediate response the other day when I imposed on our old friendship with a selfish request, and for going to the trouble of writing an introduction to Yoshida Trading, Incorporated, for me. I can't tell you how much receiving such warm and encouraging support so soon after my arrival in Japan means to me.

I extend to you my heartfelt thanks.

Today we visited Yoshida Trading (to which you introduced me) and met with Managing Director Suzuki and others, and we had a friendly discussion regarding the matter of a business tie-up with their company. They told us that they would favorably consider our proposal, which made me extremely happy.

I will send you a more detailed report of the results later, but wanted first to say thank you for your help and give you this interim report of our progress.

Please take care of yourself in this unsettled season.

Sincerely yours ⑤

留意事項

1) 面談した相手だけでなく、面談できるように紹介してくれた方に対しても面談結果を報告する礼状を出します。その際には、ものごとの成り行きや将来どうしたいかを書き加えると、こちらの感謝の気持ちを出すことができます。

2) 個人的な関係で紹介してもらった場合には、格式張った文章よりも親しみを加えた表現のほうが望ましいと言えます。

1. You write a thank you letter not only to the party you met but also to the party who introduced you, reporting on the results of the meeting. When you do this, it is advisable to include something about the development of things and what you hope to do in the future, thus enabling you to convey your feelings of gratitude. ⑥

2. When writing to someone you know on a personal basis, it is better to write in a friendly manner, rather than using formal language.

第5課　面談を終えて礼状や報告を書く●73

② The Situation

The situation addressed by each letter is explained here.

③ The Main Text

From the date and addressee to the closing greeting, each letter is presented in its proper and complete form. There has also been no attempt to simplify the letters by substituting *hiragana* for more difficult kanji. There are many ways to use both hiragana and kanji, and companies and individuals also have their own styles, so rather than trying to simplify the language, these diverse writing styles have been included. Please consult part six of the appendix for a list of words and expressions often used in business letters that can be written in a number of ways.

④ Vocabulary List

A list of special expressions and difficult words used in business letters is provided, along with the English translations.

⑤ English Translation of Letters

The book contains an English translation of each letter and the accompanying notes. In order to express the meaning of the original Japanese, an effort has been made to provide a literal or word-for-word translation into English. Although we have tried to avoid awkward expressions as much as possible, there are a number of Japanese set phrases used in formal correspondence for which there are no natural English equivalents. Also, there are a number of words (such as なお and つきましては) that are translated in different ways, depending on the context.

⑥ Explanatory Notes

In the explanatory notes section there is a discussion of points that may need special attention when reading and writing certain letters, and basic points that must be understood regarding individual letters.

(3) The "Flow and Model Sentences" Section

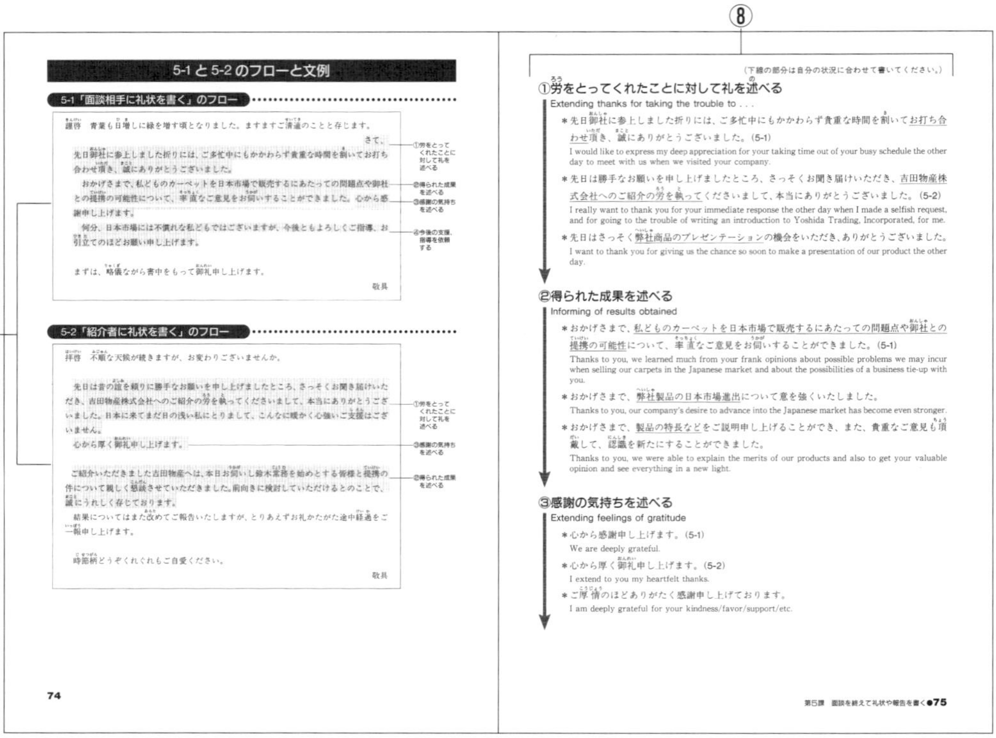

⑧

⑦

5-1と5-2のフローと文例

5-1「面談相手に礼状を書く」のフロー

謹啓　青葉も日増しに緑を増す頃となりました。ますますご清適のことと存じます。

さて、

先日御社に参上しました折りには、ご多忙中にもかかわらず貴重な時間を割いてお打ち合わせ頂き、誠にありがとうございました。 — ①労をとってくれたことに対して礼を述べる

おかげさまで、私どものカーペットを日本市場で販売するにあたっての問題点や御社との提携の可能性について、率直なご意見をお伺いすることができました。 — ②得られた成果を述べる

心から感謝申し上げます。 — ③感謝の気持ちを述べる

何分、日本市場には不慣れな私どもではございますが、今後ともよろしくご指導、お引立てのほどお願い申し上げます。 — ④今後の支援、指導を依頼する

まずは、略儀ながら書中をもって御礼申し上げます。

敬具

5-2「紹介者に礼状を書く」のフロー

拝啓　不順な天候が続きますが、お変わりございませんか。

先日は昔の誼を頼りに勝手なお願いを申し上げましたところ、さっそくお聞き届けいただき、吉田物産株式会社へのご紹介の労を執ってくださいまして、本当にありがとうございました。日本に来てまだ日の浅い私にとりまして、こんなに暖かく心強いご支援はございません。 — ①労をとってくれたことに対して礼を述べる

心から厚く御礼申し上げます。 — ③感謝の気持ちを述べる

ご紹介いただきました吉田物産へは、本日お伺いし鈴木常務を始めとする皆様と提携の件について親しく懇談させていただきました。前向きに検討していただけるとのことで、誠にうれしく存じております。 — ②得られた成果を述べる

結果についてはまた改めてご報告いたしますが、とりあえずお礼かたがた途中経過をご一報申し上げます。

時節柄どうぞくれぐれもご自愛ください。

敬具

74

（下線の部分は自分の状況に合わせて書いてください。）

①労をとってくれたことに対して礼を述べる

Extending thanks for taking the trouble to . . .

* 先日御社に参上しました折りには、ご多忙中にもかかわらず貴重な時間を割いてお打ち合わせ頂き、誠にありがとうございました。(5-1)
  I would like to express my deep appreciation for your taking time out of your busy schedule the other day to meet with us when we visited your company.
* 先日は勝手なお願いを申し上げましたところ、さっそくお聞き届けいただき、吉田物産株式会社へのご紹介の労を執ってくださいまして、本当にありがとうございました。(5-2)
  I really want to thank you for your immediate response the other day when I made a selfish request, and for going to the trouble of writing an introduction to Yoshida Trading, Incorporated, for me.
* 先日はさっそく弊社商品のプレゼンテーションの機会をいただき、ありがとうございました。
  I want to thank you for giving us the chance so soon to make a presentation of our product the other day.

②得られた成果を述べる

Informing of results obtained

* おかげさまで、私どものカーペットを日本市場で販売するにあたっての問題点や御社との提携の可能性について、率直なご意見をお伺いすることができました。(5-1)
  Thanks to you, we learned much from your frank opinions about possible problems we may incur when selling our carpets in the Japanese market and about the possibilities of a business tie-up with you.
* おかげさまで、弊社製品の日本市場進出について意を強くいたしました。
  Thanks to you, our company's desire to advance into the Japanese market has become even stronger.
* おかげさまで、製品の特長などをご説明申し上げることができ、また、貴重なご意見も頂戴して、認識を新たにすることができました。
  Thanks to you, we were able to explain the merits of our products and also to get your valuable opinion and see everything in a new light.

③感謝の気持ちを述べる

Extending feelings of gratitude

* 心から感謝申し上げます。(5-1)
  We are deeply grateful.
* 心から厚く御礼申し上げます。(5-2)
  I extend to you my heartfelt thanks.
* ご厚情のほどありがたく感謝申し上げております。
  I am deeply grateful for your kindness/favor/support/etc.

第5課　面談を終えて礼状や報告を書く●75

After the second example letter in each lesson, the section "フローと文例" (Flow and Model Sentences) are provided, in which the structure of the letters are analized.

⑦ The "Flow" of Sentence Structures

The structure of the first and second sample letters used to illustrate the business stage being discussed in each chapter are presented in a flow chart. The sentences in the main body of each letter, following the introductory sentences, are divided into numbered sections, and an analysis of the sentence structure is provided. By grasping the flow of the sentence structure in each chapter, the reader will learn how to smoothly read and write the business correspondence in Japanese.

⑧ Model Sentences

Following the numbered sentences in the "flow" section, several frequently used sentences that appear in business letters are given as models. The reader is able to quickly grasp what kind of sentence should be used in each situation. A word or phrase that is underlined indicates the parts that must be changed or rewritten, according to different circumstances. The reader may then use the sentence just as it appears or change the relevant underlined part to an expression that best suits their own situation. Sentence patterns that are frequently used for specific purposes are presented under the title ～の書き方 (How to write ～).

Sentences that are taken from the text of the letters in the chapter are indicated in parentheses at the end of the model sentence, for example, (5-2).

3 Concluding Sections

(1) Appendix: Words and Phrases

Special vocabulary regularly used in business correspondence, ways of referring to oneself and one's business associates, expressions used in giving and receiving, and the multiple ways authors use kanji and kana are provided in handy reference lists. Please consult this resource when you are reading and writing business letters.

(2) Letter Index

The types of letters covered in this book are organized according to purpose. This will be a handy reference to consult when you are seeking a model letter for one you are writing for a particular purpose.

- Letters primarily used for social exchanges.
- Letters primarily used to exchange information.
- Letters used to exchange information and to prompt a response or action by the other party.
- Letters used to exchange information and to solicit the feelings or viewpoint of the other party or to communicate one's own feelings.
- Other types of letters.

(3) Vocabulary Index

Words and phrases included in the vocabulary list of each letter, and other important vocabulary explained in the "Basics of Japanese Business Letters," are listed in *a-i-u-e-o* order.

ビジネス文書の基本

実際のビジネス文書には、企業によって個人によって、レイアウト、表記、語句・表現の使い方などにおいてさまざまなバリエーションがあります。本書でもそういう点で数多くのバリエーションを取り上げていますから、ご自分で書く際の参考にしてください。ただし、そういう多くのバリエーションのなかにも共通する重要なポイントがあります。それは、次の二つです。

1. **簡潔でわかりやすい文書形式を持っていること**
2. **適切な通信方法を取ること**

このいずれが欠けても円滑な業務の遂行に支障を生じます。

そこで次に、重要な役割を担うビジネス文書に共通するこれらの要素について明らかにしておきます。

1 「簡潔でわかりやすい文書形式」とはどのような文書形式か？

1－1 文書全体の基本形を守ること

ビジネス文書にはどこに何をどう書くか、その決まった一般的な形があります。通常用いられる横書き、あいさつ・招待状などに使われる縦書き、それぞれ次のような形が一般的です。

■横書き文書の基本形

営総第○○○号❶
平成○年○月○日❷

○○○○○○○株式会社
　○○支社長　○○○○殿❸

○○○○○○○株式会社
○○○部長　○○○○○❹㊞

○○○○○○○○○○○の件❺

❻頭語　❼初めのあいさつ……………………………………………。
さて、……………………………………………………………。…………………………
……………………………。……………　❽本　文　………………………………………
…………………………………………………………………………………………………
…………………………。
❾終わりのあいさつ……………………………………。

❿結語

⓫記

1.……………………………………………………………………
2.……………………………………………………………………

❿以上

⓬同封物：…………………………

⓭追記………………………………………………………………

❿再拝

■縦書き文書の基本形

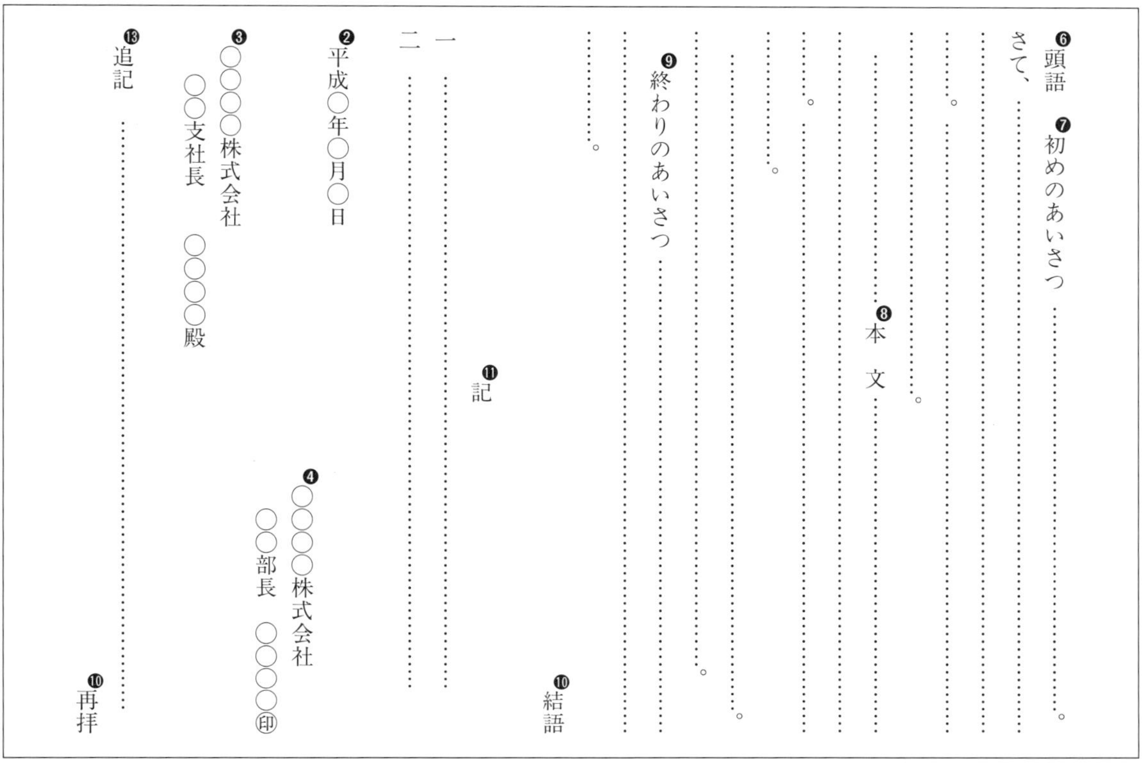

❶発信番号

発信元の組織が大きく発信文書の数が多い場合は、番号をつけます。初めに発信元の部署名を、次に文書の通し番号を書きます。たとえば、営業部･総務課発信ならば「営総第123号」などと書きます。(縦書きの場合は、発信番号を書かないことがあります。)

❷日付

横書きの場合、文書右上に日付を書きます。年号は西暦でも元号でもかまいませんが、社内で統一されているはずですからそれにならいます。縦書きの場合は、差出人の前に書きます。

❸宛名

横書きでは、文書左上に宛名を書きます。(住所は通信することの多い相手先の場合は省略します。) 縦書きの場合は、最末尾に書きます。

宛名につける敬称の例

殿……………名前につける最も一般的な敬称
様……………個人的な文書の場合
ご一同様……ある部署の全員を指す場合
各位…………ある部署の部員・課員めいめいに宛てる場合
御中 …………会社、団体、部署宛ての場合社内文書では、「専務」「営業部長」など役職名のみ書く場合、それに「専務殿」「営業部長殿」などと「殿」を加える場合、さらに「鈴木専務」「山田営業部長」などと個人名を用いる場合があります。

❹差出人

横書きの場合、文書右上に差出人名を書きます。そして、名前の最後に重なるように押印します。縦書きの場合は、宛名の右に書きます。

❺件名

20字以下のできるだけ短いことばで、「～の件」「～のこと」と、その文書の目的や内容が即座にわかるようなタイトルをつけます。場合によっては、「～の件(ご通知)」「～の件(ご依頼)」「～のこと (ご照会)」などと (　　) 内にはっきりと文書内容を示したり、下線を引いて強調することもあります。ただし、単なるあいさつ状の場合は、件名をまったく省略してしまうことがあります。

❻頭語

「初めのあいさつ」とともに、必ず書くことば。次にその例を紹介しておきますが、その中でも最も一般的なのは「拝啓」です。ただし、社内文書では省略するのが普通です。

拝啓、謹啓、恭啓、謹白、謹呈、拝呈……一般的な例
前略、急啓、冠省……特に急ぎで、時候のあいさつなどを省略して本文に入るとき
拝復、拝答、復啓……返事を書くとき

❼初めのあいさつ

普通、①**時候**（季節）**のあいさつ**、②**慶賀**（先方が健康であり、またますます発展していることを祝う）**のあいさつ**、③**日ごろの厚意に対する感謝**、の三つの部分からなります。ただし、社内文書では省略するのが一般的です。

①時候のあいさつの例

月	通常の表現	やや柔らかい、個人宛て文書などに使われる表現
1	初春、新春、厳寒	初春とはいえ厳しい寒さが続いておりますが、
2	立春、余寒、春寒	梅のつぼみもようやくほころんでまいりましたが、
3	早春、春暖、春分	日増しに暖かさがましてまいりましたが、
4	陽春、温暖、桜花	花便りも伝わる今日この頃ですが、

5	新緑、若葉、薫風	+の候、	吹く風も夏めいてまいりましたが、
6	初夏、梅雨、長雨		梅雨のうっとうしい季節でございますが、
7	盛夏、猛暑、大暑		連日厳しい暑さが続きますが、
8	晩夏、残暑、初秋		残暑がなお厳しい今日この頃ですが、
9	秋冷、秋色、秋涼		秋の気配が次第に濃くなってまいりましたが、
10	仲秋、紅葉、秋晴		灯火親しむ頃となりましたが、
11	晩秋、落葉、向寒		朝夕はめっきり冷え込む季節でございますが、
12	寒冷、初冬、師走		年の瀬もいよいよ押し迫ってまいりましたが、

＊なお、季節に関係なくいつでも使える便利な表現として、「時下」という表現があります。文書の冒頭に「時下」とし、すぐに慶賀のあいさつ、日ごろの厚意に対する感謝のことばを続けます。

②慶賀のあいさつの例

基本パターン

A	（におかれましては）、ますます	B	のことと、お慶び申し上げます。
A	（におかれましては）、ますます	B	の段、大慶に存じます。

Aに入るもの	Bに入るもの
●個人あて● 貴台（かなり高い地位の人の場合） 貴殿（最も一般的な表現） 貴兄（親しい関係にあるとき） 貴職（相手の企業内の立場を特定するとき）	ご健勝、ご清祥
●企業あて● 貴社（最も一般的な表現） 貴店（先方の名称が「～店」の場合） 貴行（先方が銀行の場合）	ご清栄、ご発展、ご隆昌、ご繁栄
●部署のメンバーあて● 各位、皆様方、ご一同様	ご健勝、ご清祥

③日ごろの厚意に対する感謝を表す表現の例

平素は 日頃は 毎度	＋	格別の 一方ならぬ	＋	ご高配 お引き立て ご愛顧 ご厚情 ご厚誼	＋	を賜り、 にあずかり、	＋	厚く御礼申し上げます。 誠にありがたく存じます。

❽本文

最重要伝達事項を盛り込む部分。改行して「さて」「早速ではございますが」「ところで」などのことばで始めます。最も一般的なのは「さて」ですが、「さて」は単に改行するだけでなく、行末から始めることがあります。また、「私」「弊社」などで文を始める場合も、行の最初からではなく行末から書くことがあります。

各段落の最初は、１字下げてもまったく下げなくてもどちらでもかまいませんが、一つの文書の中では統一させます。また、社外文書では「～でございます」「～ております」などのスタイルで書きますが、一般の社内文書では「～である」などのように「です・ます」でないスタイルで書くこともあります。

❾終わりのあいさつ

文書を終えるためのあいさつですが、単にあいさつの意味合いだけではなく、「念押し」の役割も果たします。次に、その例を紹介しておきます。

●書状によることのことわり

本来は実際に会ってしなければならない用事を、手紙で済ますときの終わりのあいさつ

まずは、 右、 以上、	＋	略儀ながら とりあえず	＋	書中、 書中をもって、 書中をもちまして、	＋	ご挨拶 ご報告 ご依頼 ご通知 ご案内 ご一報 お詫び 御礼	＋	申し上げます。 まで。

↑

二つ以上の場合は「かたがた」でつなぐ。

例）ご挨拶かたがたご報告申し上げます。

●急ぐことのことわり

本来ならば十分にあいさつしたり詳しく話をしたりすべきなのに、そのようなことを省略して急いで連絡するときの終わりのあいさつ

（まずは、）取り急ぎ、	＋	当用のみ（申し上げます）。 要用のみ（申し上げます）。 確認まで。 御礼まで。 ご連絡まで。 ご回答まで。 ご返書まで。

↑
二つ以上の場合は「かたがた」でつなぐ。

例）確認かたがた御礼まで。

●健康や活躍を祈ることば

相手の健康やこれからの活躍を祈ったり、相手の企業の発展を祈ったりする終わりのあいさつ

時節がらご自愛のほど、 ご多幸を ますますのご活躍を ますますのご繁栄を	＋	お祈り申し上げます。

⑩結語

文書の最後に必ず書くことば。次の例のように、必ず「頭語」と対で使われます。ただし、社内文書では頭語とともに省略することがあります。

敬具、敬白……「拝啓」「謹啓」「恭啓」、「拝復」「拝答」「敬復」などの頭語を用いたとき
草々、不一……「前略」「急啓」「冠省」などの頭語を用いたとき
再拝……………追って書きの後。社内では、「了」「完」とする場合もあります。
以上……………記書きの後、あるいは全文書の最後。特に、重要な文書では後から他の人に何かつけ加えられることがないよう、そこが文書の最後であることを示すために必ず書きます。同じ目的で「以下、余白」という書き方もあります。

⓫記書き

文書の要点をよりわかりやすくするために、内容を項目ごとに分けて書く部分。本文中あるいは結語の後に1～2行程度あけ、中央に「記」と書き、さらに行を改めて箇条書きで書きます。社内はもちろん、社外に出す文書でも「～である」のスタイルで書くのが普通です。そして最後に、横書きの場合は右隅に、縦書きの場合は最末尾に「以上」と結語を書いておきます。

⓬同封物リスト

同封物などがあるときは、それをリストにしてまとめておきます。結語の後に1～2行程度あけ、「同封物」「添付書類」などと書き、さらに行を改めて箇条書きで書きます。

⓭追って書き

本文で書き切れなかったことや特に確認しておきたいことなどがあった場合に、文書の最後につけ加えます。

以上が文書各部分の留意事項ですが、その他、

- **文書全体を見やすいレイアウトにする。**
- **文章を書いた後の余白が、上下・左右でバランスがとれるよう文章を書き出す位置、1行あたりの字数、行数などに留意する。**

といったことも「簡潔でわかりやすい文書形式」に必要なことがらです。

1−2 封筒の宛名書きで留意することがら

封筒の宛名書きで留意することは、次の２点です。

- **相手の住所・社名・部署名・肩書きなどは省略せず正式なものを用いること。**
- **相手の名前を封筒の中心に置き、やや大きめに書くこと。**

次に、その例を紹介しておきます。

■横書きの例

160-0022
東京都新宿区新宿3-2-1
日本貿易ビル４階

田中商事株式会社
営業部長　鈴　木　一　郎　殿

S&Aコーポレーション日本支社
〒100-0004 東京都千代田区大手町1-2-1
平成ビルディング８階
TEL(03)3211-4567　FAX(03)3211-0880

- 先方の肩書き・名前を、中央に、大きく目立つように書く。
- 先方の肩書きは、「営業部長　鈴木一郎殿」でも「鈴木一郎　営業部長殿」でもどちらでもよい。
- 宛先が部署名など組織の場合は、「殿」「様」などではなく、「御中」とする。

■縦書きの例

(オモテ)

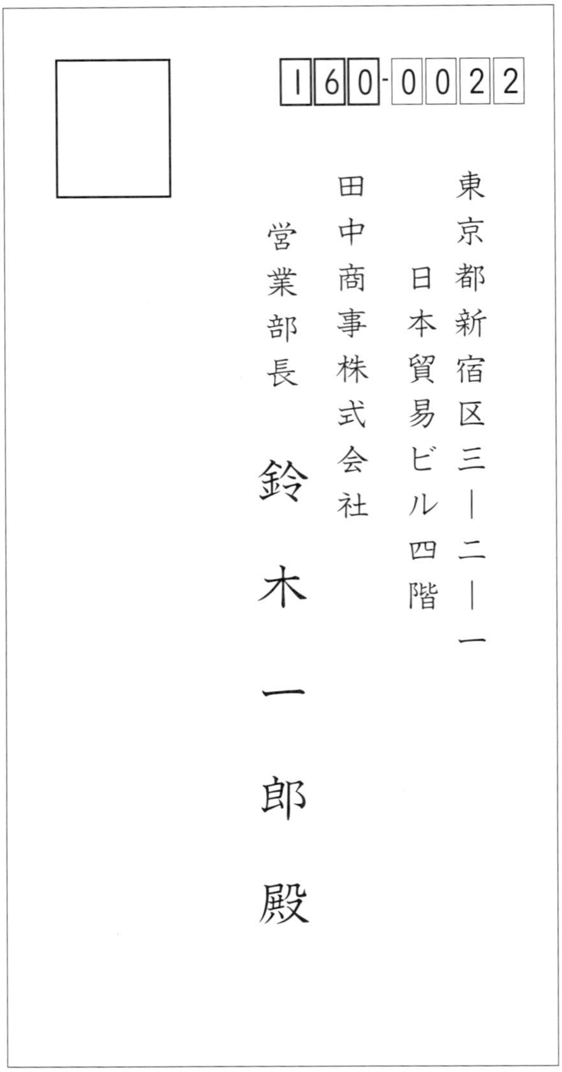

(ウラ)

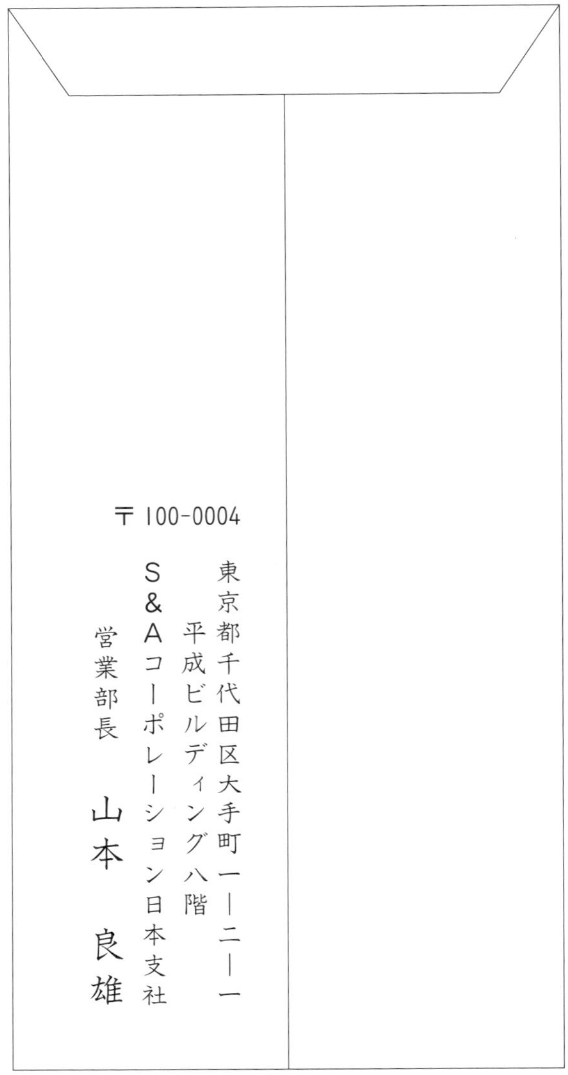

・数字はアラビア数字・漢数字どちらでもよい。
・差出人は封筒裏左下に書く。
・文書が横書きの場合、縦長封筒でも宛名を横書きにする場合がある。

1－3 理解しやすい文書であること

文書を簡潔で理解しやすくすることは、次のような工夫によって実現されます。

●文書を短くする

一文書は、資料などを除きできるかぎり1ページに納(おさ)めます。そして、内容を3段落程度にまとめます。さらに、各文をなるべく、2行以下で50～60字以下、「、」が三つ以下、構文が単純なものにします。

●内容をシンプルにする

一つの文書には一つの用件だけ書くようにします。やむを得ず複数の用件を書く場合は箇条書きにするなど短く簡単にまとめます。箇条書きにする場合には、次のことに留意します。

・重要なものから順に並べ、番号をつける。

・各文は長くとも20～30字程度にする。

・文末は名詞止めの形、あるいは「である」の形を用いる。

また、結論は明確に示します。そのために、最初の段落に結論を、第2～3段落にその理由やそうなった経緯(けいい)・それに対する意見・要望(ようぼう)を書くという書き方もあります。文学的な表現・どちらとも取れるあいまいな表現・長過ぎる修飾語・流行語・社内だけで用いる表現などは避けます。

2「適切な通信方法」とは何か？

2－1 同位者(どういしゃ)の原則を守ること

対外文書では、双方(そうほう)の企業の規模(きぼ)が大きく違わない限り、原則として、同位者から同位者への形で文書のやり取りをします。すなわち、課長職からは課長職へ、部長職からは部長職へ、部署からは部署へといったやり取りです。また、文書や封筒などの宛名(あてな)を書くときには、先方の所属(しょぞく)や役職を書いた場合にはこちらも所属・役職を書きます。

2－2 正式なやり取りは文書で行うこと

最近はファックス・電子メールなども一般的になりましたが、正式なやり取りは文書で行うことには変わりありません。電話及び面談で口頭でなされたやり取りも、改めて文書をやり取りして内容を確認します。

2－3 適切な文書の書き方をすること

社内用と社外用の用紙は区別し、特に外部に対してはレターヘッド入りのＡ４版またはＢ５版を縦長に用います。

■レターヘッド見本

S&A

S&Aコーポレーション日本支社
〒100-0004　東京都千代田区大手町1-2-1 平成ビルディング8階
TEL(03)3211-4567　FAX(03)3211-0880

また、最近のビジネス文書はワープロやコンピュータで打つのが一般的ですが、誤字・脱字・当て字などがないよう十分気をつけます。特に、先方の企業名・部署名・役職名・氏名さらに日時や金額に誤りがないか十二分に留意します。手書きの場合には、楷書ではっきり書きます。

さらに、先方とこちらとの関係・その場の状況などを考慮し、それにふさわしい敬意を持つ語句・表現を用いるようにします。

Basics of Japanese Business Letters

Business letters, while conforming to certain patterns, vary in layout, way of writing, phrasing, and style according to the company and person writing them. This book, therefore, provides several variations on each type for you to refer to when writing your own letters. All these variations have, however, two points in common: they are written in a simple, easy-to-understand format and they use the most appropriate means of communication for each situation.
Letters that lack those traits will be obstacles to efficiently carrying out business. Thus, let us look at those two vital traits.

1 What is a simple, easy-to-understand format?

1-1 Adhering to a basic letter format

A set format exists for what goes where in a business letter. While most utilitarian letters are written horizontally and more ceremonial ones, such as greetings and invitations, vertically, both are made up of much the same parts that are used in a set order.

■ Basic horizontal format

営総第○○○号❶
平成○年○月○日❷

○○○○○○○株式会社
　○○支社長　○○○○殿❸

○○○○○○○株式会社
○○○部長　○○○○○❹㊞

○○○○○○○○○○の件❺

❻頭語(とうご)　❼初めのあいさつ……………………………………。
さて、……………………………………………………。……………………
……………………。……………　❽本　文　………………………………
…………………………………………………………………………………
…………………………。
❾終わりのあいさつ……………………………。
❿結語(けつご)

⓫記(き)
1.……………………………………………………
2.……………………………………………………
❿以上

⓬同封物(どうふうぶつ)：……………………

⓭追記(ついき)…………………………………………………
❿再拝(さいはい)

■ Basic vertical format

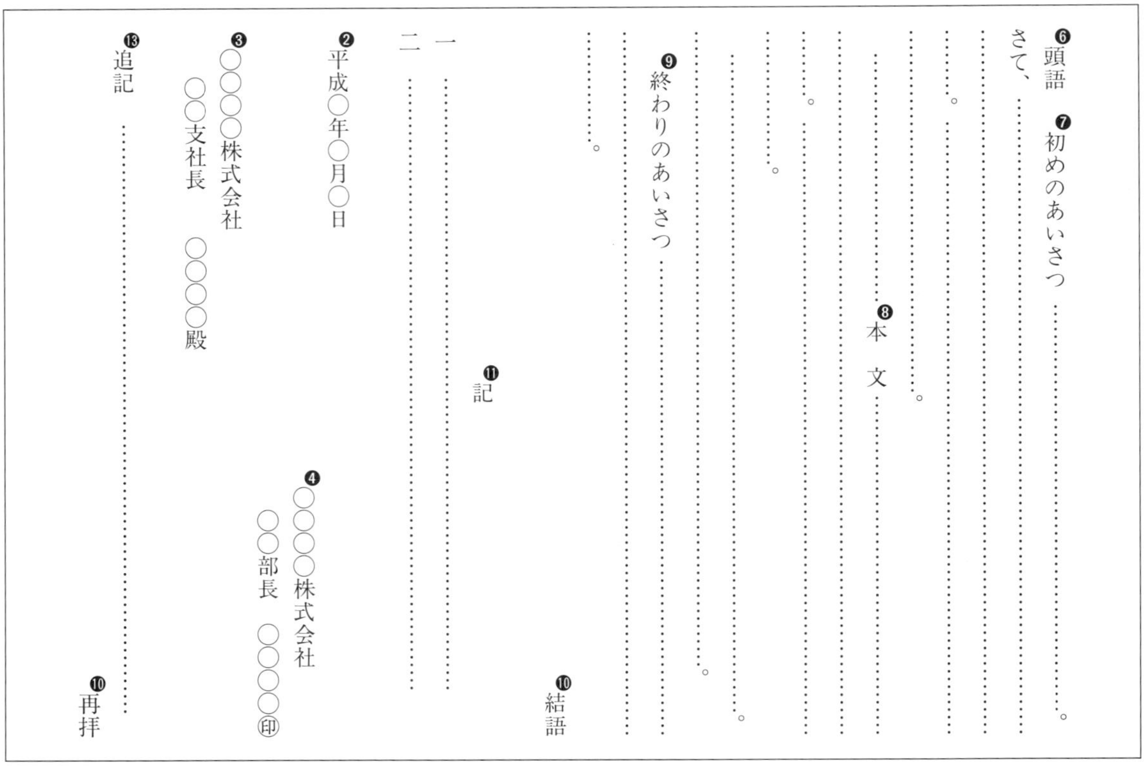

❶ Document number

Large organizations that send out many letters and other documents usually number them. The name of the section sending the document is followed by the document number. For example, a letter from the general affairs section of the sales department is labeled "Sales: General 123." (Sometimes vertical format letters do not have a document number.)

❷ Date

The date goes on the upper right-hand side for horizontal format letters, and before the name of the sender when using the vertical format. The year may be written in the Western or Japanese format, but check your company's in-house style and conform to it.

❸ Recipient

In the horizontal format, the recipient's address and name are on the upper left-hand side. (If you write to the same person frequently, you may omit the address.) The address and name come at the end in vertical format letters. Be sure to use the right form of address after the name:

殿(どの) …………(Mr./Ms.) The most generally used term of respect
様(さま) …………(Mr./Ms.) Use when the letter is private, or addressed to a specific individual
ご一同様(いちどうさま) … Use to refer to everyone in the department in question
各位(かくい) ……… Use to refer to each member of the department in question individually
御中(おんちゅう) ……… Use to refer to a company, organization, or department

In in-house documents, sometimes only the recipient's title is used: 専務 (Managing Director) or 営業部長 (Manager of the Sales Department), for example. It is possible to combine that title with the formal 殿 (e.g., 専務殿; 営業部長殿) or with the person's surname (e.g., 鈴木専務; 山田営業部長).

❹ Sender

The name of the sender is placed at the upper right of horizontal format letters, with the seal impressed to overlap it. In the vertical format, the sender's name comes to the right of the recipient's name.

❺ "件名" (Re:)

Similar to the use of "Re: . . ." in memos, "件名" states, in 20 characters or fewer, what the letter is about. The most general formats end with の件 or のこと (both equivalent to "Re:"). Depending on the content of the letter, it is underlined for emphasis, or ご通知 (announcement), ご依頼 (request), or ご照会 (inquiry) may be added in parentheses after ～の件 or ～のこと.

It may be omitted from letters of greeting.

❻ Salutations

This part of the letter, roughly equivalent to "Dear . . . ," should not be omitted, except in in-house communications. The most commonly used form is 拝啓.

General-purpose forms: 拝啓, 謹啓, 恭啓, 謹白, 謹呈, 拝呈
Forms signaling an abbreviated note excluding the seasonal greetings: 前略, 急啓, 冠省
Forms used in replies to letters: 拝復, 拝答, 復啓

❼ Opening greeting

The opening greeting usually consists of three parts: a seasonal reference, a hope for the recipient's continued health and prosperity, and a statement of gratitude for help and consideration, in that order. Generally, however, these are omitted with in-house letters.

① *Examples of seasonal greetings*

Month	Standard expressions		Expressions used for personal letters, etc.
January	初春、新春、厳寒		初春とはいえ厳しい寒さが続いておりますが、 Although the calendar says spring, the weather continues to be cold, . . .
February	立春、余寒、春寒		梅のつぼみもようやくほころんでまいりましたが、 The plum blossoms are at last beginning to bloom . . .

March	早春(そうしゅん)、春暖(しゅんだん)、春分(しゅんぶん)		日増し(ひまし)に暖かさがましてまいりましたが、 It is growing warmer every day . . .
April	陽春(ようしゅん)、温暖(おんだん)、桜花(おうか)		花便り(はなだより)も伝わる今日この頃ですが、 During this season when news of the cherry blossoms reaches us . . .
May	新緑(しんりょく)、若葉(わかば)、薫風(くんぷう)		吹く風も夏めいてまいりましたが、 The breezes are becoming more summer-like . . .
June	初夏(しょか)、梅雨(ばいう)、長雨(ながあめ)	＋の候(こう)、	梅雨(つゆ)のうっとうしい季節でございますが、 During this gloomy rainy season . . .
July	盛夏(せいか)、猛暑(もうしょ)、大暑(たいしょ)		連日厳しい暑さが続きますが、 As this sultry weather continues . . .
August	晩夏(ばんか)、残暑(ざんしょ)、初秋(しょしゅう)		残暑がなお厳しい今日この頃ですが、 The summer heat remains with us . . .
September	秋冷(しゅうれい)、秋色(しゅうしょく)、秋涼(しゅうりょう)		秋の気配(けはい)が次第に濃(こ)くなってまいりましたが、 It is gradually feeling more like fall . . .
October	仲秋(ちゅうしゅう)、紅葉(こうよう)、秋晴(しゅうせい)		灯火(とうか)親しむ頃となりましたが、 The nights are drawing in . . .
November	晩秋(ばんしゅう)、落葉(らくよう)、向寒(こうかん)		朝夕はめっきり冷え込む季節でございますが、 The mornings and evenings are turning crisp . . .
December	寒冷(かんれい)、初冬(しょとう)、師走(しわす)		年の瀬(せ)もいよいよ押し迫(せま)ってまいりましたが、 As the year draws to a close . . .

(「の候」＝during the season of)

＊ An extremely handy phrase that can be used in any season is 時下(じか), “at present”; write it at the beginning of the opening greeting, and then move directly into expressing your hopes for the recipient’s health and your gratitude for the kindness/support he/she usually gives to you.

② *Examples of congratulatory greetings*

Basic Pattern

(The following 1 and 2 hold the basic meaning of “Allow me to express my congratulations on your good health and well-being.”)

A	(におかれましては)、ますます	B	のことと、お慶び(よろこび)申し上げます。
A	(におかれましては)、ますます	B	の段(だん)、大慶(たいけい)に存じます。

Words for A	**Words for B**
● To an individual ●	
貴台(きだい) (For those of a high rank)	ご健勝(けんしょう)、ご清祥(せいしょう)
貴殿(きでん) (The most commonly used form)	

貴兄 (For someone with whom you are on friendly terms) 貴職 (When specifying the recipient's position in his/her company)	
● To a company ● 貴社 (The most commonly used form) 貴店 (When company name ends in ～店) 貴行 (When writing to a bank)	ご清栄、ご発展、ご隆昌、ご繁栄
● To a department or group ● 各位、皆様方、ご一同様	ご健勝、ご清祥

③ *Expressions of gratitude for the recipient's constant kindness*

平素は 日頃は 毎度	+	格別の 一方ならぬ	+	ご高配 お引き立て ご愛顧 ご厚情 ご厚誼	+	を賜り、 にあずかり、	+	厚く御礼申し上げます。 誠にありがたく存じます。

❽ The body of the letter

The body of the letter includes, of course, the important information you are communicating. It begins on a new line and with a phrase indicating a change of topic, such as さて (now), 早速ではございますが (forgive my abruptness, but), or ところで (by the way). さて is the most generally used and is often written at the end of a new line. Also, in cases where the text starts with 私 (I), 弊社 (my company), and so on, there are times when this is not written at the beginning but at the end of a line.

The start of each paragraph can be indented or not, but be consistent within any one letter.

A letter to someone outside your company will be written in the more formal *de gozaimasu,* or *te orimasu* style, while in-house documents are sometimes written in the *de aru* style.

❾ Closing greeting

The closing greeting is more than a final greeting: it also serves to wrap up what it is you are trying to communicate. A few examples will show how this works.

● *Apologizing for a written communication*

Use one of these phrases when you are doing by letter something you should really do in person.

まずは、 右、 以上、	＋	略儀(りゃくぎ)ながら とりあえず	＋	書中(しょちゅう)、 書中をもって、 書中をもちまして、	＋	ご挨拶(あいさつ) ご報告 ご依頼 ご通知 ご案内 ご一報(いっぽう) お詫(わ)び 御礼(おんれい)	＋	申し上げます。 まで。

↑

* If you use more than one of the above, combine them with かたがた.
For example: ご挨拶かたがたご報告申し上げます。
(These are the items I want to report to you, while also thanking you for your cooperation.)

● *Apologizing for haste*

Use these when you are hurriedly writing about something that should be discussed thoroughly and with proper formality.

(まずは、) 取り急ぎ、	＋	当用(とうよう)のみ (申し上げます)。 要用(ようよう)のみ (申し上げます)。 確認まで。 御礼まで。 ご連絡まで。 ご回答まで。 ご返書まで。

↑

* If your letter includes more than one of the above, combine them with かたがた.
For example: 確認かたがた御礼まで。
(These are the items I want to confirm, while also thanking you for your cooperation.)

● *Expressing hopes for health and active participation in the future*

A conclusion that ends by expressing hopes for the recipient's health, active participation (in business dealings), and the company's development include:

時節(じせつ)がらご自愛(じあい)のほど、 ご多幸(たこう)を ますますのご活躍(かつやく)を ますますのご繁栄(はんえい)を	＋	お祈(いの)り申し上げます。

⑩ Complimentary close

This part of the letter, roughly equivalent to "sincerely yours," must be included at the end of letters addressed to people outside your company. As the examples below show, the complimentary close is paired with the salutation. In in-house letters, however, it may be omitted, along with the salutation.

敬具、敬白	When using salutations such as 拝啓, 謹啓, 恭啓, 拝復, 拝答 and 敬復.
草々、不一	When using salutations such as 前略, 急啓 and 冠省.
再拝	Used after a postscript. In in-house messages, you may use 了 or 完.
以上	This phrase, meaning "ends" or, roughly, "that's all," is used at the end of a document, particularly if it is an important one to which you do not wish another person to make additions. 以下、余白 is used in the same way.

⑪"記書き" (Writing specifics)

This part of the letter, written as an itemized listing, makes main points of the letter easier to understand. After the complimentary close, or within the letter itself, leave about one or two lines and write 記 in the center of the page, and then begin a new line and write the itemized outline. It is usual with both internal and external letters to use the *de aru* style. Conclude the letter with 以上: For letters written in the horizontal style, this should be written in the bottom right-hand corner; for those written vertically, write it as the conclusion at the very end.

⑫ Listing enclosed items

When enclosing items with a letter, attach a list of those items. Leave a couple of lines and write 同封物 (enclosed items), 添付書類 (attached documents), and so on, after the complimentary close, then write the list on a new line by the itemized format.

⑬ Postscript

In cases where there are things you couldn't finish in the text or something you especially wanted to confirm, add them at the end of the text.

Also note the following for writing a simple, easy-to-understand letter:

* The overall layout of the letter should be easy to read.
* Be sure to obtain a balance between the written part of the letter and the white spaces at the top, bottom and sides, and pay attention to the positioning of the sentences, the number of words per line and the number of lines, etc.

1-2 Things to pay attention to when writing the address on the envelope

There are two points to pay attention to when writing the address on the envelope:

* Use in full the other party's address, company and department name, title, and so on.
* Place the addressee's name at the center of the envelope, and write it a little bigger than the rest of the information.

■ An example in the horizontal style

160-0022
東京都新宿区新宿3-2-1
日本貿易ビル4階

田中商事株式会社
営業部長　鈴　木　一　郎　殿

S&Aコーポレーション日本支社
〒100-0004 東京都千代田区大手町1-2-1
平成ビルディング8階
TEL(03)3211-4567　FAX(03)3211-0880

* Write the other party's title/name in the center and in large print so that it stands out.
* You can write the other party's title either in the "name + position" or "position + name" patterns.
* In the case where the addressee is not a person but an organization, such as a department, section, etc., do not write 殿 or 様 but 御中.

■ An example in the vertical style

(the face side)

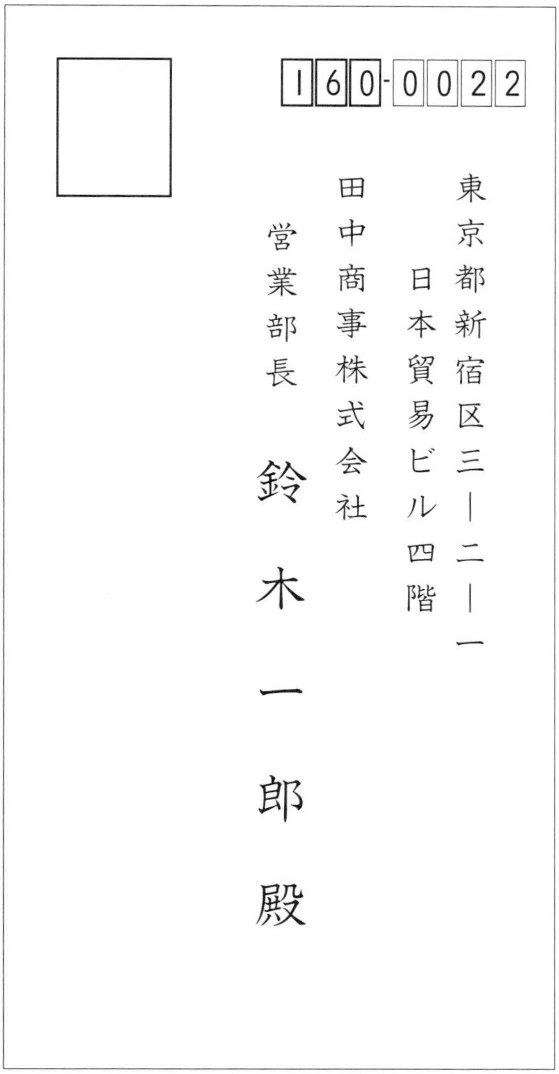

(the reverse side)

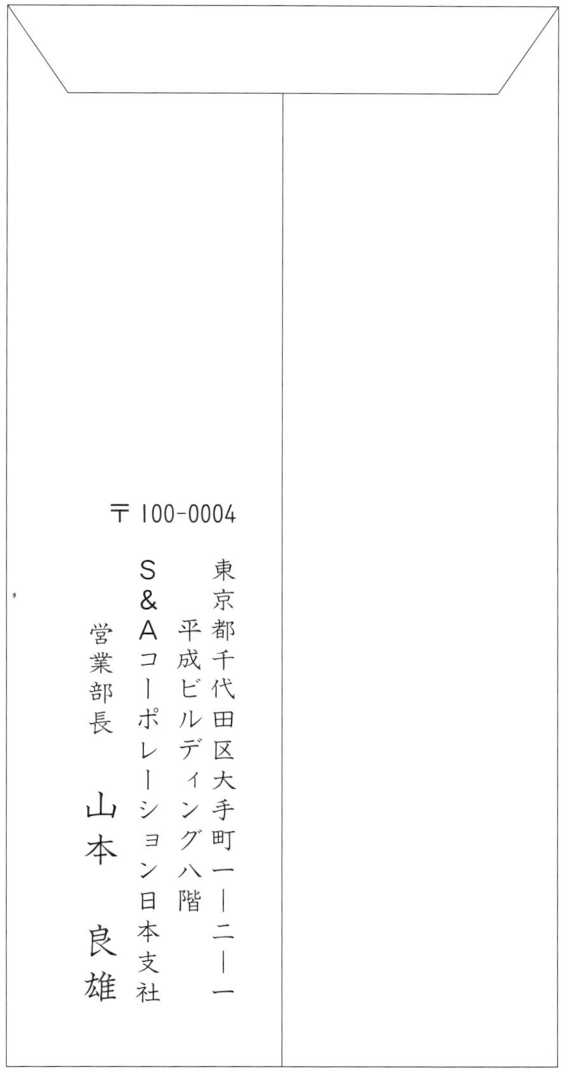

* Numbers can be written using either Arabic or Chinese numerals.
* The sender's name is written on the reverse side at the bottom left-hand side.
* In cases where the letter is written in the horizontal writing style, there are occasions when the same style is also used when writing on a long, vertical envelope.

1－3 Making the letter easy to understand

A concise, easy-to-understand letter can be realized through the following points:

● *Keep the letter short*
Providing you can leave out any additional materials, keep a letter down to one page. Then summarize the contents in about three paragraphs. Furthermore, use simple sentence structures: Keep each sentence to no more than two lines; with no more than 50-60 characters; and containing no more than three commas.
● *Keep the content simple*
In any one letter write about only one business matter. In cases where writing about more than one matter cannot be avoided, it should be arranged in a short and simple itemized format. For this latter case, pay attention to the following points:
—Arrange matters in order of importance and number them.
—Keep each sentence to a maximum of 20-30 characters
—End each sentence with a noun, or use the *-de aru* form.
Also, put forward the conclusion clearly. In order to do so, write the conclusion in the first paragraph, and the reasons or the circumstances bringing the letter about, your opinion, and your hopes in the second and third paragraphs.

Avoid using any flowery phrases, phrases that could be taken as vague, long modifying words, "in" words, phrases only used within the company, and so on.

2 What is the "proper method of correspondence"?

2－1 Keeping the "same rank" principle

As long as there is no big difference in the scale of the two companies, as a principle, letters sent outside your company are exchanged between persons of the same rank. That is to say, section chiefs send letters to section chiefs, department managers to department managers, and a certain section to the same equivalent section. Also, when writing the address on an envelope or a letter, in cases where you have written the other party's position and section, also write your own position and section.

2－2 A formal interaction is undertaken by writing

Recently, fax and e-mail have become a more general way of interacting, but for formal interactions letters are still used. Even when discussions have been held verbally, by telephone, or by direct talks, the content of those talks is confirmed once more by letter.

2－3 Writing a letter correctly

There is a difference between the paper used for internal and external letters, especially regarding letterhead paper for outside use, where A-4 (296×210mm) or B-5 (256×182mm) paper is used lengthwise.

■Letterhead sample

S&A

S&Aコーポレーション日本支社
〒100-0004　東京都千代田区大手町1-2-1 平成ビルディング8階
TEL(03)3211-4567　FAX(03)3211-0880

Also, recently, business letters are generally typed by word processor or computer, but great care should be made to ensure that there are no misused characters, omitted words, and phonetic equivalents. Particular attention must be paid to the addressee's name, business name, section name, and position. Furthermore, pay careful attention to ensure no mistakes are made with the date and amounts of money. For handwritten letters, write in a clear, printed style.

Furthermore, use respectful words and phrases which are appropriate for the circumstances/relationship between yourself and the other party.

第1課

新しい部署に赴任する

Arriving at a new post

勤務地や勤務する部署が変わったときは、今までお世話になった関係先やこれからお世話になる関係先に異動のあいさつをする必要があります。

離任の前にはそれまでのお礼を兼ねて、また着任後には自己紹介を兼ねて取引先や関係先にあいさつをして回ります。これを「あいさつ回り」といいますが、あいさつ回りに行けないところには、あいさつ状を出す必要があります。

あいさつ状は、新しく会社を作った、新しい任務についた、担当が変わった、会社の名称を変更したなど、関係先に通知を兼ねてその旨のあいさつをするための文書ですが、そのついでに会社を紹介したり、組織の変更を案内したりするといいでしょう。

ビジネス文書では、一般的に、どのような目的でどのような内容の文書であるかを１行に集約して「件名」を書くのが普通ですが、あいさつ状とか慶弔の文書などには件名を記さないのが通例です。

When your place of employment or position changes, it is necessary to inform previous business contacts who were helpful to you then and those who may prove helpful in your new position.

Additionally, before leaving a post, visit those you previously did business with to express your thanks.

It is also necessary to go around and introduce yourself to those you will be doing business with and to other related parties after arriving at your new post. These are known as あいさつ回り, or "paying courtesy visits." However, in cases where such a visit is not possible, it is necessary to send out a letter of introduction.

This letter is sent to those connected to your work to inform them that you are starting at a new company, you are starting a new position, your responsibilities have changed, your company name has changed, etc. Additionally, this is also an appropriate time to inform others of such matters as organizational changes and to introduce the company.

Generally speaking, the objective and content of a business letter is usually written in a one-line precis (件名(けんめい)), but this is not necessary in a letter of introduction or in letters of congratulations or condolences.

1-1 着任のあいさつをする
Extending greetings at your new post

アメリカのインテリア・家具の製造販売会社のＳ＆Ａ社のスミスは、日本支社長に着任のため来日し、あいさつ状を作ります。

Mr. Smith, who works for S&A Corporation (an American furniture and home furnishings manufacturing and marketing company), comes to Japan to become the manager of the company's Japan Office. He writes a letter introducing himself.

私儀：pertaining to personal matters　～在勤中：while working in ～　厚情：kindness　何にも代え難い：there is nothing else　任地：position　従来にも増しまして：even more than before　鞭撻：encouragement　概要：profile　設立：establishment　事業内容：description of business　～一般：general ～　要望に応える：answer to (your) wishes

S&Aコーポレーション　概要

☆本　社　米国　ニューヨーク市

日本支社　〒一〇〇-〇〇〇四　東京都千代田区大手町一の二の一

平成ビル八階　八〇一号室

電話　〇三-三二一一-四五六七（代表）

☆本社設立年月日　一九二六年二月一日

☆資本金　八千二百万米ドル

☆売上高　一億二千万米ドル　一九九八年十二月期

☆事業内容　インテリア並びに家具一般……特にカーペットには優れた製品を多数用意しお客様のご要望にお応えしております

☆従業員　二千五百名

留意事項

1) 責任者や上位職にある人が新しい部署に赴任したときは、あいさつ状をなるべく早く出します。特に重要な客先には書状とは別にあいさつ回りをします。

2) あいさつ状には、新任地名と新所属や新役職名を書き、新しい任務での努力の決意を表して友好関係を作るとともに、今後の援助をお願いしたい旨を書きます。また、前任地で受けた支援に対してお礼のことばをつけ加えることがあります。

3) あいさつ状は、これから仕事の上で付き合いが多くなる相手の企業で、差出人と同等の地位にある人を中心に出します。

4) 会社の知名度が低いときは、会社の概要をいっしょに書くことがあります。

1. When you assume a senior position, you should send out a letter introducing yourself as soon as possible. In addition to sending this letter, you should make formal and individual visits to introduce yourself to all important customers.

2. Include the address of your new place of business and your new assignment, including your official title, in your introductory letter. Also express your determination to do a good job, your hope that a friendly relationship will be established, and your request for the other party's support. It may be appropriate to express appreciation for their support while you were working at your former location.

3. Introductory letters should be addressed to the businesses of those with whom you expect to have a great many dealings, focusing on persons at a similar level in their company as the sender.

4. When the recipient does not know much

拝啓　時下ますますご清栄のこととお慶び申し上げます
平素は格別のご高配を賜り厚く御礼申し上げます
さて　私儀
このたび　S&Aコーポレーション　日本支社長を命じられ　この程着任致しました
ニューヨーク本社在勤中は　一方ならぬご厚情とご指導を賜り誠に有り難く
厚く御礼申し上げます
日本で皆様にご挨拶できますこと　私にとり何にも代え難い喜びであります
新しい任地で心を新たに努力致す所存であります
何卒従来にも増しまして　ご指導ご鞭撻を賜りますようお願い申し上げます
まずは略儀ながら書中をもって　ご挨拶申し上げます

敬具

平成○年○月

S&Aコーポレーション
日本支社長　H・G・スミス

5) 離任・着任のあいさつ状の日付は、「月」までで「日」は書かないことが多く、日付を書くときは「○月吉日」などと書きます。

6) あいさつ状などの儀礼的な文書には、伝統的な縦書きの書式がまだ多く使用されています。ていねいな文書では筆を使って1通ずつ書きますが、毛筆で書くときはもちろん縦書きとなります。最近は印刷で横書きの書式も増えてきています。その際差出人が上位職にある場合は、毛筆体の活字を使い、句読点を省略することがあります。

7) 特にお世話になった相手には、印刷した書状に自筆で手書きの添え書きをしてお礼の気持ちを表すことがあります。

8) 最初のあいさつから用件に移る際、これから用件に入りますという意味で「さて」を、縦書きの行の下または横書きの行の右端に書くことがあります。1行あけて用件を書き出す場合もあります。

about a certain business, you may want to include a brief profile of your company.

5. When sending a letter of notification about either leaving or starting, a position, often only the month is written (omit the day). When writing the date, you might use 吉日 (a lucky day) along with the name of the month.

6. In formal letters, such as the introductory letter, the traditional vertical style of writing is generally used. It is courteous to write each letter separately using a calligraphy brush. Letters written in this manner are always written vertically. Recently, there has been an increase in the number of introductory letters typed horizontally and printed by machine. If, as a high-ranking person, you utilize this method, you might use a font that resembles brush writing and omit punctuation marks.

7. When sending printed introductory letters, adding a hand-written note to those with whom you have personal acquaintance expresses a feeling of gratitude.

8. When moving from the opening greetings to matters of business, さて (now) can be written at the bottom of a column (in the case of vertical style) or at the right edge of a line (in the case of horizontal style). You sometimes insert an extra line or column before getting down to business.

Salutations: At this time, allow me to express my congratulations on your good health and well-being. I sincerely appreciate your exceedingly kind and continuing consideration.

With regard to my situation,

I was recently appointed manager of the Japan Office of S&A Corporation and have just arrived to take up that position.

Allow me to express my deep gratitude for the extreme kindness and guidance you gave me while I was working at the main office in New York.

I cannot think of anything that could bring me more joy than being able to greet all of you here in Japan.

I endeavor to make a fresh start as I assume this new position in a new place.

It is my hope that you will provide even more guidance and encouragement than you have in the past. Please accept these informal greetings by letter.

Sincerely yours

Date (year, month)

S&A Corporation
Japan Office Manager H. G. Smith

Profile of S&A Corporation

☆ Headquarters: New York City, NY, U. S. A.
Japan Office: 100-0004 Tokyo-to, Chiyoda-ku, Otemachi 1-2-1, Heisei Bldg., Room #801
TEL: (03) 3211-4567 (Main switchboard)

☆ Headquarters established: February 1, 1926

☆ Capital investment: $82 million (U.S.)

☆ Sales: $120 million (U.S.) (December 1998)

☆ Description of business: general furniture and home furnishings; we especially carry a large number of fine carpets in response to our customers' wishes.

☆ Number of employees: 2,500

1-2 会社組織の変更の通知を兼ねた着任のあいさつ状を書く

Introducing yourself and notifying of a change in company organization

S&A社は、東京支店を日本支社に昇格させました。スミスは、新しく日本支社長として着任し、また支店が支社に昇格した旨のあいさつ状を作ります。

The Tokyo office of S&A Corporation has been upgraded to become the company's Japan Office. Mr. Smith has assumed the position of the new office manager, and the following is a letter of introduction and notification of that change of status.

199○年○月○日

東京商事株式会社

営業部長　小　川　　正　殿

S&A コーポレーション

日本支社長　ハワード　G. スミス

拝啓

時下、春暖の候、ますますご清祥のこととお慶び申し上げます

弊社製品については毎々格別のご愛顧を頂き厚く御礼申し上げます

さて

この度　S&Aコーポレーションでは　東南アジア地区、とりわけ日本における販売促進のため　4月1日をもって従来の東京支店を日本支社に昇格し　私　ハワード　G. スミスが支社長としてこの程着任致しました

日本には過去何度か伺いご挨拶の機会を得ておりますが　家族同伴での赴任は今回が初めてであります　いろいろ不慣れの点も多いことと存じますが　皆様のご鞭撻を得てご愛顧にお応えしたいと存じます

いずれ改めてご挨拶に参上致しますが　とりあえず支社昇格のご報告と着任のご挨拶まで申し上げます

敬　具

格別のご愛顧：your special support　とりわけ：more specifically; especially　販売促進：sales promotion　従来の：past　昇格する：upgrade　～の機会を得る：have the opportunity to ～　～同伴：accompanied by ～　赴任：assuming a new position　不慣れの点：lack of experience　鞭撻を得る：get (your) encouragement　愛顧に応える：respond to (your) support

Date (year, month, day)

Tokyo Shoji, Incorporated
Sales Department Manager Ogawa Tadashi (Mr.)

S&A Corporation
Japan Office Manager Howard G. Smith

Salutations:
At this time, allow me to congratulate you on your good health and well-being in this warm spring season.
I wish to sincerely thank you for your continued special support of our company's products.
Now, to promote sales in the South East Asia region, more specifically in Japan, S&A Corporation has upgraded its Tokyo office to become the Japan Office as of April 1, and I, Howard G. Smith, have just arrived to assume the position of office manager.
I have had the opportunity to greet you a number of times in the past when I visited Japan on business, but for the first time I have brought my family to be with me on this assignment. I know that my lack of experience will come out in many ways, but I hope to be able to receive your encouragement and respond to your support.
I will soon call on you to convey my greetings formally, but for the time being, please accept this as a notice of the upgrading of our office and of my arrival here.

Sincerely yours

留意事項

1) 自分が新任務に着任(ちゃくにん)したことを述(の)べて今後の支援(しえん)を願う旨(むね)を書きます。
2) 会社組織に変更(へんこう)がある場合、相手に知っておいてもらうため、あいさつ状の中でもそのことを書きます。
3) 関係先に親しみを持ってもらうために、家族同伴(どうはん)で来たとか、これまでに出張でお世話になっていたなどの状況を付け加えて書くことがあります。
4) あいさつ状は普通、自分と同位同職者を中心に出すことが多いので、任務や目的、時には経営の置かれている環境など、自分の役職に応じた内容にします。そして、くだけた表現は避け、フォーマルな形で書きます。
5) また、相手が親しい場合でも、これから新しい任務・生活が始まるという意味で、ていねいな表現にします。
6) 文書は、用紙の大きさや文の長さと上下左右の余白のバランスを考えて字配りをします。

1. After writing that you have just arrived at your new job, express your desire for support in the future.
2. When a change in company organization is involved, inform the recipient of the letter of such in the body of the letter.
3. To enable the related party to feel a sense of closeness, include something about your family accompanying you on this assignment, or how you enjoyed working with them when you visited on previous business trips, or something similar.
4. Introductory letters are usually sent to persons of the same rank or position, so it is important to consider your duties, objectives, and sometimes the environment of your operation when deciding what to write concerning your official position. Keep your letter formal, avoiding expressions of familiarity.
5. Even when the addressee is an acquaintance, use polite expressions to show that this is the start of a new position.
6. The size of the paper, length of the letter, and top, bottom, and side margins around the text should be considered in order to achieve a balanced effect.

1-1と1-2のフローと文例

1-1「着任のあいさつをする」のフロー

拝啓　時下ますますご清栄のこととお慶び申し上げます
平素は格別のご高配を賜り厚く御礼申し上げます
さて　私儀
このたび　S&Aコーポレーション　日本支社長を命じられ　この程着任致しました
ニューヨーク本社在勤中は　一方ならぬご厚情とご指導を賜り誠に有り難く
厚く御礼申し上げます
日本で皆様にご挨拶できますこと　私にとり何にも代え難い喜びであります
新しい任地で心を新たに努力致す所存であります
何卒従来にも増しまして　ご指導ご鞭撻を賜りますようお願い申し上げます
まずは略儀ながら書中をもって　ご挨拶申し上げます

敬具

①新役職と着任月日を報告する

②これまでの支援に対して礼を述べる

③仕事への意欲を述べる＋今後の支援、指導を依頼する

1-2「会社組織の変更の通知を兼ねた着任のあいさつ状を書く」のフロー

拝啓

時下、春暖の候、ますますご清祥のこととお慶び申し上げます

弊社製品については毎々格別のご愛顧を頂き厚く御礼申し上げます

さて

この度　S&Aコーポレーションでは　東南アジア地区、とりわけ日本における販売促進のため　4月1日をもって従来の東京支店を日本支社に昇格し　私　ハワード　G. スミスが支社長としてこの程着任致しました

日本には過去何度か伺いご挨拶の機会を得ておりますが　家族同伴での赴任は今回が初めてであります　いろいろ不慣れの点も多いことと存じますが　皆様のご鞭撻を得てご愛顧にお応えしたいと存じます

いずれ改めてご挨拶に参上致しますが　とりあえず支社昇格のご報告と着任のご挨拶まで申し上げます

敬具

①新役職と着任月日を報告する

③仕事への意欲を述べる＋今後の支援、指導を依頼する

（下線の部分は自分の状況に合わせて書いてください。）

①新役職と着任月日を報告する

Reporting a new position and the date of arrival at that position

＊私儀　このたび　S&Aコーポレーション　日本支社長を命じられ　この程着任致しました　(1-1)

With regard to my situation, I was recently appointed manager of the Japan Office of S&A Corporation and have just arrived to take up that position.

＊この度　S&Aコーポレーションでは　4月1日をもって従来の東京支店を日本支社に昇格し　私　ハワード　G.　スミスが支社長としてこの程着任致しました　(1-2)

S&A Corporation has upgraded its Tokyo office to become the Japan Office as of April 1, and I, Howard G. Smith, have just arrived to assume the position of office manager.

＊私こと　このたび○月○日付をもちまして日本支社勤務を命ぜられ　過日着任致しました　(1-3)

On a personal note, on (month, day), I received the assignment to work at our Japan Office, and I arrived a few days ago to assume that position.

②これまでの支援に対して礼を述べる

Extending thanks for support received so far

＊ニューヨーク本社在勤中は　一方ならぬご厚情とご指導を賜り誠に有り難く厚く御礼申し上げます　(1-1)

Allow me to express my deep gratitude for the extreme kindness and guidance you gave me while I was working at the main office in New York.

＊ニューヨーク本社総務部在勤中の三年間　大過なく勤務できましたことは　ひとえに皆様のご厚情のお陰と深く感謝申し上げます　ここに改めてお礼申し上げます　(1-3)

The fact that I was able to serve creditably during the three years I worked in the general affairs department of our headquarters in New York is entirely due to your kindness, and I want to express my deep appreciation for this. I am taking this opportunity to express my thanks.

＊ニューヨーク在勤中のご厚誼に対し深謝申し上げます。

I want to express my deep gratitude for your kindness during my employment in New York.

③仕事への意欲を述べる + 今後の支援、指導を依頼する

Expressing one's hopes regarding work and requesting further support and guidance from now on

＊新しい任地で心を新たに努力致す所存であります　何卒従来にも増しまして　ご指導ご鞭撻を賜りますようお願い申し上げます　(1-1)

I endeavor to make a fresh start as I assume this new position in a new place. It is my hope that you will provide even more guidance and encouragement than you have in the past.

＊いろいろ不慣れの点も多いことと存じますが　皆様のご鞭撻を得てご愛顧にお応えしたいと存じます　(1-2)

I know that my lack of experience will come out in many ways, but I hope to be able to receive your encouragement and respond to your support.

＊新任地におきましても全力を尽くす所存ですので　今後ともよろしくご指導の程お願い申し上げます　(1-3)

I intend to do my utmost in this new position and therefore request your guidance again in the future.

1-3 離任(りにん)のあいさつをする

Giving notification when leaving a post

スミスは日本支社勤務を命じられ着任(ちゃくにん)しましたが、前任地ニューヨークの関係先に、在任中お世話になった旨(むね)の礼状を書きます。

Having been appointed to his new post, Mr. Smith arrives at S&A's Japan Office. He now writes a letter of thanks to someone who helped him during his time in office at his previous place of employment in New York.

拝啓(はいけい)　時下(じか)ますますご清祥(せいしょう)のこととお慶(よろこ)び申し上げます　さて　私こと
このたび○月○日付をもちまして日本支社勤務を命ぜられ　過日着任(かじつちゃくにん)致し
ました
ニューヨーク本社総務部在勤中の三年間　大過(たいか)なく勤務できましたことは
ひとえに皆様のご厚情(こうじょう)のお陰と深く感謝申し上げます
ここに改(あらた)めてお礼申し上げますとともに　新任地におきましても全力を尽(つ)く
す所存ですので　今後ともよろしくご指導の程お願い申し上げます
なお　ニューヨーク本社総務部長の後任としては　J・D・モルガンが執務(しつむ)
致しますので　私同様のご愛顧(あいこ)ご鞭撻(べんたつ)の程お願い申し上げます
まずは書中をもってご挨拶(あいさつ)申し上げます
敬具

平成○年○月○日

S&Aコーポレーション
日本支社長　H・G・スミス
〒一〇〇-〇〇〇四　東京都千代田区大手町一―二―一
電話（〇三）三二一一―四五六七（代表）
FAX（〇三）三二一一―〇八八〇

私こと：pertaining to personal matters　～日付(にちづけ)をもちまして：on ～ (date)　過日(かじつ)：a few days ago　着任(ちゃくにん)する：arrive to assume a new position　～在勤中：while working in ～　大過(たいか)なく勤務する：serve creditably　厚情(こうじょう)のお陰：due to your kindness; in light of your kindness　新任地：new position　全力を尽(つ)くす：do one's utmost　所存：intention　後任：successor　執務(しつむ)する：work　～同様の：in the same way as ～　愛顧(あいこ)：support　鞭撻(べんたつ)：encouragement

Salutations: Allow me to congratulate you on your good health and well-being at this time.

On a personal note, on (month, day), I received the assignment to work at our Japan Office, and I arrived a few days ago to assume that position.

The fact that I was able to serve creditably during the three years I worked in the general affairs department of our headquarters in New York is entirely due to your kindness, and I want to express my deep appreciation for this.

While taking this opportunity to express my thanks, I also want you to know that I intend to do my utmost in this new position, and therefore request your guidance again in the future.

I would also like to inform you that J. D. Morgan will succeed me as head of the general affairs department at the headquarters in New York. I ask that you extend to him the same support and encouragement you gave to me.

I extend to you my greetings through this letter.

Sincerely yours

Date (year, month, day)

S&A Corporation
Japan Office Manager H. G. Smith

100-0004 Tokyo-to, Chiyoda-ku, Otemachi 1-2-1
TEL: (03) 3211-4567
FAX: (03) 3211-0880

留意事項

1) 離任のあいさつ状は、仕事でお世話になった人、親しくお付き合いをした人を中心に出します。

2) あいさつ状は、できるだけ離任の前に関係先に届くように出しますが、出せなかった場合は、新任地に着いたらすぐに出すようにします。

3) 離任のときは、新しい赴任先と新役職についても書きます。そして、これまで世話になったお礼を述べるとともに後任者を紹介し、その人に対する支援を依頼します。

4) 前任者の離任と後任者の着任のあいさつを、1通の見開きの用紙の左右にそれぞれ印刷して出すことがあります。

1. Departing letters are sent to persons to whom you are indebted in your work and those with whom you have worked closely.

2. These letters should be sent before leaving your post, if at all possible; however, if this cannot be done, send them as soon as you can after you arrive at your new position.

3. Include information about your new position and responsibilities. Express your appreciation for the recipient's help, while also introducing your successor and requesting their continuing support of him or her.

4. Sometimes the departing letter for the person leaving and the introductory letter for the successor are printed on facing halves of the same sheet of paper.

1-4 ファックスで名刺(めいし)の印刷を注文する
Ordering the printing of business cards by fax

S&A日本支社の支社長付き秘書はスミス支社長のあいさつ回りに必要な名刺(めいし)を作るために、書体・納期(のうき)などを指定した注文書をファックスで送ります。

The secretary to Mr. Smith, the manager of the Japan Office of S&A Corporation, orders business cards by fax, which the manager will need when making introductory visits to customers. The fax specifies such things as the type of font to be used and the deadline for delivery.

199◯年3月22日

有限会社東京印刷
営業課 武田次郎 殿

S&Aコーポレーション
日本支社 秘書 渡辺美智子（印）

名刺(めいし)作成依頼の件

下記名刺の印刷をお願いします。

記

①印刷見本（両面印刷）

表面

> S&Aコーポレーション日本支社
>
> 支社長 ハワード G. スミス
>
> 〒100-0004 東京都千代田区大手町1-2-1
> 平成ビル8階 801号室
> 電話：03-3211-4567（代）
> FAX：03-3211-0880

裏面
(文字は
イタリック体)

> *S&A Corporation*
>
> *Howard G. Smith*
>
> *Manager, Japan Office*
>
> *Rm. #801, Heisei Bldg.*
> *1-2-1, Otemachi, Chiyoda-ku,*
> *Tokyo 100-0004*
> *Phone: 03-3211-4567*
> *Fax: 03-3211-0880*

②紙質(ししつ)： 白色(はくしょく)上質紙で、なるべく薄手(うすで)のもの
③印刷の色： 黒色(こくしょく)で字が盛(も)り上がって見えるもの
④枚数： 500枚
⑤納期(のうき)： 3月27日(金)まで

本件につき、折り返し確認の連絡をお願いします

以上

有限会社：limited (liability) company　イタリック体：italics　上質紙：high-quality paper　薄手（うすで）：lightweight　盛（も）り上がって見える：stand out　納期（のうき）：delivery date　折り返し：by return (post)

March 22, 199_

Tokyo Printing, Ltd.
Sales Section, Takeda Jiro (Mr.)

S&A Corporation
Japan Office Secretary Michiko Watanabe (seal)

RE: Request for printing business cards

Please print business cards according to the following:

Details

1. Sample for printing (print on both sides)
   Front

   Back (use italics)

2. Paper quality: white high-quality paper, as lightweight as possible
3. Color of ink: black ink that stands out on the page
4. Quantity: 500 cards
5. Delivery date: no later than March 27 (Friday)

Please respond as soon as possible to confirm the details of this order. (the end)

留意事項

1) あいさつ回りには名刺（めいし）の交換が欠かせないので、着任（ちゃくにん）前か着任と同時に新しい名刺を準備します。

2) 名刺の発注（はっちゅう）は、書体、紙質（ししつ）、印刷形式、数量、納期（のうき）など希望する内容を指定します。その際、見本をつけたほうが確実です。

3) 名刺は、日本では自己紹介の際に使われます。相手の氏名の確認のほか、住所や電話・ファックス番号などの記録と、今後の連絡のために非常に便利です。最近は電子メールのアドレスなども書きます。

4) 名刺に社章を型押ししたり、自分の顔写真を貼り付けたりすることがあります。

1. As the exchange of business cards is essential when making introductory visits to customers, new business cards must be prepared either before you assume a new job or as soon as you arrive.

2. Designate font, quality of paper, layout, number of cards needed, and deadline for delivery on the order form. It is best to attach a sample as well.

3. Business cards are customarily used in self-introductions in Japan. They are handy in confirming the name of the person you are meeting, as well as serving as a record of the person's address and phone and fax numbers. Many people now include e-mail addresses.

4. Sometimes the company emblem or your photograph is included on the card.

1-5 着任を祝う電報を打つ
Sending a congratulatory telegram for assuming a new position

S&A社の取引先である山田家具の山田社長は、スミス日本支社長の着任を祝って電報を打ちます。
Mr. Yamada, the president of Yamada Furniture Corporation, one of S&A Corporation's clients, sends a telegram congratulating Mr. Smith on his appointment as office manager of S&A's Japan Office.

トウキョウト　チヨダク　オオテマチ　1-2-1
　エス　アンド　エイ　コーポレーション
　　ニホンシシャチョウ　　エイチ　ジー　スミス　殿

「祝」
　エス　アンド　エイ　コーポレーション　ノ　ニホンシシャチョウ　トシテ　ゴフニン　ノ　オモムキ　ウケタマワリマシタ。オメデトウ　ゴザイマス。
　ニホン　モ　フケイキ　ノ　サイチュウ　デ、ゴショウバイ　ニモ　イロイロ　ゴクロウ　ガ　オオイト　オモイマスガ、ニューヨーク　ホンシャ　デノ　ゴケイケン　ヲ　イカシタ　ジュウオウ　ノ　ゴカツヤク　ト　ゴハッテン　ヲ　ココロカラ　オイノリモウシアゲマス。

ヤマダ　カグ　カブシキガイシャ
シャチョウ　ヤマダ　エイサク

〔漢字電報の例〕

東京都　千代田区　大手町　1-2-1
　S&Aコーポレーション
　　日本支社長　H. G. スミス　殿
「祝」
　S&Aコーポレーションの日本支社長としてご赴任の趣承りました。おめでとうございます。
　日本も不景気の最中で、ご商売にもいろいろご苦労が多いと思いますが、ニューヨーク本社でのご経験を生かした縦横のご活躍とご発展を心からお祈り申し上げます。

山田家具株式会社
社長　　山田栄作

赴任：assuming a new position　～の趣：to the effect that ～　苦労が多い：many difficulties　～を生かす：make use of ～；put ～ to use　縦横の活躍：wide range of activities

Tokyo-to, Chiyoda-ku, Otemachi 1-2-1
S&A Corporation
Japan Office Manager H. G. Smith (Mr.)

"Congratulations"
I received the message concerning your appointment as Japan Office Manager of S&A Corporation. Congratulations.
With Japan now in the midst of a recession, I imagine you will experience many difficulties in your business, but I pray that you will be able to put your experience in the New York office to use to bring about an expansion of activities and new business development.

Yamada Furniture Corporation
President Yamada Eisaku

留意事項

1) 本来はお祝いやお悔やみは文書にしたほうがていねいですが、最近はほとんどが電報で行われるようになりました。電報には目的に応じた特別の図柄の用紙や封筒が用意されています。電報は配達日時の指定ができます。

2) 通常の電報は字数を少なくするために簡潔な表現の文にしますが、祝電や弔電は十分にこちらの気持ちが伝わるように、普通の手紙文のような省略のない文章とします。ただ、時候のあいさつは除きます。

3) 最近はレタックスといって、出した人の書いた字体や絵などがそのまま相手に届けられるファックス形式の電報や、通常はカタカナである電報を漢字交じりの電文とする漢字電報もあります。レタックスは、郵便局から出しますが、カタカナ電報や漢字電報はNTTに電話でも受け付けてもらうことができます。

4) 電話で電文を伝えるときは、同じ発音で意味が違うことば「同音異義語」がありますので、注意が必要です。

1. Originally, it was considered more polite to send handwritten letters of congratulations or condolence, but recently almost all such messages are sent by telegram. Special paper and envelopes are used for telegrams, depending on the purpose of the letter. The date and time for delivery of the telegrams can be specified.

2. To keep the length of a regular telegram to a minimum, concise expressions are used; in the case of congratulatory or condolence telegrams, however, you may use ordinary sentence forms. Please note that season-related greetings should be omitted.

3. Recently, a new type of telegram called a lettax, a hybrid letter-fax, has become available, in which messages and pictures prepared by the sender can be transmitted as they are. Telegrams are usually sent using *katakana*, but there are also telegrams that now include both kanji and kana. You must go to a post office to send a lettax, but *katakana* and kanji telegrams can be sent by telephoning the NTT office.

4. When sending a telegram by phone, it is important to remember that confusion can occur because many words in Japanese sound the same but have different meanings.

社外 確認する〈注文請書〉 confirmation of an order

1-6 名刺印刷の受注を確認する

Confirming the receipt of an order for business cards

東京印刷はS&A日本支社から支社長の名刺の印刷の注文を受けて、その確認のため注文請書を作成します。

Tokyo Printing received an order from S&A Corporation's Japan Office for the manager's business cards and sent back a written acknowledgment to confirm the receipt of the order.

注 文 請 書

平成○年３月22日

エス アンド エイ コーポレーション
日 本 支 社 (秘 書) 御 中

〒103-0000 東京都 中央区 八重洲 3-5-1
☎ 03-3804-7911
FAX 03-3804-7910
有 限 会 社 東 京 印 刷
営 業 課 (印)

御社よりの平成○年３月22日付のご注文書記載のご注文を下記の通りお請け致しました。

記

1) ご注文用紙： 松印 1号 名刺 (特漉薄手上質紙 白地)
2) 枚数： 500枚
3) 字体： 英文はイタリック
4) 納期： 平成○年３月27日 (金)
5) お見積金額： 金15,000円也 (単価 金3,000円／100枚)
6) その他： 黒刷り、両面、特急仕上、浮き出し印刷
その他 貴見本の通り

以 上

注文請書：acknowledgment of an order　有限会社：limited (liability) company　記載：description　特漉：specially made (paper)　薄手：lightweight　上質紙：high-quality paper　字体：font　納期：delivery date　見積金額：estimated cost　也：(used after price figures)　単価：unit price　浮き出し印刷：embossed print

Acknowledgment of an order

Date (year, March 22)

S&A Corporation
Messrs. Japan Office (Secretary)

103-0000 Tokyo-to, Chuo-ku, Yaesu 3-5-1
TEL: 03-3804-7911
FAX: 03-3804-7910
Tokyo Printing, Ltd.
Business Department (seal)

We received your order dated March 22, 199_, with the following specifications:

1. Paper quality: Matsu Brand #1, business card paper (high-quality, lightweight, specially made paper, white)
2. Quantity: 500 cards
3. Font: use italics on English
4. Deadline: March 27, 199_ (Friday)
5. Estimated cost: 15,000 yen (unit price: 3,000 yen per 100 cards)
6. Other: print in black, on both sides, special (fast) order, embossed print
   The rest as in your sample.

(the end)

留意事項

1)大切な注文を受けた場合、間違いのないよう、請書(うけしょ)を書いて注文の内容と条件や仕様(しよう)などの確認をします。この文書は名刺の受注(じゅちゅう)の簡単なものの請書の例ですが、大きな規模の印刷や工事の受注には、必ず細部まで確認するための請書を書きます。

1. When receiving an important order, always confirm the contents, terms, and specifications of the order with a written acknowledgment. This example is a simple acknowledgment of the business card order, but when writing one for a large-scale printing job or construction project, it is absolutely vital to write clearly and in detail.

1-7 名刺(めいし)の納入(のうにゅう)代金の請求書(せいきゅう)を書く

Writing an invoice requesting payment for business cards

東京印刷は注文された名刺(めいし)の納入(のうにゅう)と同時に、代金の請求書(せいきゅう)を提出します。

Tokyo Printing submits an invoice for payment when they deliver the business cards.

<u>請(せい)　求(きゅう)　書</u>

平成○年 3 月 27 日

エス　アンド　エイ　コーポレーション

日　本　支　社　(秘　書)　御(おん)　中(ちゅう)

〒103-0000　東京都　中央区　八重州 3-5-1

☎　03-3804-7911

FAX　03-3804-7910

有　限　会　社　東　京　印　刷

代表取締役(とりしまりやく)　只　野　三　平 (印)

(経理課)

金　壱(いち)　万　五　千　円　也(なり)

但(ただ)し、平成○年 3 月 27 日納入名刺(のうにゅうめいし) 500 枚代金として

(特急、特漉薄手(とくすきうすで)上質紙、浮(う)き出し印刷)

①お支払期日：　平成○年 4 月末日

②お支払方法：　松竹梅銀行丸ノ内支店　普通預金口座

×××－××××××××　振込

上記金額をご請求申し上げます

以　上

有限会社：limited (liability) company　壱(いち)：one　也(なり)：(used after price figures)　但(ただ)し～代金として：for ～ costs　特漉(とくすき)：specially made (paper)　薄手(うすで)：lightweight　上質紙：high-quality paper　浮(う)き出し印刷：embossed print　支払期日：payment due date　普通預金口座：ordinary account　振込：transfer

Invoice

Date (year, March 27)

S&A Corporation
Messrs. Japan Office (Secretary)

103-0000 Tokyo-to, Chuo-ku, Yaesu 3-5-1
TEL: 03-3804-7911
FAX: 03-3804-7910
Tokyo Printing, Ltd.
Representative Director, Tadano Sanpei (seal)
Accounting Department

Fifteen thousand yen
for 500 business cards delivered March 27, 199_ [special (rush) order; high quality, thin (lightweight), specially-made paper, embossed printing]
(1)Payment due: last day of April, 199_
(2)Payment method: Deposit in Shochikubai Bank, Marunouchi Branch, Ordinary Account, Account Number xxx-xxxxxxx

This serves as an invoice for the above amount.

(the end)

留意事項

1) 請求書(せいきゅうしょ)は、納品(のうひん)と同時、または納品後に提出します。
2) 請求書には、いつ納入(のうにゅう)した何の代金かを明示します。
3) 支払いの方法について、期日や振り込みの銀行口座など代金決済(けっさい)に必要な事項を書きます。現金で支払いを受けるときは、支払い期限のみ書きます。
4) 請求書は、大きな組織では特に、金銭出納(きんせんすいとう)の事務手続きのために必要となります。小口(こぐち)現金決済のときは、請求書は省略(しょうりゃく)して、1-8の例のような領収書(りょうしゅうしょ)ですませることがあります。

1. An invoice is submitted to the party placing the order either at the same time the merchandise is delivered or immediately afterward.
2. The invoice specifies when the order was delivered and what money is owed.
3. With respect to the method of payment, all information needed for settling the payment, such as deadline and bank account number, is included on the invoice. When receiving cash for the order, the deadline alone is written.
4. Especially when the party placing the order is a large organization, invoices are necessary for the office handling of money. When settling small amounts of cash, the invoice is omitted and the account is simply settled with a receipt, as in example 1-8.

社外 領収書 receipt

1-8 名刺の代金の領収書を書く

Writing a receipt for payment of business cards

東京印刷は支払いを受けた名刺の代金の領収書（受領書）を発行します。

Tokyo Printing issues a receipt upon receiving payment for business cards.

領　収　書

平成○年4月30日

エス　アンド　エイ　コーポレーション
日　本　支　社　御　中

〒103-0000　東京都　中央区　八重州 3-5-1
☎　03-3804-7911
FAX　03-3804-7910
有　限　会　社　東　京　印　刷
代表取締役　只　野　三　平（印）

金　壱　万　五　千　円　也

但し、平成○年3月27日納入名刺500枚代金として

上記金額正に領収致しました

以　上

有限会社：limited (liability) company　壱：one　也：(used after price figures)
但し～代金として：for ～ costs　正に：correctly

Receipt

Date (year, April 30)

S&A Corporation
Messrs. Japan Office

103-0000 Tokyo-to, Chuo-ku, Yaesu 3-5-1
TEL: 03-3804-7911
FAX: 03-3804-7910
Tokyo Printing, Ltd.
Representative Director Tadano Sanpei (seal)

Fifteen thousand yen

The above correctly received in payment for 500 business cards delivered March 27, 199_
(the end)

留意事項

1) 金銭(きんせん)の受け取りは「受領(じゅりょう)書」(確かに受け取ったということを証する書類)ともいいますが、「領収(りょうしゅう)書」(または「領収証」)が一般的表現です。物品の場合は「受領書」の表現が用いられ、同じ様式で書かれます。

2) 領収書は、代金と引き替えに、入金した日付で発行します。

3) 領収書・受領書には、何の代金か、何の受け取りかを明示します。

4) 領収書は、支払った側では経理と税務(ぜいむ)処理上絶対必要な書類です。

1. Although we also call the receipt of a payment "受領(じゅりょう)書" (a document proving that you have received payment), the general term is "領収(りょうしゅう)書" (or "領収証"). However, in the case of receipt of goods, the former is used.

2. The receipt is directly exchanged for payment, and it notes the date payment was received.

3. An explanation of what the payment is for and what has been received is clearly stated on the receipt.

4. Receipts are documents essential to the party making payment for accounting and tax purposes.

第2課

業務が始まり取引先を探す

Starting a business and looking for business associates

新しい支店を開設したり、新しい業務を始めたり、取引先を探したりする場合、その方面のことをよく知っている人や会社を紹介してもらってから行動したほうが効果的なことがあります。

紹介には、文書で紹介してもらう場合と紹介する旨を簡単に名刺などに書いてもらう場合があります。もらった紹介状は、アポイントを求める文書に添付して送る場合と面会するときに持参する場合とがあります。依頼を受けた人が先方に電話でその旨を伝えて紹介するという簡単な方法もありますが、この課では文書と名刺による紹介の仕方を学びます。

Before opening a new office or business, or finding companies to do business with, asking someone to introduce you to a person or company well acquainted with the field is an effective move.

There are cases where you will ask that person to introduce you through a letter or by asking him/her to write simply the purpose of the introduction on a business card, etc. In some instances, you will send the letter of introduction attached with a letter asking for an appointment, and, in other instances, you will take it with you when you meet. Another simple method is for the person receiving the request for an introduction to communicate the purpose of the introduction by telephone, but in this section we will learn how to make that introduction by means of letters and business cards.

2-1 新規取引先の紹介を依頼する

Requesting an introduction to new business associates

インテリア・家具会社のS&A社日本支社は新しい支社長のスミスを迎えて、新規開拓の仕事を始めました。スミスは、知り合いである東京商事の小川部長に、カーペットの拡販に力となる販売代理店を紹介してもらいたいと、依頼状を書きます。

The Japan Office of S&A Corporation, an American furniture and home furnishings company, has just welcomed Mr. Smith as its new manager, and has started to develop a new business. Mr. Smith writes to his acquaintance, Mr. Ogawa, a manager at Tokyo Shoji, asking him to introduce a sales agent, which would strengthen his company's attempts to increase carpet sales.

199○年○月○日

東京商事株式会社
　営業部長　小　川　　正　殿

S&Aコーポレーション
日本支社長　H. G. スミス（印）

新規取引先ご紹介方ご依頼の件

拝啓　陽春の候、ますますご清祥のこととお喜び申し上げます。いつも格別のご厚情を賜り、誠にありがとうございます。

さて、先日お話し申し上げました通り、弊社は目下、新製品「デュクロン」の拡販のため適当な提携先を求めておりますが、あいにく日本の市場には不慣れなため、どこが適当か判断がつきかねております。

つきましては、貴社の幅広いご交際先の中から日本地区におけるカーペットの販売代理店として優良な企業をご紹介いただけますよう、ぜひお願い申し上げます。

ご紹介先につきましては、ご一報いただければ、お伺いいたしまして細部のお話を承りたく存じます。

ご多用のところ、誠に勝手なお願いを申し上げまして恐縮ですが、何分ともよろしくお願いいたします。

また、ご参考までに、弊社のパンフレットその他の資料を同封させていただきました。

まずは書中ご依頼申し上げます。

敬具

同封物：1　S&Aコーポレーション　会社概要　3部
　　　　2　製品カタログ　3部

以上

新規：new　～方：regarding ～　目下：now　拡販：expansion sales　適当な提携先：appropriate company with which to tie up　あいにく：unfortunately　不慣れ：lack of experience　判断がつきかねる：not be able to judge　幅広い交際先：wide association (with other companies)　販売代理店：sales agent　ご一報いただく：contact (me)　参考までに：for your reference　同封する：include　概要：profile

---

Date (year, month, day)

Tokyo Shoji, Incorporated
Sales Department Manager Ogawa Tadashi (Mr.)

S&A Corporation
Japan Office Manager Howard G. Smith (seal)

RE: Request for introduction to new business associates

Salutations: Allow me to congratulate you on your good health and well-being as the sun brightens each spring day. I thank you deeply for always showing me kindness.

And now, as I mentioned in our conversation the other day, our company is looking for an appropriate company with which to tie up to expand our sale of a new product called Dukelon, but unfortunately we are inexperienced in the Japanese market and not able to make a judgment as to who might be appropriate.

Knowing that you have extensive association with companies in Japan, I am therefore writing to request that you recommend a top-rated sales agent for carpets.

If you will contact me, I will be happy to visit you and receive detailed information regarding the company to which you are going to introduce us.

I am sorry to trouble you with this selfish request when I know you are extremely busy, but I would appreciate any assistance you can give.

I am including here copies of my company's pamphlets and other introductory materials for your reference.

I am first putting this request in writing.

Sincerely yours

Enclosures: 1. Profile of S&A Corporation (3 copies)
2. Product catalog (3 copies)

(the end)

留意事項

1) 依頼するときは、目的、背景、依頼する内容、希望条件など、先方がどのような相手を紹介すればよいのかの判断の基準となる要件を明確に書きます。

2) あくまでも、先方の好意による紹介を求めるのですから、文章もていねいな表現で書きます。

1. When writing a request like this, provide a clear description of purpose, background, contents of the request, and desired conditions so that the other party will have enough criteria to assist them in deciding who to recommend.

2. Remember that your request for a rec-

3) 先方が依頼に応じて検討しやすいように、こちらの会社の概要や製品を説明する資料など必要なものを添付します。「同封物」「添付資料」などと書いて添付物の内容とその数量など明細を記します。簡単な資料のときは、単に「同封物あり」などとだけ書くことがあります。

4) 一方的に先方の好意に頼る場合は、文中に「再度お願いする」と書くことがあります。これは、先方の業務に関係しない依頼や上位者に対する依頼で特別に迷惑や手間をかけるときに、こちらがこのようなお願いをして非常に恐縮しているという姿勢を示すとともに、こちらの希望がそれだけ強いことを印象づける効果があります。

5) 軽い依頼や先方にあまり負担をかけないような依頼、先方の職務の一部に属する依頼、当方との取り引きに関係した依頼、親しい間柄での依頼などのときは「再度依頼する」ということばは必要ありません。

ommendation is wholly dependent on the goodwill of the other party, so use polite expressions.

3. To make it easier for the other party to decide how to respond to your request, include a brief profile of your company and materials explaining your products. When enclosing materials, indicate such in your letter by writing 同封物 (enclosures) or 添付資料 (attachments), along with an explanation, including how many of each is enclosed. When enclosing simple documents, you may write only 同封物あり (enclosures included).

4. When you are making a completely one-sided request, there are times when you should include an extra “please” in your letter. When it is a request not directly related to the other party’s work, or when the other party is of a higher rank than you, especially when your request will cause an inconvenience or take extra time and effort, you should exhibit a proper recognition of the obligation. This will also be effective in strengthening the impression your request makes.

5. It is not necessary to write a second “please” in letters of request when the request is a simple one, or when it is related to one part of the other party’s job, or when related to dealings between you and the other party, or when you are close to the other party.

社外　依頼する　request

2-2 取引先を指定して、紹介を依頼する
Choosing business associates and requesting introductions

S&A社のスミス日本支社長は、カーペットの拡販にあたりいろいろな情報から吉田物産と提携したいと考えています。スミスは、吉田物産の山田部長を知ってはいますが、あまり親しくありません。そこで、以前から親しい東京商事の小川部長に、自分を山田部長に紹介してほしいと依頼します。

Mr. Smith, manager of the Japan Office of S&A Corporation, in his desire to expand carpet sales, thinks from what he has heard that he'd like to link up with Yoshida Trading. He is acquainted with Mr. Yamada, the manager of Yoshida Trading, but he does not know him very well. He therefore asks Mr. Ogawa, an old acquaintance and manager of Tokyo Shoji, for an introduction to Mr. Yamada.

総第○○○号
平成○年○月○日

東京商事株式会社
　営業部長　小川　正　殿

S&Aコーポレーション
日本支社　支社長　　(英文サイン)
(Howard G. Smith)

新規取引先のご紹介につきご依頼の件

拝啓　時下いよいよご清祥のことと大慶に存じます。
　平素は格別のお引立てをいただきまして、ありがたく御礼申し上げます。
　さて、先日は貴社をお訪ねいたしまして、５年ぶりに貴台のお元気なご様子に接し、懐かしく、また心強く存じました。今後とも公私にわたりご厚情のほど、改めてお願い申し上げます。
　その節お話し申し上げましたが、弊社は、インテリア、特にカーペットの新製品「デュクロン」の極東での販売拡大を当面の全社的目標としております。
　この間、調査・検討の結果、現在弊社としては、有力な新規取引先として吉田物産とカーペットの取り引きを望んで参りました。実は、吉田物産の山田営業部長とは、貴社のシスコのパーティの席上で名刺交換をしたことがあります。ただ、あまり深いお付き合いはありませんでした。
　そこで、この際、貴台のお力添えにより、山田部長に対し弊社をご紹介願えれば、まことに幸いに存じます。
　ご参考までに、弊社の会社案内など同封ご送付させていただきました。

　なお、よろしければ、ご紹介のご名刺をいただきに参上いたしますので、ご連絡下さいますよう重ねてお願い申し上げます。　敬具

(添付書類)	1．会社案内パンフレット	3部
	2．各製品カタログ	3部

以上

新規：new　貴台：you　～に接する：see ～; meet ～　公私にわたり：in both official and private affairs　厚情のほど：your kindness　極東での販売拡大：sales increase in East Asia　当面の全社的目標：company's overall objective at this time　有力な：influential　～の席上：on the occasion of ～　力添えにより：with (your) help　参考までに：for your reference　同封：include　参上する：visit　添付書類：attached documents

General Document #______
Date (year, month, day)

Tokyo Shoji, Incorporated
Sales Department Manager Ogawa Tadashi (Mr.)

S&A Corporation
Japan Office Manager (signature in English)
(Howard G. Smith)

RE: Request for introduction of new distributor

Salutations: Allow me to congratulate you on your good health and well-being at this time.

I want to express my deep appreciation for your constant and special support.

Seeing how healthy you were the other day and meeting again after five years had gone by filled me with nostalgia as well as encouragement. I request your continued kindness on both an official and personal basis.

When we met, I mentioned that our company's overall objective at this time is to increase the sale of home furnishings, especially our new carpet, Dukelon, in East Asia.

As a result of investigation and study, our company would like to establish a business relationship with the influential Yoshida Trading at this time, as a new distributor for our carpets. Actually, I met and exchanged business cards with Mr. Yamada, the Sales Department Manager of Yoshida Trading, at your party in San Francisco. I have not, however, had any close dealings with him.

This is why I would be grateful now if you could help me by introducing my company to Manager Yamada.

For your information, I am enclosing my company profile, etc.

If it is convenient, I would like to visit you to obtain one of your business cards, which will introduce me, so I also request that you inform me whether this would be possible or not.

Sincerely yours

Attached documents: 1. Company pamphlet (3 copies)
2. Product catalogs (3 copies)

(the end)

留意事項

1) 紹介してもらいたい相手が、名刺交換をした程度の間柄であまり親しくない相手のときは、双方を知る第三者に紹介をしてもらってから会ったほうが相手も安心しますし、ビジネス上の話もしやすくなります。

2) この手紙のように紹介を依頼する相手と自分が個人的に親しければ、「懐かしく、また心強く存じました」のように、堅苦しくない親しみをこめた表現を加えることも効果的です。

3) 終わりのあいさつや初めのあいさつは、必ず書かなければならないものとは限りません。簡略化したり省略することがあります。特に親しい間柄では、堅苦しさを避けることもあって、表現はていねいでも文章の構成は、すべてのパターンを踏まずに書くことがあります。

4) 紹介を依頼することは大事なことがらですから、紹介の依頼には改まって出向いてお願いするか、出向くことができないときは書状で依頼することになります。書状によることのことわりは、特に親しい間柄などでは、その記載を省略することがあります。

1. At times when you are not so well acquainted with the person to whom you would like to be introduced, or you only know him/her from a time when business cards were exchanged, getting a third party, who is acquainted with both sides, to make the introduction will not only put the other party at ease but also help the ensuing business talks go more smoothly.

2. If, as in the case of this letter, you are a personal friend of the person from whom you are requesting an introduction, you may add an informal friendly phrase like, "I am filled with nostalgia as well as encouragement."

3. It is not always necessary to write opening and closing greetings. There are times when simplification and omission are used, especially when the other party is someone you know well; in order to avoid formality, even when polite expressions are used, write the letter without just going through the whole pattern of letter composition.

4. Since requesting an introduction is an important matter, either go out formally and make the request, or, if that is not possible, make the request by letter. In cases where the other person is particularly well known to you, an apology for writing the request by letter can be omitted.

2-1と2-2のフローと文例

2-1「新規取引先の紹介を依頼する」のフロー

新規取引先ご紹介方ご依頼の件

拝啓　陽春の候、ますますご清祥のこととお喜び申し上げます。いつも格別のご厚情を賜り、誠にありがとうございます。

さて、先日お話し申し上げました通り、弊社は目下、新製品「デュクロン」の拡販のため適当な提携先を求めておりますが、あいにく日本の市場には不慣れなため、どこが適当か判断がつきかねております。

①紹介を依頼するいきさつを説明する

つきましては、貴社の幅広いご交際先の中から日本地区におけるカーペットの販売代理店として優良な企業をご紹介いただけますよう、ぜひお願い申し上げます。

②紹介を依頼する

ご紹介先につきましては、ご一報いただければ、お伺いいたしまして細部のお話を承りたく存じます。

③連絡方法を知らせる

ご多用のところ、誠に勝手なお願いを申し上げまして恐縮ですが、何分ともよろしくお願いいたします。

⑤再度、依頼する

また、ご参考までに、弊社のパンフレットその他の資料を同封させていただきました。

④同封書類の案内をする

まずは書中ご依頼申し上げます。

敬具

同封物：1　S&Aコーポレーション　会社概要　3部
　　　　2　製品カタログ　3部

以上

2-2「取引先を指定して、紹介を依頼する」のフロー

新規取引先のご紹介につきご依頼の件

拝啓　時下いよいよご清祥のことと大慶に存じます。

平素は格別のお引立てをいただきまして、ありがたく御礼申し上げます。

さて、先日は貴社をお訪ねいたしまして、5年ぶりに貴台のお元気なご様子に接し、懐かしく、また心強く存じました。今後とも公私にわたりご厚情のほど、改めてお願い申し上げます。

その節お話し申し上げましたが、弊社は、インテリア、特にカーペットの新製品「デュクロン」の極東での販売拡大を当面の全社的目標としております。

この間、調査・検討の結果、現在弊社としては、有力な新規取引先として吉田物産とカーペットの取り引きを望んで参りました。実は、吉田物産の山田営業部長とは、貴社のシスコのパーティの席上で名刺交換をしたことがあります。ただ、あまり深いお付き合いはありませんでした。

①紹介を依頼するいきさつを説明する

そこで、この際、貴台のお力添えにより、山田部長に対し弊社をご紹介願えれば、まことに幸いに存じます。

②紹介を依頼する

ご参考までに、弊社の会社案内など同封ご送付させていただきました。——④同封書類の案内をする

なお、よろしければ、ご紹介のご名刺をいただきに参上いたしますので、ご連絡下さいますよう重ね（かさ）てお願い申し上げます。——③連絡方法を知らせる

敬具

（添付（てんぷ）書類）　1．会社案内パンフレット　3部

2．各製品カタログ　3部

以上

（下線の部分は自分の状況に合わせて書いてください。）

①紹介を依頼するいきさつを説明する

Explaining the reason for the request for an introduction

②紹介を依頼する

Requesting an introduction

＊貴社の幅広いご交際先の中から日本地区におけるカーペットの販売代理店として優良な企業をご紹介いただけますよう、ぜひお願い申し上げます。(2-1)

Knowing that you have extensive associations with companies in Japan, I am therefore writing to request that you recommend a top-rated sales agent for carpets.

＊貴台（きだい）のお力添（ちからぞ）えにより、山田部長に対し弊社（へいしゃ）をご紹介願えれば、まことに幸（さいわ）いに存じます。(2-2)

I would be grateful if you could help me by introducing my company to Manager Yamada.

＊貴社お取引先の中から、私どもの販売提携（ていけい）代理先として適当な企業をご紹介頂（いただ）きたくお願い申し上げます。

I am writing to you to request that you introduce us to an appropriate company among your customers who could act as a distributor for us.

③連絡方法を知らせる

Notifying of contact procedures

＊ご紹介先につきましては、ご一報（いっぽう）いただければ、お伺（うかが）いいたしまして細部のお話を承（うけたまわ）りたく存じます。(2-1)

If you will contact me, I will be happy to visit you and receive detailed information regarding the company to which you are going to introduce us.

＊よろしければ、ご紹介のご名刺（めいし）をいただきに参上いたしますので、ご連絡下さいますよう重（かさ）ねてお願い申し上げます。(2-2)

If it is convenient, I would like to visit you to obtain one of your business cards, which will introduce me, so I also request that you inform me whether this would be possible or not.

＊お電話いただければ、お伺（うかが）いし、ご紹介先につきお話をお聞かせいただきたく存じます。

If you would please telephone me, I will be happy to visit you to learn about the company being introduced.

④同封書類の案内をする

Explaining enclosed documents

＊ご参考までに、弊社(へいしゃ)のパンフレットその他の資料を同封させていただきました。(2-1)

I am including here copies of my company's pamphlets and other introductory materials for your reference.

＊ご参考までに、弊社(へいしゃ)の会社案内など同封ご送付(そうふ)させていただきました。(2-2)

For your information, I am enclosing my company profile, etc.

＊同封資料をご参考までにお送り申し上げました。

I am sending the enclosed documents for your reference.

⑤再度、依頼する

Repeating the request

＊ご多用のところ、誠(まこと)に勝手なお願いを申し上げまして恐縮(きょうしゅく)ですが、何分ともよろしくお願いいたします。(2-1)

I am sorry to trouble you with this selfish request when I know you are extremely busy, but I would appreciate any assistance you can give.

＊手前勝手(てまえがって)なお願いではございますが、何分のご高配(こうはい)を賜(たまわ)りたくお願い申し上げます。

I know this is a selfish request, but I would appreciate any help you can give.

＊お手数をおかけして恐(おそ)れ入りますが、なにとぞよろしくお願いいたします。

I am sorry to trouble you, but I would appreciate your assistance.

2-3 紹介の依頼に対して、取引先を推薦(すいせん)する

Responding to a request to recommend business associates

東京商事の小川部長は、以前から親しいS&A日本支社長のスミスからカーペットの販売代理店を紹介してほしいとの依頼を受けました。そこで、適当な販売提携候補(ていけいこうほ)の企業を推薦(すいせん)する手紙を書きます。

Manager Ogawa of Tokyo Shoji received a request from Mr. Smith, an old acquaintance who is now manager of the Japan Office of S&A Corporation, to introduce to him a sales agent for carpets. Mr. Ogawa writes a letter recommending an appropriate candidate.

199◯年◯月◯日

S&Aコーポレーション
日本支社長　ハワード　G. スミス　殿

東京商事株式会社
営業部長　小　川　　正（印）

インテリア製品の販売提携(ていけい)先ご紹介の件

冠省(かんしょう)

先般来(せんぱんらい)ご依頼を受けておりました貴社インテリア製品の日本における販売提携先についていろいろ検討の結果、候補(こうほ)として次の3社をご推薦致(すいせんいた)したく。

①株式会社　インテックス
〒176-0003　東京都　練馬区　羽沢 5-5-8
☎ 03-2339-6101
資本金：5,000万円
売上高(だか)：12億円
従業員：80名
担当：営業部長　　高橋　吉男

②高島インテリア株式会社
〒130-0021　東京都　墨田区　緑 5-6-3
☎ 03-6634-0261
資本金：1,500万円
売上高：7億円
従業員：10名

担当：業務部長　森田　稔

③吉田物産株式会社

〒150-0000　東京都　渋谷区　青山 6-1-2

☎03-3716-9042

資本金：１億 4,000万円

売上高：107億 5,000万円

従業員：120名

担当：営業部長　山田　栄三

各社の特徴は、

①「㈱インテックス」は中堅のインテリア関係の会社で、主として東北、北海道方面に実績を持っています。どちらかと言うと、家具に強いと言えましょう。

②「高島インテリア㈱」は、小粒で従業員も少ないですが、小回りが利いて東京地区ではなかなかの実績を持っております。

③「吉田物産㈱」は、規模も陣容も揃った会社で、インテリア、家具双方に幅広い活動と国内全域に実績を持っております。

いずれもそれぞれの特徴を持ち、日本に新しい販売網の展開を志す貴社の良い伴侶となりましょう。

提携条件については、各社それぞれの要求があることと存じますので、コンタクトの上、貴社の要望に沿う社をご選定になりますよう申し添えます。

まずは、ご連絡まで。　当用のみ。

草　々

販売提携先：sales associate　先般来：recently　中堅：mid-size　～関係：～related　主として：especially; mainly　～方面：region of ～　実績を持っている：have good results　小粒：small (company)　小回りが利く：versatile; flexible　なかなかの～：quite ～　規模：scale　陣容が揃う：have a number of good staffers　双方：both　幅広い活動：extensive activity　いずれも：any (of the companies)　販売網の展開：developing a sales network　志す：aim　良い伴侶：good partner　提携条件：conditions of a tie-up　コンタクトの上：after contacting　要望に沿う：meet demands　ご選定になる：choose; select　申し添える：additionally ask/say

Date (year, month, day)

S&A Corporation
Japan Office Manager Howard G. Smith (Mr.)

Tokyo Shoji, Incorporated
Sales Department Manager Ogawa Tadashi (seal)

RE: Introduction of possible home furnishings distributor with whom to tie up

I hasten to inform you of the following:

After careful consideration of your recent request for possible home furnishings distributors with whom your company might establish a relationship to pursue sales in Japan, I have decided to recommend the following three companies:

1. Intex, Incorporated
   176-0003 Tokyo-to, Nerima-ku, Hanezawa 5-5-8
   TEL: 03-2339-6101
   Capital investment: 50 million yen
   Sales: 1.2 billion yen
   Number of employees: 80 persons
   Person responsible: Sales Department Manager Takahashi Yoshio

2. Takashima Interior, Incorporated
   130-0021 Tokyo-to, Sumida-ku, Midori 5-6-3
   TEL: 03-6634-0261
   Capital investment: 15 million yen
   Sales: 700 million yen
   Number of employees: 10 persons
   Person responsible: Business Director Morita Minoru

3. Yoshida Trading, Incorporated
   150-0000 Tokyo-to, Shibuya-ku, Aoyama 6-1-2
   TEL: 03-3716-9042
   Capital investment: 140 million yen
   Sales: 10.75 billion yen
   Number of employees: 120 persons
   Person responsible: Sales Department Manager Yamada Eizo

Characteristics of each company:

1. Intex, Inc., is a mid-sized home furnishings company showing good results, especially in the Tohoku and Hokkaido regions. It is, if anything, a little stronger in the furniture line.
2. Takashima Interior, Inc., is a small company with only a few employees, but it is versatile and has performed quite well in the Tokyo area.
3. Yoshida Trading, Inc., is a sizable company and has a number of good staffers, with extensive activity in both furniture and home furnishings, showing good performance in all regions of the country.

Anyway, each of the companies, with its special characteristics, would make a good partner for you, as you aim to develop a new sales network in Japan.

As each of the companies has its own demands with respect to conditions for a tie-up, I ask you to make your selection after contacting them to see if they fit your specifications.

To begin, I am providing you with this information for your immediate use.

Sincerely yours

留意事項

1) 事務的な返事なので、初めのあいさつなどは省略(しょうりゃく)します。

2) 求めに応じて会社を紹介したり推薦(すいせん)したりするときは、企業規模(きぼ)や経営内容などその企業の大体の様子がわかる資料といっしょに、紹介・推薦する理由を添(そ)えて回答します。

3) 紹介あるいは推薦した企業には「紹介をした」「推薦をした」ということを連絡するのが礼儀(れいぎ)です。その際には、なるべく推薦した理由や相手企業の状況と資料を添付(てんぷ)して連絡します。

4) 本文の前に書く季節のあいさつや慶賀(けいが)のことばは、親しい間柄(あいだがら)や同じ用件で何度もやり取りする場合では省略しますが、そのときは「前略(ぜんりゃく)」「冠省(かんしょう)」などの頭語(とうご)を、「草々(そうそう)」「不一(ふいつ)」などの結語(けつご)と組み合わせて使用します。

5) この手紙のように親しい間柄のときには、「致(いた)したく存じます」の「存じます」を除いた表現を用いることができます。社内文書のときも同様の表現を使うことができます。

1. As this is a business-related reply, an opening greeting may be omitted.

2. When introducing or recommending a company in response to a request, include materials that provide a general idea of the business, such as its size and management style, along with why you are introducing or recommending that business.

3. It is polite to contact companies that you have introduced or recommended to a company, which requested the intoroduction, to inform them of what you have done. At this time, you should include as much information as possible on the reason for the recommendation, adding details on the company and other data.

4. Seasonal greetings or words of congratulations are omitted when you are close to the other person or when you communicate with them repeatedly on the same business matter. Instead of those greetings, you may use salutations like 前略(ぜんりゃく) or 冠省(かんしょう) (I hasten to inform you that . . .) along with complimentary closes such as 草々(そうそう) or 不一(ふいつ) (sincerely yours).

5. When writing to a person with whom you have a close relationship, as in the case of this letter, it is possible to use expressions that do away with such polite words as 存じます of 致したく存じます. You may do the same when writing in-house communications.

2-4 紹介状を書く
Writing letters of introduction

東京商事の小川部長は、S&A社のスミス日本支社長からの紹介してほしいという希望に応じ、吉田物産の山田部長宛(あて)にスミス支社長の紹介状を書きます。

Having received a request for introductions from Mr. Smith, manager of the Japan Office of S&A Corporation, Manager Ogawa of Tokyo Shoji writes a letter of introduction addressed to Mr. Yamada, manager of Yoshida Trading.

199○年○月○日

吉田物産株式会社
　営業部長　山田栄三殿

東京商事株式会社
　営業部長　小川　正（印）

<u>ハワード　G. スミス氏ご紹介の件</u>

拝啓(はいけい)　平素(へいそ)は格段(かくだん)のご愛顧(あいこ)を頂(いただ)きありがとうございます。

さて、S&A社のハワード　G. スミス氏をご紹介申し上げます。同氏は、この程S&A社の日本支社長として赴任(ふにん)されました。スミス氏と私とはアメリカ駐在(ちゅうざい)当時からの知人で、米国では家族ぐるみの付き合いをしていました。

S&A社は、カーペットの製造、販売で著名な会社で、最近新しいカーペットを日本市場で拡販(かくはん)するにあたり、東京に直轄(ちょっかつ)の支社を設(もう)けることになりました。しかし、先日、スミス氏より、日本での知名度(ちめいど)が低いため、提携(ていけい)先を求めたいとの相談を受けました。そこで、支店網(もう)も充実し実力のある貴社を紹介させていただきました。

いずれ、本人より連絡があると思いますので、その節はなにとぞよろしくお願いいたします。

まずは、突然でご迷惑(めいわく)ながら紹介のお知らせまで。

敬具

赴任(ふにん)する：assume a new position　～駐在(ちゅうざい)当時から：since the time (I) was working in ～　家族ぐるみの：with all the family　著名な：famous　拡販(かくはん)する：expand sales　直轄(ちょっかつ)：direct control　設(もう)ける：open; establish　知名度(ちめいど)が低い：not be well known　提携(ていけい)先を求めたい：want to tie up with other companies　支店網(もう)：branch network　充実している：fruitful　いずれ：soon; sometime

Date (year, month, day)

Yoshida Trading, Incorporated
Sales Department Manager Yamada Eizo (Mr.)

Tokyo Shoji, Incorporated
Sales Department Manager Ogawa Tadashi (seal)

RE: Introducing Mr. Howard G. Smith

Salutations: Thank you for your superb, ever-present support.

Now, allow me to introduce Mr. Howard G. Smith of S&A Corporation. Recently, he assumed the responsibility of the Japan Office Manager of S&A Corporation. I got to know Mr. Smith when working in the United States, at which time our families did many things together.

S&A Corporation is famous for the manufacture and sale of carpets. In order to expand sales of a new line of carpet in the Japanese market, it recently opened an office directly controlled in Tokyo. The other day, Mr. Smith came to me asking that I introduce possible companies he might approach, because his company is not well known in Japan. I took the liberty of introducing your company, with its fruitful branch networking system and capabilities.

In any case, I think you will be hearing from him soon, and ask that you kindly listen to his request.

Anyway, I am writing to inform you of my action, realizing that this is a sudden request and that it may interfere with your busy schedule.

Sincerely yours

留意事項

1) このような紹介状は、紹介を依頼した人が紹介先に会うときに持参するか、面談の約束を求める文書に添えて送ります。

2) 紹介状には、紹介する会社または人物がどのような会社・役職の人で、何を求めているかを書きます。また、紹介状を書いた人と紹介状を渡した会社や人との関係についても簡単に触れます。

3) 文書による紹介状はフォーマルなものです。したがって、紹介状を出したほうでも紹介を依頼した人や紹介先に対して、紹介したことについて責任を持つことになります。

1. This type of letter of introduction is either presented to the person being introduced at the time of the meeting or sent with the letter requesting an opportunity to have a meeting.

2. In a letter of introduction, tell something about the company and/or individual, such as what type of company it is or the official position of the individual, and what it is that they are seeking. Briefly mention your relationship with the company or individual.

3. A written introduction is a very formal document. Because of this, the person issuing the letter has an obligation to both the person requesting the introduction and to the one being introduced.

2-5 名刺による紹介状を書く

Writing introductions using business cards

東京商事の小川部長は、吉田物産の山田部長宛の紹介状を名刺に書き込んで、紹介の依頼者であるスミス支社長に渡します。

Manager Ogawa of Tokyo Shoji writes an introduction to Manager Yamada of Yoshida Trading on one of his business cards and gives it to Manager Smith as he requested.

吉田物産(株) 山田営業部長殿
S&A社のスミス支社長をご紹介いたします.
私の古くからの友人です. 新規客先開拓に
意欲を燃やしています.
話をお聞き頂ければ
幸です.

東京商事株式会社

営業部長　小川　正

〒105-0001　東京都港区虎ノ門1-1-8
電話　03-3545-2468
FAX　03-3545-2470

S&A社のスミス支社長をご紹介します.
御社との取引を希望されています.
よろしくご引見下さい.

東京商事株式会社

営業部長　小川　正

6/10

〒105-0001 東京都港区虎ノ門一-一-八
電話 03-三五四五-二四六八
FAX 03-三五四五-二四七〇

吉田物産株式会社
山田営業部長殿

新規客先開拓：development of a new market　意欲を燃やす：eager to do　引見：meet

Yoshida Trading, Incorporated, Sales Department Manager Yamada (Mr.)
Allow me to introduce S&A Corporation's Japan Office Manager Smith. He has been a friend of mine for many years. He is eagerly seeking to develop a new market. I would be grateful if you would listen to his explanation.
(seal) (month, day)

Allow me to introduce Manager Smith of S&A Corporation. He desires to do business with your company. I would appreciate it if you would meet him.
(signiture) (month, day)

Yoshida Trading, Incorporated
Sales Department Manager Yamada (Mr.)

留意事項

1) 名刺による紹介は、急ぐ場合（依頼を受けてその場で書く場合）、簡単に紹介する場合、紹介する人が紹介先と親しい間柄にある場合などに用います。

2) 名刺による紹介は正式な形ではありませんが、紹介の効果は文書による紹介と同じです。ただし、文書の場合は相手が会社・個人のいずれの場合も使えるのに対して、名刺によるときは個人から個人への紹介に用いられるのが普通です。

3) 名刺では書き込みの余白が少ないので、単に「紹介します」とだけ記したり、依頼者の希望を簡単に書いたりするなど、決まった形式はありません。しかし、「誰を紹介するのか」と「宛先」は必ず書き、さらに「どのような希望を持って会いにいくのか」「紹介状の持参者と名刺を書いた本人との関係」などが簡単にでも書いてあると、面談を受けるほうはどのような対応をしたらよいかがわかりやすくなります。宛先は、名刺のわかりやすい場所にはっきり書きます。

4) 名刺には、コメントを書いた月日を記入し、本人が書いた証拠に名刺の自分の名前の下に捺印またはサインをするのが普通です。

5) 名刺は、そのままで依頼者に渡す場合と、名刺用の小封筒に入れて渡す場合とがあります。

1. Introductions using business cards are used when time is of the essence (i.e., when writing at the same time as the request), when a simple introduction will suffice, or when the writer has a close relationship with the person being introduced.

2. Business card introductions are not considered formal, but they can be as effective as formal letters of introduction. Whereas letters may be used in the case of either companies or individuals, business card introductions are usually used only when introducing individuals.

3. Because business cards usually have very little space on which to write, you sometimes simply write "Introduction," or you may include a brief note about the nature of the request. There are no specific rules about what must be included. You must, however, indicate who is being introduced to whom, and if it is possible to include such information as why they seek the interview and how they are related to you, it will be helpful at the time of the interview. Write the addressee's name clearly in a prominent place on the card.

4. Indicate the present date on your business card. You usually affix your seal or signature below your name to show that you wrote the introduction.

5. Sometimes you give the business card directly to the individual requesting it; sometimes you place it in a small envelope before giving it.

第3課

取引先の信用情報を集める

Gathering credit information on possible business associates

ビジネスに必要なさまざまな情報を入手するために、社内や社外に対して問い合わせ、その提供を求めます。その際に使われる文書を照会文といいます。

一般にビジネスの照会文では、取引条件、在庫・入出荷状況、価格、見積りなどの営業関係のほか、市況や景気の見通し、財務・経理などの経営内容、人事、資産など、照会する内容は多岐にわたります。

In order to get various information crucial to your business, it is necessary to make inquiries within and outside the company. The type of letter used at this time is called 照会文(しょうかいぶん) (a letter of inquiry).

Generally, a letter of inquiry for business purposes will be used to investigate various matters, including:

- sales-related matters, such as the conditions of your business, incoming and outgoing stock, prices, and estimates;
- future market and business prospects;
- management contents (financial affairs, accounting, and so on);
- personnel affairs;
- property;

and so on.

社外 問い合わせる〈照会文〉 inquiry

3-1 調査機関に信用状況を問い合わせる

Asking an investigation agency about a credit standing

S&A社では提携にふさわしい会社を選定するため、候補企業の信用状況を調べることになりました。S&A社の山崎調査部長は、調査専門機関である帝国商工リサーチに対して、提携候補の高島インテリア社の信用状況を照会する手紙を書きます。

To enable it to choose a suitable company to tie up with, S&A Corporation decided to collect data on the credit standing of candidates. Mr. Yamazaki, director of S&A Corporation's investigation department, writes a letter to Teikoku Shoko Research inquiring into the credit standing of Takashima Interior, one of the candidates being considered.

調第○○○号
平成○年○月○日

株式会社 帝国商工リサーチ 御中

S&Aコーポレーション日本支社
調査部長 山崎文夫（印）

信用調査ご依頼の件

拝啓 貴社ますますご隆昌の段大慶に存じます。

さて、下記企業に関して、別記事項の調査をお願いします。

敬具

記

1．調査対象：高島インテリア株式会社
〒130-0021 東京都墨田区緑 5-6-3 （☎03-6634-0261）
資本金 1,500万円、 売上高 7億円、 従業員 10名

2．調査事項：
⑴経営者のリーダーシップ、人格、経営組織、経営方針
⑵過去3年の業績、売上高、営業利益、経常利益の推移
⑶今後の業績予想
⑷金融機関との取引状況、同社に対する評価
⑸主な業務取引先、取引実績、同業者間の評価
⑹企業としての特色、取引上の特記留意事項

3．調査報告の提出、支払い：
「特急」扱いとし、調査が済み次第、報告書を提出するとともに、改めて口頭にて補足報告を願いたい。
費用は、先般お打合せのとおり、525,000円（消費税込み）とする。
調査完了後、請求書を当社あて送付のこと。

以上

（写）弊営業部、経理部

別記事項：matters written elsewhere　対象：subject　人格：character　経営方針：management policies　業績：performance; business results　経常利益：ordinary (recurring) profit　推移(すいい)：changes　業績予想：estimated future performance　金融(きんゆう)機関：financial institutions　評価：evaluation　取引実績：business performance　同業者間：among traders in the same field　特記留意事項：special matters of consideration　報告の提出：handing in a report　支払い：payment　～扱いとする：handle as ～　～が済(す)み次第：as soon as ～ is completed　口頭(こうとう)にて：verbally　補足(ほそく)報告：supplementary report　先般(せんぱん)打合せのとおり：as already agreed　消費税込み：consumption tax included　当社あて送付(そうふ)のこと：please send (invoice) to our company

Investigation Document # ＿＿＿＿＿
Date (year, month, day)

Teikoku Shoko Research Corporation
To Whom It May Concern:

S&A Corporation, Japan Office
Investigation Department Manager Yamazaki Fumio (seal)

RE: Request for Credit Check

Salutations: I imagine you are extremely happy with your company's growing prosperity.
Now, I request that you investigate the following items for the company, as shown below.

Sincerely yours

Details

1. Subject of investigation: Takashima Interior, Incorporated
130-0021 Tokyo-to, Sumida-ku, Midori 5-6-3 (TEL: 03-6634-0261)
Capitalization: 15 million yen; Sales: 700 million yen; Number of employees: 10 persons

2. Items to investigate:

(1) Leadership of the management, their character, management structure, management policies
(2) Changes in performance, amount of sales, sales profit, and ordinary profit in the past three years
(3) Projected future performance
(4) Condition of their dealings with financial institutions, their evaluation of the company
(5) Evaluation of major business associates, business performance, and evaluation by other traders in the same field
(6) Special characteristics of their business and special matters of consideration in their dealings

3. Deadline and payment for fees for investigation report:

Please handle this as a rush order and submit a report to us as soon as your investigation is completed. We would also like to ask you for a supplementary verbal report.
As already agreed, we will pay 525,000 yen (consumption tax included).
Please invoice us as soon as you have completed the investigation.

(the end)

Copies: Sales Department, Accounting Department of S&A Corporation

留意事項

1) 調査機関に対してはこちらが客なので、本文の前後のあいさつ的なことばは簡潔な表現としたり、その一部または全部を省略することがあります。

2) 照会することがらは、必要項目を箇条書きで、できるだけ具体的に書きます。一般的に、信用状況の調査は、特定した会社の資本金、会社の履歴、役員の氏名と経歴、営業の内容とその状況や成績、取引先の内容、経理や財務の状況、金融機関や同業者や取引先の評価と評判、今後の見通しなどの項目について行われます。しかし、民間の調査機関では、一般に、あらかじめ定型的な調査項目とその標準的な費用が決められているので、定型パターンによるときは特記事項以外は省略します。外部に依頼するときは、調査の目的や理由を述べてしまうと、企業の意図や方針を明らかにしてしまうので触れません。

3) 調査報告の提出期日を明示します。特に急ぐときは期日の指定をせず、至急報告を求める「特急」などと指定します。

4) 信用調査関係文書は、一般的に関係以外の部署の人には見せてはいけない文書である「部外秘」として取り扱われます。

5) 文書のコピー（写）の配布先は、例のように文章の最後に書く場合、1ページめの左上に書く場合、宛名の下に書く場合など、企業によってさまざまです。

6) 記書きの文章は、「です・ます」調ではなく「である」調で書いてもかまいません。

1. Writing as a customer requesting assistance from an investigation agency, you should use concise expressions in the greeting-type phrases that come before and after the main text of the letter. At times, you may choose to eliminate all or part of these greetings.

2. When making an inquiry, itemize the information you want, being as specific as possible. Generally speaking, an inquiry into credit standing includes the following information about a specific company: capital investments; the company's history; the names and experience of its directors; description of its business, including status and performance; description of business associates; status of accounting and financial affairs; evaluation and reputation of the company by financial institutions, other traders in the same field, and business associates; and projections for the future. When using a private investigation agency, however, categories of inquiry are already set, and standard fees for such inquiries are fixed. Therefore, when using the set pattern, you may omit any special items not on the set list. When making a request outside your company, do not mention the objective of or reason for the investigation, as this would reveal the purpose and policy of the company.

3. The date by which the report is to be submitted should be specified. If you have an order that needs to be done quickly, do not designate a deadline, but designate it as a 特急 (rush order).

4. Documents related to credit status are generally designated as 部外秘(ぶがいひ) (confidential) and are not to be seen by anyone other than the person (or post) concerned.

5. As in this letter, you may note at the end of a letter where copies of it have been sent; this can also be noted in the upper left-hand corner of the first page or below the addressee's name. Different companies follow different practices.

6. You can use the *de aru* (plain) forms of verbs instead of the *desu* and *masu* (polite) forms for the "記書(きが)き" section.

3-2 社内の調査部に信用状況を問い合わせる
Asking your company's investigation department about a credit standing

S&A社の山本営業部長は、提携候補にあがった高島インテリア社に関する信用状況を問い合わせる社内照会文書を書きます。

Mr. Yamamoto, sales department manager of S&A Corporation, writes an in-house memo of inquiry to the investigation department manager, asking them to investigate the credit standing of Takashima Interior, which will help in the selection of a possible business associate.

営第○○○号
平成○年○月○日

調　査　部　長　殿

営　業　部　長　(印)

信用調査の件（依頼）

かねて当部において下記企業に対し取引交渉中のところ、このほど具体的な取引条件の打ち合わせに入ることとなったので、改めて別記事項に関して貴部による調査をお願いいたしたく、よろしくお取り計らい願う。

記

1．調査企業

高島インテリア株式会社

〒130-0021　東京都墨田区緑 5-6-3　（☎03-6634-0261）

2．調査事項

(1)会社組織、経営方針
(2)金融機関との取引状況
(3)インテリア業界での同社の特色、評価
(4)財務諸表の推移、今後の業績見通し
(5)その他特記事項

3．調査期限

○月○日までにお願いしたい。

なお、同社に関し、当部において入手済みの別添資料をご参照願う。

以　上

（添付資料）会社経歴書、会社案内、商品カタログ　　各1部

完

取引交渉中：in the middle of business negotiations　具体的な条件：concrete conditions　打ち合わせに入る：enter consultations　別記事項：matters written elsewhere　取り計らい：take care of; deal with　経営方針：management policies　金融機関：financial institutions　〜業界：world of 〜 trade　評価：evaluation　財務諸表の推移：changes in financial statements　業績見通し：performance prospects　期限：deadline　入手済み：already obtained　別添資料：attached materials　参照：refer　添付資料：attached materials　経歴書：company history

Sales Document # ＿＿＿＿＿
Date (year, month, day)

The Honorable Manager, Investigation Department

Sales Department Manager (seal)

RE: Credit standing inquiry (request)

We are already involved in negotiations to establish a business relationship with the company noted below, but as we have now entered consultations regarding concrete conditions for a relationship, we would like to request that your department conduct an inquiry into the matters listed below. We appreciate your taking care of this for us.

Details

1. Subject of investigation:
   Takashima Interior, Incorporated
   130-0021 Tokyo-to, Sumida-ku, Midori 5-6-3 (TEL: 03-6634-0261)
2. Items to investigate:
   (1) Company structure, management policies
   (2) Condition of their dealings with financial institutions
   (3) Special characteristics and evaluation of the company by others in the home furnishing trade world
   (4) Changes in financial statements, prospects for future performance
   (5) Other items worthy of mention
3. Investigation deadline
   Please complete your investigation by (month, day). Please refer to the attached materials related to this company that we have already obtained.

(the end)

(Attached materials) company history, company profile, product catalog (one each)

(the end)

留意事項

1) 社内の部門に対する照会ですから、照会の理由や目的を書いてその意図を明確にし、必要とする調査事項を明示します。

2) 参考となる資料があればそれも添付して、先方が十分な調査活動が行えるようにします。

3) 社内に対する文書には、外部に出す文書と違い、頭語や結語・あいさつを省き要件のみを簡潔に述べます。

1. Since this is an inquiry addressed to a department within the writer's company, state the reason and objective for the inquiry and clearly note the purpose. Specify the items that you want investigated.

2. If you have materials that would be helpful in their research, include them with your request.

3. Letters written to persons within the company are different from those written to

また、「です・ます」調ではなく「である」調を用いたり敬語を省いたりすることがありますが、各企業ごとに書き方が決まっています。

4) 社内文書の終わりには「以上」「完」「了」などと書きますが、追記(ついき)をした時は同じ用語を使わずに、「以下余白(よはく)」など別のものを使用します。

persons on the outside. Leave out salutations, complimentary closes, and greetings, and write only the nature of your business in a concise manner. At times, you may use the *de aru* (plain) form of verbs, instead of the *desu* and *masu* (polite) forms. You need not use polite or honorific forms. Each business has its own way of writing, which includes specific customs, jargon, expressions, and style.

4. At the conclusion of in-house memos, write 以上 or 完 or 了, each of which means "the end." When adding a postscript, you should also end it with a phrase meaning "the end," but not the same one that you used at the end of the letter, e.g., 以下余白.

3-1と3-2のフローと文例

3-1「調査機関に信用状況を問い合わせる」のフロー

信用調査ご依頼の件

拝啓(はいけい)　貴社ますますご隆昌(りゅうしょう)の段大慶(たいけい)に存じます。

さて、下記企業に関して、別記事項の調査をお願いします。 ——②調査を依頼する

敬具

記

1．調査対象：高島インテリア株式会社
〒130-0021　東京都墨田区緑 5-6-3　(☎ 03-6634-0261)
資本金　1,500 万円、　売上高(だか)　7 億円、　従業員 10 名

2．調査事項：
(1)経営者のリーダーシップ、人格、経営組織、経営方針
(2)過去 3 年の業績、売上高、営業利益、経常利益の推移(すいい)
(3)今後の業績予想
(4)金融(きんゆう)機関との取引状況、同社に対する評価
(5)主な業務取引先、取引実績、同業者間の評価
(6)企業としての特色、取引上の特記留意事項

(中　略)

——③記——調査依頼内容

以上

(写(うつし))　弊(へい)営業部、経理部

3-2「社内の調査部に信用状況を問い合わせる」のフロー

信用調査の件（依頼）

かねて当部において下記企業に対し取引交渉中のところ、このほど具体的な取引条件の打ち合わせに入ることとなったので、改(あらた)めて別記事項に関して貴部による調査をお願いいたしたく、よろしくお取り計(はか)らい願う。

——①調査を依頼するいきさつを説明する
——②調査を依頼する

記

1．調査企業
高島インテリア株式会社
〒130-0021　東京都墨田区緑 5-6-3　(☎ 03-6634-0261)

2．調査事項
(1)会社組織、経営方針
(2)金融(きんゆう)機関との取引状況
(3)インテリア業界での同社の特色、評価

(中　略)

——③記——調査依頼内容

以　上

(添付(てんぷ)資料)　会社経歴書、会社案内、商品カタログ　　各 1 部

完

①調査を依頼するいきさつを説明する

Explaining reasons for the request of an investigation

②調査を依頼する

Requesting an investigation

* 下記企業に関して、別記事項の調査をお願いします。(3-1)［専門調査機関に依頼する場合］
  I request that you investigate the following items for the company, as shown below. [In the case of making a request to an investigation agency.]

* 別記事項に関して貴部による調査をお願いいたしたく、よろしくお取り計(はか)らい願う。(3-2)［社内の場合］
  We would like to request that your department conduct an inquiry into the matters listed below. [In the case of an in-house inquiry.]

* お手数ではございますが、下記企業について至急(しきゅう)ご調査の上、ご回答くださいますようお願い申し上げます。［金融(きんゆう)機関、取引先などの場合］
  I am sorry to trouble you, but would you please make an urgent investigation into the company listed below and send us a reply upon completion. [In the case of a financial institution or a business client.]

③記――調査依頼内容（調査対象、調査事項、報告期限、費用の確認、回答日時、など）

Description—contents of the investigation request (object of the investigation, issues to be investigated, confirmation of fee, report deadline, etc.)

〈調査依頼内容の書き方〉

How to write the contents of an investigation request

* 調査が済(す)み次第、報告書を提出するとともに、改(あらた)めて口頭補足(こうとうほそく)報告**を願いたい**。(3-1)
  Please submit a report to us as soon as your investigation is completed. We would also like to ask you for a supplementary verbal report.

* ○月○日までに**お願いしたい**。(3-2)
  Please complete your investigation by (month, day).

* 費用は、先般(せんぱん)お打合せのとおり、525,000円**とする**。(3-1)
  As already agreed, we will pay 525,000 yen.

* 調査完了後、請求書(せいきゅうしょ)を当社あて送付(そうふ)**のこと**。(3-1)
  Please invoice us as soon as you have completed the investigation.

3-3 信用照会に対し、調査の報告をする（調査機関の報告）
Report from the investigation agency on a credit standing

帝国商工リサーチは、S&A社から照会された情報について、次のような文書を添えて調査報告書を提出します。
Teikoku Shoko Research, a credit investigation agency, submits the following letter along with the report of the investigation they were asked to do by S&A Corporation.

企調第 ○○○ 号
平成○年○月○日

S&Aコーポレーション日本支社
　調査部長　山崎文夫殿

株式会社　帝国商工リサーチ
企業調査第一部長　田島秀雄（印）

調査ご報告の件

拝復　貴社には、ますますご隆昌のこととお喜び申し上げます。
　毎度格別のお引立てを賜り厚く御礼申し上げます。
　さて、○月○日付調第○○○号貴信をもってご照会をいただきました高島インテリア株式会社に係わる調査の件につきまして、下記の通りご報告申し上げます。
　なお、来る○日午前10時、本件につき口頭ご説明に参上いたしたく、ご了承のほど願い上げます。
　とりあえず書中ご報告申し上げます。

敬具

記

［総合所見］
　経営者、従業員の結束は堅く、財務内容、金融機関の取引関係も良好であります。販売網は、特に首都圏の中堅企業や学校関係に強く、フットワークの利く仕事ぶりは、広く安定した評価を得ています。
　詳細は、別添の報告書をご参照願います。

以　上

（添付書類）「高島インテリア株式会社」調査報告書　　1部

口頭説明：verbal explanation　参上する：visit　了承のほど：acknowledging　総合所見：general observations　結束が堅い：closely united　財務内容：financial conditions　金融機関：financial institutions　販売網：sales network　首都圏の中堅企業：mid-sized companies in the Tokyo Metropolitan area　～関係：～ related　フットワークが利く：can maneuver more effectively　安定した評価を得る：attain a consistently good reputation　詳細：details　別添の：attached　参照：refer　添付書類：attached documents

---

Business Investigation Document # ＿＿＿＿＿
Date (year, month, day)

S&A Corporation, Japan Office
Investigation Department Manager Yamazaki Fumio (Mr.)
Teikoku Shoko Research Corporation
First Business Investigation Department Manager Tajima Hideo (seal)

RE: Report of investigation

Salutations: I imagine you are extremely happy with your company's growing prosperity.
Allow me to express our deep appreciation for the gift of your continued special support.
And now, with regard to your communication of (month, day), letter # ＿＿＿＿＿, concerning an inquiry of Takashima Interior, Incorporated, I offer the following report.
In addition, on (day) at 10:00 A.M., I will visit you to give a verbal explanation of the report. For this I ask your acknowledgment.
In the meantime, I am sending you this written report.　Sincerely yours

Details

[General observations]
The management and employees are closely united, and their financial condition and relationship with financial institutions are both favorable. Its sales network is especially strong in mid-sized businesses and schools in the Tokyo metropolitan area. They can maneuver effectively in business, and thus attain a consistently good reputation over a wide area.
For details, please refer to the attached report.

(the end)

Attached documents: [Takashima Interior, Incorporated] investigation report—1 copy

---

留意事項

1)例のように、総合所見の要点を簡潔に書くことは、報告を受ける側ではそのだいたいの内容をあらかじめ把握する上で大変参考になります。

2)文書に書き切れない状況や所見などを、口頭で補足することがあります。

1. As in this example, concise general observations provided by the agency give excellent background information to the recipients of the report.

2. Circumstances and observations that will not fit on the letter accompanying the report are sometimes conveyed verbally.

3-4 信用照会に対し、調査の報告をする（社内調査部の報告）

Report from your company's investigation department on a credit standing

調査部は、営業部から照会を受けた提携候補の高島インテリア社について、内外の調査情報を集め、次のような文書を添えて報告書を提出します。

In response to the request by the sales department related to Takashima Interior, a candidate for business associate, the investigation department of S&A Corporation gathered materials already available, as well as those obtained from an outside investigation, and submitted them along with this letter.

調第　〇〇〇　号

平成〇年〇月〇日

営業部長　山　本　良　雄　殿

調査部長　山　崎　文　夫（印）

信用調査の件（報告）

〇月〇日付営第〇〇〇号貴信をもって照会のあった高島インテリア株式会社の信用調査の件に関し、下記の通り報告するので、よろしくお取り計らい願う。

なお、かねてお打ち合わせの通り、既提携先の状況・提携条件等については、貴部においてしかるべくご検討ありたい。

記

1．調査意見の総括

業績は、順調に推移しており、財務内容・資金繰りも安定している。小回りの利くフットワークにより評価は高く、提携先として信頼性があるものと考えられる。(具体的内容は、添付資料を参照。)

2．調査内容

主として貴信指摘の調査事項(1)～(5)について調査を行った。

3．調査方法

取引金融機関や同業者の情報による他、営業の実態については、当部聞き込みにより補足した。

以　上

(添付資料)　1．調査意見書　1部

2．調査部「調査資料」　1部

取り計らい：deal with　既提携先：present associates　～条件：conditions of ～　しかるべく：as you see fit; properly　ご検討ありたい：want/hope ～ to consider　総括：summary　業績：performance　順調に推移する：moving/progressing smoothly　財務内容：financial affairs　資金繰りが安定している：fund management is stable　小回りが利く：can maneuver more effectively　フットワーク：footwork　評価：evaluation　信頼性がある：be trustworthy　添付資料：attached materials　参照：refer　指摘：pointing out　事項：matters; issues　取引金融機関：financial institutions dealt with　実態：actual condition　聞き込み：gathering of information　補足する：supplement

---

Investigation Document # ＿＿＿＿＿
Date (year, month, day)

Sales Department Manager Yamamoto Yoshio (Mr.)

Investigation Department Manager Yamazaki Fumio (seal)

RE: Credit standing (report)

With regard to your communication of (month, day), letter # ＿＿＿＿＿, concerning the credit standing of Takashima Interior, Incorporated, I offer the following report. Please deal with it as you see fit.

As we already discussed, with regard to the candidate's present associates and possible terms for a tie-up, and so on, I hope your department will examine the information as you see fit.

Details

1. Summary of comments on the inquiry
   Performance is moving in a favorable direction; their finances and fund management are stable. They are highly rated because they can maneuver effectively in business, and I feel they can be trusted as a business associate. (For a detailed report, refer to the attached materials.)
2. Contents of investigation
   Our investigation dealt mainly with points (1) through (5) of your request.
3. Method of investigation
   In addition to information from financial institutions they deal with and others in similar businesses, we ourselves gathered supplementary material related to the actual condition of their sales.

(the end)

Attachments: 1. Comments on the investigation—1 copy
2. Investigation Department (investigation materials)—1 copy

留意事項

1) 社内だけでは調査に限度がある場合、社外の調査機関からも情報を集めて報告をまとめます。

2) 客観的な資料のほかに、担当部署としての主観的な意見があれば、それを添えて報告することがあります。

3) 社内文書ですからあいさつは省略します。また、「です・ます」調ではなく「である」調で書くことがあります。

1. When the information available within a company is too limited, information is gathered from outside sources and a report is then assembled.

2. When subjective opinions from the responsible department are available in addition to objective data, they are sometimes included with the report.

3. This is an in-house memo, so greetings are omitted; that may mean using the *de aru* (plain) form instead of the *desu* or *masu* (polite) forms.

第4課

交渉を希望する相手先に面談を申し入れる

Proposing a meeting to discuss negotiations

手紙のやり取りだけでは不十分で、会って話を聞きたいことがあります。面談したい相手に対しては、アポイントを取ってから会うのが礼儀です。アポイントには、口頭で取る場合と文書によって申し入れる場合とがあります。

簡単なことやそれほど重要でない場合、時間的に余裕のない場合、こちらが相手先と対等な立場（会社の規模が同じで先方とこちらが同位同職である場合など)、事務的な打ち合わせの場合、よく知っている親しい間柄の場合、秘書を通して申し入れる場合などのときには電話ですませることもありますが、大切な問題である場合や初対面の場合、先方が役職者の場合などは面談の目的も明らかに記して、文書で申し入れることが礼儀にかなったやり方です。

When an exchange of letters alone is insufficient, a meeting where you can talk directly to the company in question is desirable. As far as the party you are hoping to hold talks with is concerned, it is courteous to make an appointment beforehand. Depending on the circumstances, the appointment can be made verbally or by letter.

Appointments may be made by phone in the following situations: when you have a simple request; when it is simply not necessary to write a letter; when you are pressed for time; when the person you are dealing with is on an equal standing as yourself (for example, he/she performs similar duties in a firm of equal size as your company); when the arrangements are of a clerical nature; when you know the person you will deal with well; or when you are making the appointment through a secretary, and so on. It is more courteous, however, to apply for an appointment in writing, clearly stating your purpose for the proposed meeting, if the meeting involves a particularly important matter, if this is a first meeting, or the other party is in a managerial post, etc.

社外 依頼する request

4-1 紹介を受けた提携候補会社に面談を申し入れる

Proposing a meeting with a possible candidate for an affiliation

S&A社のスミス日本支社長は、東京商事の小川部長に紹介してもらった吉田物産の山田部長との、販売提携に関する面談のアポイントを取る文書を作ります。

Mr. Smith, manager of the Japan Office of S&A Corporation, composes a letter proposing an appointment to discuss a sales tie-up with Mr. Yamada, manager of Yoshida Trading, who was introduced to him by Mr. Ogawa, manager of Tokyo Shoji.

199○年○月○日

吉田物産株式会社

営業部長　山田　栄三　殿

S&Aコーポレーション

日本支社長　H. G. スミス（サイン）

アポイントご依頼の件

謹啓　新緑の候、益々ご清栄のこととお慶び申し上げます。

さて、

このたびは突然お手紙を差し上げますこと、失礼をお許し下さい。

私どもは米国ニューヨーク市に本社をおき、家具及びカーペットの製造、販売を致しておりますが、この程日本支社を設け、日本市場での販売を開始する運びとなりました。その際、弊社としましては、日本国内ではぜひ貴社との提携により拡販を図りたいと存じまして、東京商事の小川部長殿にお願いを致し、ご紹介いただきました。

つきましては、弊社の商品の内容などをご披露申し上げたく、ぜひ一度ご都合のよろしい日時にご面談の機会を持たせていただきたく存じます。

お差支えなければ、来週早々当方からお電話にて改めてご都合をお伺い致したく存じますので、何分のご高配を賜りますようお願い申し上げます。

まずは、当用のみ申し上げます。

敬具

追って、弊社及び取扱い製品の簡単なご紹介のパンフレットを同封させて頂きましたので、ご覧願えれば幸いに存じます。

同封物：　S&Aコーポレーション　会社概要　一部

製品カタログ　一部

以上

設(もう)ける：open; establish　～運びとなる：be at the stage of ～　披露(ひろう)する：show; announce　差支(さしつか)えない：have no objections; not be inconvenient　～早々：early (part of the week/month/year/etc.)　高配(こうはい)を賜(たまわ)る：receive your kind consideration　同封する：enclose　ご覧(らん)願う：please take a look　概要(がいよう)：profile

Date (year, month, day)

Yoshida Trading, Incorporated
Sales Department Manager Yamada Eizo (Mr.)

S&A Corporation
Japan Office Manager H. G. Smith (signature)

RE: Request for an appointment

Salutations: I rejoice that you are increasingly well and prospering during this season of new green around us.

Now,

excuse my impoliteness for suddenly sending a letter at this time.

We are a company based in New York City, specializing in the manufacture and sale of furniture and carpets. We recently opened an office in Japan and are at the stage of launching a sales program in the Japanese market. As we do so, we as a company would like to expand our sales in Japan with a tie-up with your company. Mr. Ogawa, manager of Tokyo Shoji, in response to our request, introduced you to us.

In this regard, we would very much like to have the opportunity to meet with you at your convenience to introduce our products.

If you have no objections, I will contact you by phone early next week to inquire as to when it might be convenient (to meet). Thank you.

This is all I will say at this time.

Sincerely yours

P.S. I am enclosing a simple pamphlet introducing our company and the products we carry. Please take a look at them.

Enclosures: S&A Corporation, profile of the company—1 copy
Product catalog—1 copy

(the end)

留意事項

1)紹介をしてもらっている場合でも、アポイントを取らないで突然訪問するのは失礼です。あらかじめ文書で(あるいは電話で)誰の紹介か、どんな目的で面談を求めるのかを伝え、相手の都合のよい日時を確かめ、約束をしてから訪問します。

2)仲介者(ちゅうかいしゃ)の紹介状は、アポイントを求める文書に添付(てんぷ)するか、会うときに持参(じさん)します。

3)依頼状にこちらの会社についての説明や参考資料を添付しておけば、先方もあらかじめ検討することができて効率的な面談になります。

1. Even when you have received an introduction, it is extremely impolite to show up for a visit without first making an appointment. You must request a meeting in writing (or by phone), stating who introduced you and why you want to meet the other party. After checking the other person's availability, set up the appointment and then make your visit accordingly.

2. The letter of introduction written by your go-between may be sent with the letter requesting the interview or taken with you when you visit.

3. Sending an explanation of your com-

4)同封物がある時は、その旨を記します。記載方法は、「同封物」「添付資料」などと記して明細を書くか、例のように追伸として述べるか、いずれでもさしつかえありません。簡単な資料や文書の本文中で同封を言及してあれば、「同封物あり」とだけ記すこともあります。

pany and other pertinent materials and a statement of the purpose of the meeting ahead of time will allow the other party to prepare, thus leading to a more effective meeting.

4. When you enclose other materials, mention it in the letter. It makes no difference whether you do this by listing materials under 同封物 (enclosures) or 添付(てんぷ)資料 (attachments), or by adding a postscript, as in this example. If the enclosures are self-explanatory, or if you refer to them in the body of the letter, simply writing 同封物あり (enclosures included) is sufficient.

4-2 取り引きのない相手に機器売り込みの面談を申し入れる

Proposing a meeting to promote products with a company you have not dealt with before

コンピュータ関連の販売会社である東京システム販売は、まだ取り引きのないS&A社に関連機器の売り込みをしようとして、面談のアポイントを求める文書を書きます。

Tokyo System Sales, a company that sells computers and related equipment, writes a letter to S&A Corporation, with which they have not yet done business, requesting a meeting to discuss possible sales of their equipment.

199○年○月○日

S&Aコーポレーション日本支社
営業部長　山　本　良　雄　殿

東京システム販売株式会社
営業部長　代　々　木　　進（印）

ご挨拶に参上致したい件

拝啓　貴社ますますご清栄のこと慶賀申し上げます。

さて、

突然本状を差し上げます非礼お許し下さい。実は、東京商事株式会社営業部長 小川　正様のご紹介でご挨拶申し上げます。

私どもはYMN社のグループ会社として同社製のコンピュータとその関連機器並びに関連ソフトの販売を取り扱っておりますが、このほど東京商事様にホストコンピュータと関連システムの納入が決まり、現在鋭意作業を取り進めさせて頂いている所でございます。

伺いますと、御社の支社長様と小川部長様とはご親交があるとのことで、また御社では新製品の販路拡張に取り組まれているとも洩れ承っておりますが、情報や事務処理の迅速化、省力化には充分ご検討のことかと存じます。

つきましては、この機会に改めてご挨拶を兼ね、弊社製品の特徴並びにアプリケーションの状況などご参考に供し、今後の御社のご処理にお役に立ちたく存じております。

できますれば一度ご都合のよろしき日時にぜひ参上させて頂きたく、後刻改めてご都合をお伺い申し上げますので、その節は宜しくご高配賜りたくお願い申し上げます。

まずは取り急ぎ書中にて申し上げます。　敬具

追伸　ご覧いただいているとは存じますが、弊社にて取り扱い致しておりますコンピュータ関連機器とOA機器、それらのソフト群のカタログを同封貴覧に供します。　再拝

参上する：visit　非礼：impoliteness　関連機器：related equipment　取り扱う：handle; deal with　納入：supply; delivery　作業を取り進める：proceed with work　伺いますと：I hear that ～　親交がある：be on friendly terms (with)　販路拡張に取り組む：be engaged in developing markets　洩れ承る：learn; get wind of　処理の迅速化：increasing speed (of handling)　省力化：saving energy; power saving　～を兼ねる：～ and at the same time　参考に供する：offer for your reference; show　後刻：later　ご高配賜りたく：want to ask for your kind consideration　～群の～：a set of ～　同封：enclose　貴覧に供する：offer for you to look at

Date (year, month, day)

S&A Corporation, Japan Office
Sales Department Manager Yamamoto Yoshio (Mr.)

Tokyo System Sales, Incorporated
Sales Department Manager Yoyogi Susumu (seal)

RE: Desire to pay a formal visit

Salutations: May I congratulate you on your increasing health and prosperity.

Now, please forgive the impolite suddenness of this letter. Actually, I am writing to you through the introduction of Mr. Ogawa Tadashi, sales department manager of Tokyo Shoji, Incorporated.

We are members of the YMN group of companies and, as such, deal with computers, computer-related equipment, and software made by that group. Recently, Tokyo Shoji decided to have us supply them with a new host computer and related systems, and we are now diligently in the process of installing it for them.

I heard that the office manager of your company is a close friend of Manager Ogawa's, and that your company is now engaged in developing markets for a newly developed product. I wonder if you have considered a means of increasing speed and saving energy as you deal with information- and office-related tasks.

In this regard, I would like the opportunity to visit and at the same time tell you about the special characteristics of our products and their applications for your reference, with the hope that they might be useful to your company in the future.

If possible, I would like to visit you at your convenience. I will contact you later to inquire as to when it might be convenient, so I ask for your kind consideration at that time.

I hasten to write this.

Sincerely yours

P.S. You may have already seen these, but I am enclosing catalogs of our computer and office equipment and software for you to look at.

Thank you again.

留意事項

1) これまで付き合いのなかった相手には、突然手紙を出す失礼のおわびをするとともに、突然面談を申し入れる理由を詳しく書きます。

2) 紹介をしてもらっているときは、誰から紹介を受けているかを記します。

1. When writing to a party with whom you have never dealt before, first apologize for the suddenness of your letter, and then give a detailed explanation of why you are proposing an interview.

2. When you have received an introduction to the other party, explain who it is that

3) こちらの話を聞くことによって相手先はどんなメリットが期待できるのか、また、こちらは今までどの企業と取り引きしているかの実績を相手に示し、信頼感と関心を持たせるようにします。

4) 先方の検討の参考に、こちらの会社の概要(がいよう)や、面談時の目的に関係する資料を添付(てんぷ)します。

suggested you contact them.

3. By hearing your explanation, the other party should be able to tell what benefits they can expect to receive, what other companies you do business with, etc., thus awakening their interest and trust.

4. Include for the other party's examination your company's profile and materials relating to the purpose of the talks.

4-1と4-2のフローと文例

4-1「紹介を受けた提携候補会社に面談を申し入れる」のフロー

アポイントご依頼の件

謹啓　新緑の候、益々ご清栄のこととお慶び申し上げます。

さて、

このたびは突然お手紙を差し上げますこと、失礼をお許し下さい。

①突然手紙を出す非礼をわびる

私どもは米国ニューヨーク市に本社をおき、家具及びカーペットの製造、販売を致しておりますが、この程日本支社を設け、日本市場での販売を開始する運びとなりました。その際、弊社としましては、日本国内ではぜひ貴社との提携により拡販を図りたいと存じまして、東京商事の小川部長殿にお願いを致し、ご紹介いただきました。

②自社紹介をする

③面談を依頼するいきさつを説明する

つきましては、弊社の商品の内容などをご披露申し上げたく、ぜひ一度ご都合のよろしい日時にご面談の機会を持たせていただきたく存じます。

④面談を申し入れる

お差支えなければ、来週早々当方からお電話にて改めてご都合をお伺い致したく存じますので、何分のご高配を賜りますようお願い申し上げます。

⑤連絡方法を知らせる

まずは、当用のみ申し上げます。

敬具

追って、弊社及び取扱い製品の簡単なご紹介のパンフレットを同封させて頂きましたので、ご覧願えれば幸いに存じます。

同封物：　S&Aコーポレーション　会社概要　一部
　　　　　製品カタログ　一部

以上

4-2「取り引きのない相手に機器売り込みの面談を申し入れる」のフロー

ご挨拶に参上致したい件

拝啓　貴社ますますご清栄のこと慶賀申し上げます。

さて、

突然本状を差し上げます非礼お許し下さい。実は、東京商事株式会社営業部長 小川正様のご紹介でご挨拶申し上げます。

①突然手紙を出す非礼をわびる

③面談を依頼するいきさつを説明する

私どもはYMN社のグループ会社として同社製のコンピュータとその関連機器並びに関連ソフトの販売を取り扱っておりますが、このほど東京商事様にホストコンピュータと関連システムの納入が決まり、現在鋭意作業を取り進めさせて頂いている所でございます。

②自社紹介をする

伺いますと、御社の支社長様と小川部長様とはご親交があるとのことで、また御社では新製品の販路拡張に取り組まれているとも洩れ承っておりますが、情報や事務処理の迅速化、省力化には充分ご検討のことかと存じます。

③面談を依頼するいきさつを説明する

つきましては、この機会に改めてご挨拶を兼ね、弊社製品の特徴並びにアプリケーションの状況などご参考に供し、今後の御社のご処理にお役に立ちたく存じております。 ④面談を申し入れる

できますれば一度ご都合のよろしき日時にぜひ参上させて頂きたく、後刻改めてご都合をお伺い申し上げますので、その節は宜しくご高配賜りたくお願い申し上げます。 ⑤連絡方法を知らせる

まずは取り急ぎ書中にて申し上げます。 敬具

追伸　ご覧いただいているとは存じますが、弊社にて取り扱い致しておりますコンピュータ関連機器とOA機器、それらのソフト群のカタログを同封貴覧に供します。 再拝

（下線の部分は自分の状況に合わせて書いてください。）

①突然手紙を出す非礼をわびる

Apologizing for abruptly sending out a letter

＊このたびは突然お手紙を差し上げますこと、失礼をお許し下さい。(4-1)
Excuse my impoliteness for suddenly sending a letter at this time.

＊突然本状を差し上げます非礼お許し下さい。(4-2)
Please forgive the impolite suddenness of this letter.

＊突然このようなご依頼状をお届けいたしまして失礼申し上げます。
I am sorry for the impoliteness of this sudden letter of request.

②自社紹介をする

Introducing your company

③面談を依頼するいきさつを説明する（目的、紹介者など）

Explaining the circumstances surrounding your request for talks (objective, the person who introduced you, etc.)

＊弊社としましては、日本国内ではぜひ貴社との提携により拡販を図りたいと存じまして、東京商事の小川部長殿にお願いを致し、ご紹介いただきました。(4-1)
We as a company would like to expand our sales in Japan with a tie-up with your company. Mr. Ogawa, manager of Tokyo Shoji, in response to our request, introduced you to us.

＊実は、東京商事株式会社営業部長 小川　正様のご紹介でご挨拶申し上げます。(4-2)
Actually, I am writing to you through the introduction of Mr. Ogawa Tadashi, sales department manager of Tokyo Shoji, Incorporated.

＊弊社は、このたび衛星通信を利用した「配送管理システム」を開発いたしました。このシステムは、貴社の物流コスト節減と競争力強化のご要求に的確にお応えできるものと確信いたしております。
Our company has developed a "Distribution Management System," utilizing satellite communications. I am convinced that this system will be able to precisely meet your demands to reduce distribution costs and to become more competitive.

④面談を申し入れる

Proposing talks

＊弊社の商品の内容などをご披露申し上げたく、ぜひ一度ご都合のよろしい日時にご面談の機会を持たせていただきたく存じます。(4-1)

We would very much like to have the opportunity to meet with you at your convenience to introduce our products.

＊弊社製品の内容、お取引条件などにつきお話しさせていただきたく、ご面談の日時などをご指示下さいますよう、よろしくお願い申し上げます。

We would like to talk about our products and business terms. If you are interested, please indicate a time and date for a meeting.

＊弊社システム商品のプレゼンテーションの機会をいただきたく、お願い申し上げます。

We would like to request the chance to make a presentation of our company's systems products.

⑤連絡方法を知らせる

Notifying of contact procedures

＊お差支えなければ、来週早々当方からお電話にて改めてご都合をお伺い致したく存じますので、何分のご高配を賜りますようお願い申し上げます。(4-1)

If you have no objections, I will contact you by phone early next week to inquire as to when it might be convenient (to meet). Thank you.

＊後日弊社より改めてご都合のほどお伺い申し上げたく、その節はよろしくお願い申し上げます。

I will contact you in the near future to find out when it is convenient. Thank you.

＊ご都合のよい日時をご一報頂きたく、お願い申し上げます。

Please let me know of a time when it will be convenient for you (to meet).

4-3 面談を承諾する
Agreeing to a meeting

吉田物産は、S&A社が求めた面談の日取りを設定し、責任者の出席を知らせる文書を作ります。
Yoshida Trading responds to S&A Corporation's proposal by setting a date for the meeting and informing them that the responsible person(s) will attend.

営総第〇〇〇号
平成〇年〇月〇日

S&Aコーポレーション　日本支社
　支社長　ハワード　G. スミス　殿

吉田物産株式会社
　営業部長　山田　栄三（印）

ご来訪日程の件

拝復　〇月〇日付貴信拝承いたしました。誠にご丁寧なご挨拶をいただき、恐縮に存じます。

　ご紹介者の東京商事小川部長殿からは、かねてより貴社の積極的な販売姿勢や製品の優秀さについてお噂を伺っており、このたび貴社とお近づきを得られますことは、私どもにとりましても誠に喜ばしいことでございます。

　さて、お申し越しの弊社へのご来訪の件、

　〇月〇日（火）　午後2時

の日程ではいかがでしょうか。

　貴方のご都合をお聞かせいただければ幸いです。

　当日は、弊営業担当常務取締役鈴木　弘も同席させていただきますので、よろしくお願い申し上げます。
　まずは取り急ぎご連絡申し上げます。

敬具

拝承する：receive　お近づきを得る：become acquainted with　営業担当常務取締役：managing director in charge of sales

Business/General Document # ________
Date (year, month, day)

S&A Corporation, Japan Office
Manager Howard G. Smith (Mr.)

Yoshida Trading, Incorporated
Sales Department Manager Yamada Eizo (seal)

RE: Schedule for visit

Salutations: I received your letter of (month, day). I was grateful to receive such polite greetings.

I have already heard intimations of the active manner in which you conduct sales and the fine quality of your products from Mr. Ogawa, the manager of Tokyo Shoji, and I must say that we welcome the opportunity to become acquainted with your company.

Now, as to your request to visit our office,

Date (month, day) (Tuesday) 2:00 P.M.

How would this date be?

I would appreciate it if you could inform us as to whether this would be convenient.

Suzuki Hiroshi, managing director in charge of sales, will also be present that day, I hope this will be satisfactory.
I hasten to inform you of this.

Sincerely yours

留意事項

1) 面談の申し入れに対する回答には、日時と場所を明示します。

2) 面談に出席する者の役職や氏名を示せば、最大の誠意ある返事となりますし、訪問する側からすれば、どこまで突っ込んだ話ができるかの目安と準備の資料になります。

3) 単にアポイントを求められた時、日取りや時間がこちらで決められるときには日時と場所を指定して承諾の返事をします。そのような場合でも、先方の都合がこれでよいか意向を確かめ、「～の日程ではいかがでしょうか」などの表現を用います。

1. State the date, time, and place for the meeting clearly.

2. Relating the name and position of the person(s) who will be present at the meeting shows that you take it very seriously, and this will enable the visiting party to know what expectations to have for the discussions, thus helping them in their preparations.

3. When you have simply been asked for an appointment or when entrusted with deciding the date and time for an appointment, decide on a date, time, and place, and then inform the other party of your decision. But even in such a case, you should check to see if your proposal is acceptable to the other party and verify their intention, using expressions like ～の日程ではいかがでしょうか.

4-4 面談のアポイントを取り消す
Canceling an appointment

吉田物産の鈴木常務(じょうむ)は、予定外の出張をすることになったので、S&A社といったん取り決めた面談のアポイントをキャンセルし、改(あらた)めて日時を決めたいと連絡します。

Mr. Suzuki, managing director of Yoshida Trading, is forced to cancel an interview appointment he made with S&A Corporation because of an unscheduled trip out of town. He contacts them asking to change the date.

営総第〇〇〇号
平成〇年〇月〇日

S&Aコーポレーション日本支社
支社長　ハワード　G. スミス　殿

吉田物産株式会社
常務取締役(じょうむとりしまりやく)　鈴木　弘（印）

ご面会アポイントに係(かか)わる件

急啓(きゅうけい)　初夏(しょか)の候となりました。ますますご清適(せいてき)のこととお慶(よろこ)び申し上げます。

さて、〇月〇日付営本第〇〇〇号貴信をもってお申し越しのありました貴社カーペット販売に関するご面談の件について、ご連絡申し上げます。

実は、先日お打ち合わせの際、〇月〇日（火）午後2時にご来社いただきますよう申し上げておりましたところ、その後小役(しょうやく)に急に海外出張の用件ができましたため、当日不在となり、貴意(きい)に添(そ)いかねる事情となりました。
貴社の「デュクロン」には、かねてより大いに関心を持っており、お話を伺(うかが)うのを楽しみにしておりましたのに、残念に存じます。

つきましては、〇月〇日ごろ帰国後、改(あらた)めて当方より再打ち合わせのこととさせていただきたく、本件あしからずご了承(りょうしょう)のほどお願い申し上げます。

取り急ぎ書中要用のみ申し上げます。

草々

常務取締役：managing director　小役：I (“小” is used to refer to oneself or one's company, etc. “役” refers to the position of the letter writer, i.e., 常務取締役)　貴意に添いかねる：not be able to go along with your intention　～事情となる：the situation has become ～　了承のほど：understanding; acknowledging

Sales/General Document # __________
Date (year, month, day)

S&A Corporation, Japan Office
Manager Howard G. Smith (Mr.)

Yoshida Trading, Incorporated
Managing Director Suzuki Hiroshi (seal)

RE: Appointment to meet with you

Salutations: Summer has come. May I congratulate you on your continued good health.

Now, I refer to your letter dated (month, day), letter # __________, regarding the meeting to talk about the sale of your company's carpets.

Actually, the other day we discussed scheduling this meeting on (month, day) at 2:00 P.M. Since that time, however, it suddenly has become necessary for me to go abroad on business; thus, I will not be in the office on that day and will be unable to meet with you.

I have had considerable interest in your company's product Dukelon for some time, and although I very much looked forward to talking with you, it is with regret (that I cannot meet you).

In this regard, I would like to ask that we talk together again after I return home, around (month, day). I hope you will understand my situation.

I hasten to inform you of this.

Sincerely yours

留意事項

1)いったん決めた約束を取り止めたり変更することは大変な失礼にあたりますので、まずおわびをします。そして、それが予定外の出張など、やむを得ない事情によることを伝え、相手の了承を得なければなりません。
2)取り消したアポイントをどうするか、改めて日取りなどを決めるかについても書いておく必要があります。

1. As canceling or changing an appointment once it has been made is considered extremely impolite behavior, you must first apologize. Then explain that it is unavoidable because of, for example, an unexpected trip out of town, and request the recipient's understanding.
2. You must then ask what to do about the cancellation and find out whether the other party would like to reschedule.

4-5 関連会社へ打ち合わせを申し入れる

Proposing a meeting with a subsidiary

S&A社の山本営業部長は、同社の物流関係の下請(したう)け会社である大山運輸(うんゆ)の太田代表取締役(とりしまりやく)に打ち合わせの都合を聞きます。

Mr. Yamamoto, sales department manager of S&A Corporation, asks to arrange a meeting with Mr. Ota, representative director of Oyama Transportation, a distribution subcontractor for S&A Corporation.

199○年○月○日

大山運輸(うんゆ)株式会社
代表取締役(とりしまりやく) 太田 虎造 殿

S&Aコーポレーション
営業部長 山本 良雄(印)

お打ち合わせ致(いた)したき件

拝啓(はいけい) 平素(へいそ)は大変お世話になり、感謝いたします。

さて、

ご承知(しょうち)の通り、このたび弊社(へいしゃ)は東京支店を日本支社に昇格(しょうかく)、業容(ぎょうよう)の拡大を図(はか)ろうとしています。これに伴(ともな)い、弊製品の販売量の増加が予想され、その物流上の円滑(えんかつ)な処理(しょり)がさらに重要になって参ります。

つきましては、弊社の物流をもっぱらお任せしている貴社に一層(いっそう)の役務提供をお願い致したく、一度その件で忌憚(きたん)のない意見の交換をさせて頂(いただ)きたいと存じます。再来週(さらいしゅう)あたりご都合はいかがでしょうか。

勝手を申して恐縮(きょうしゅく)ですが、よろしくお願い致します。

まずは取り急ぎ用件まで。

敬具

運輸(うんゆ):transportation　代表取締役(とりしまりやく):representative director　ご承知(しょうち)の通り:as you know　昇格(しょうかく):upgrade　業容(ぎょうよう)の拡大を図(はか)る:attempt to expand business　~に伴(ともな)い:as a result (of ~)　物流上の円滑(えんかつ)な処理(しょり):smooth handling of distribution　もっぱら:entirely　一層(いっそう)の役務提供:increase services even more　忌憚(きたん)のない意見の交換:frank exchange of views　勝手を申す:take liberties

Date (year, month, day)

Oyama Transportation, Incorporated
Representative Director Ota Torazo (Mr.)

S&A Corporation
Sales Department Manager Yamamoto Yoshio (seal)

RE: Possible meeting

Salutations: I am deeply grateful for all that you do for us.

Now, as you know, we have recently upgraded our Tokyo Office to a Japan Office, in an attempt to enlarge our business. As a result, we are projecting an increase in the volume of sales of our products, and it will become even more important that their distribution be handled smoothly.

For this reason, as our company's distribution is entirely entrusted to your company, we would like to ask you to increase your services even more, and request that we meet together for a frank exchange of views on this matter. Would this be possible sometime the week after next?

I hope you will forgive my presumption in this matter, but I trust this will not cause you any inconvenience.

I hasten to inform you of this.

Sincerely yours

留意事項

1)子会社や日ごろから密接な関係にある相手に対しては、敬語などをあまり用いなくてもかまいません。

2)特に親しい遠慮(えんりょ)のいらない間柄(あいだがら)では、打ち合わせの目的を示し、あらかじめ日取りについてこちらの希望する日時や場所を申し入れてもかまいません。その時は「勝手を申して」「勝手ながら」などの表現を用いて、相手の都合を確かめずに提案することに許しを求めます。

1. When writing to a subsidiary or a company you are closely related to, you may simplify the honorific expressions.

2. When your relationship is close enough that you need not exercise restraint, it is probably acceptable for you to suggest a time and place for a meeting, after explaining the purpose of the meeting. Ask permission to make a suggestion without first checking with the other party by acknowledging that you are presuming on the relationship with expressions such as 勝手を申して or 勝手ながら (I realize I may be taking liberties, but . . .).

第5課

面談を終えて礼状や報告を書く

Writing a letter of thanks and a report after a meeting

特別にお世話になったとか大きな好意をうけた場合には、お礼の手紙を出すのが礼儀です。特に業務上で密接な関係を持つと思われるところには、必ず礼状を出して友好関係の保持に努めるようにします。それは、相手に好印象を与えるとともに、こちらの会社の品格を印象づけ今後の交渉にも好影響を与えます。

また、面談後に社内の上司や関係先に報告を書くことは、円滑な業務遂行に欠かせない一つのポイントです。

It is customary to write a letter of thanks when you have received special help or kindness. It is important to send such a letter to maintain a friendly working relationship, especially when a close connection has arisen from the work.

This will leave a good impression on the other party and remind them of the dignity of your company, which will favorably influence future negotiations.

Writing up a report on the talks for your superiors and other related parties is one essential way of ensuring business will be carried out smoothly.

5-1 面談相手に礼状を書く

Writing a letter of thanks to the person with whom you met

S&Aのスミス日本支社長は、提携(ていけい)希望相手の吉田物産の山田部長に対し、会って意見交換ができたことへの礼状を書きます。

Mr. Smith, manager of the Japan Office of S&A Corporation, writes a letter to Mr. Yamada, manager of Yoshida Trading, the company S&A are hoping to affiliate with, thanking him for meeting to exchange views about the issue.

199○年○月○日

吉田物産株式会社

営業部長　山田栄三殿

S&Aコーポレーション

日本支社長　ハワード　G. スミス（印）

謹啓(きんけい)　青葉も日増(ひま)しに緑を増す頃となりました。ますますご清適(せいてき)のことと存じます。

さて、

先日御社(おんしゃ)に参上しました折りには、ご多忙中にもかかわらず貴重な時間を割(さ)いてお打ち合わせ頂(いただ)き、誠(まこと)にありがとうございました。

おかげさまで、私どものカーペットを日本市場で販売するにあたっての問題点や御社との提携(ていけい)の可能性について、率直(そっちょく)なご意見をお伺(うかが)いすることができました。心から感謝申し上げます。

何分、日本市場には不慣れな私どもではございますが、今後ともよろしくご指導、お引立(ひきた)てのほどお願い申し上げます。

まずは、略儀(りゃくぎ)ながら書中をもって御礼(おんれい)申し上げます。

敬具

参上する：visit　～折り：when～　時間を割(さ)く：take time　～にあたっての問題点：problems which may arise when doing ～　提携(ていけい)の可能性：possibility of a tie-up　率直(そっちょく)な意見：frank opinion　引立(ひきた)てのほど：(your) support/favor

Date (year, month, day)

Yoshida Trading, Incorporated
Sales Department Manager Yamada Eizo (Mr.)

S&A Corporation
Japan Office Manager Howard G. Smith (seal)

Salutations: As more and more new leaves appear, we know that the season of green has arrived. May I congratulate you on your continued good health.

Now, I would like to express my deep appreciation for your taking time out of your busy schedule the other day to meet with us when we visited your company.

Thanks to you, we learned much from your frank opinions about possible problems we may incur when selling our carpets in the Japanese market and about the possibilities of a business tie-up with you. We are deeply grateful.

We are not yet accustomed to how the Japanese market works, and we ask for your continued guidance and support in the future.

Though this is informal, I wanted to thank you by letter.

Sincerely yours

留意事項

1) 礼状は、なるべく早く出します。

2) 訪問の当日か翌日中に相手に出す文書では、時候のあいさつを省略します。それ以上の時間が経過したときは、時候のあいさつを書きます。

3) 相手を訪問したあとに礼状を書くときは、時間を割いて会ってくれたこと、相手が意見やアドバイスをしてくれたことに対しお礼を書きます。そして、今後の計画があればさしつかえない範囲でそれを述べ、今後に対する支援をお願いし友好関係の保持の意思を伝えます。

4)「今後もよろしく」という表現は、日本語の会話や文書などで慣習的儀礼的に使われることが多いのですが、ビジネスにおいては、本来の意味で友好的な関係を維持したい意向の表現として用いられるケースが多いと言えます。

5) 仮に相手と対等の位置にある場合でも、謙遜して「指導してほしい」「支援してほしい」などの表現を用います。

6) 担当者のみが訪問したときでも、上司の名で礼状を出すほうが会社としての本当の感謝の気持ちを伝えることになり、ていねいで相手に好印象を与える文書になります。

7) 重要な要件や行事の後で、正式には自分がお礼に出向くところを文書で代用する場合には、「略儀ながら」と記します。

1. Send the "thank you" letter as soon as possible.

2. You need not include a seasonal greeting on a letter sent on the day of the meeting or the day following the meeting. Letters sent any later must include such a greeting.

3. When writing to a person after visiting them, thank them for taking the time to meet you and for expressing their opinions and giving you advice. To maintain friendly relations, if you have made plans for the future, explain them, within reasonable limits, and ask for the other party's support.

4. 今後もよろしく (a request for continued help and support in the future) is customarily used in Japanese conversation and writing as a form of good etiquette, and it basically has very little meaning. When it is used concerning business, however, we can say it is often used in its original meaning, expressing a desire to preserve friendly relations.

5. Even if you are of equal status with the other party, use humble expressions, such as "please give me your guidance" or "please assist me with your support."

6. Even when only the responsible person in the company (not the company head) visits the other party, sending a thank-you letter signed by a superior conveys a deeper expression of gratitude. Not only is it polite, but it also leaves a good impression.

7. When a letter acts as a substitute for actually going to express a formal thank you after an important business matter or event, include the phrase 略儀(りゃくぎ)ながら (dropping formalities).

5-2 紹介者に礼状を書く
Writing a letter of thanks to the person who introduced you

S&Aのスミス日本支社長は、紹介者の東京商事の小川部長に、紹介してもらった吉田物産の責任者と面談できたことをお礼のことばとともに報告します。

Mr. Smith, manager of the Japan Office of S&A Corporation, writes Mr. Ogawa, manager of Tokyo Shoji, to express thanks for introducing him to the responsible person at Yoshida Trading and to report on that meeting.

199○年○月○日

東京商事株式会社
　営業部長　小川　正　殿

S&Aコーポレーション
日本支社長　H. G. スミス（印）

拝啓　不順な天候が続きますが、お変わりございませんか。

　先日は昔の誼を頼りに勝手なお願いを申し上げましたところ、さっそくお聞き届けいただき、吉田物産株式会社へのご紹介の労を執ってくださいまして、本当にありがとうございました。日本に来てまだ日の浅い私にとりまして、こんなに暖かく心強いご支援はございません。
　心から厚く御礼申し上げます。

　ご紹介いただきました吉田物産へは、本日お伺いし鈴木常務を始めとする皆様と提携の件について親しく懇談させていただきました。前向きに検討していただけるとのことで、誠にうれしく存じております。
　結果についてはまた改めてご報告いたしますが、とりあえずお礼かたがた途中経過をご一報申し上げます。

　時節柄どうぞくれぐれもご自愛ください。

敬具

不順な天候：unsettled weather　昔の誼を頼りに：imposing on an old friendship　勝手なお願い：selfish request　～の労を執る：go to the trouble of ～　日が浅い：soon after (arrival/etc.)　心強い支援：encouraging/heartfelt support　常務：managing director　～を始めとする…：～ and . . .　提携の件：the matter of a tie-up

懇談(こんだん)する：have friendly talks　前向きに検討する：give favorable consideration　途中経過(けいか)：progress　一報(いっぽう)：informing; reporting　時節柄(じせつがら)：because of the (rainy/monsoon/unsettled/etc.) season　くれぐれも：especially (used for emphasis)　自愛：taking care of your health

Date (year, month, day)

Tokyo Shoji, Incorporated
Sales Department Manager Ogawa Tadashi (Mr.)

S&A Corporation
Japan Office Manager H. G. Smith (seal)

Salutations: I wonder how you are doing as this unsettled weather continues.

I really want to thank you for your immediate response the other day when I imposed on our old friendship with a selfish request, and for going to the trouble of writing an introduction to Yoshida Trading, Incorporated, for me. I can't tell you how much receiving such warm and encouraging support so soon after my arrival in Japan means to me.

I extend to you my heartfelt thanks.

Today we visited Yoshida Trading (to which you introduced me) and met with Managing Director Suzuki and others, and we had a friendly discussion regarding the matter of a business tie-up with their company. They told us that they would favorably consider our proposal, which made me extremely happy.

I will send you a more detailed report of the results later, but wanted first to say thank you for your help and give you this interim report of our progress.

Please take care of yourself in this unsettled season.

Sincerely yours

留意事項

1) 面談した相手だけでなく、面談できるように紹介してくれた方に対しても面談結果を報告する礼状を出します。その際には、ものごとの成(な)り行(ゆ)きや将来どうしたいかを書き加えると、こちらの感謝の気持ちを出すことができます。

2) 個人的な関係で紹介してもらった場合には、格式張(かくしきば)った文章よりも親しみを加えた表現のほうが望ましいと言えます。

1. You write a thank you letter not only to the party you met but also to the party who introduced you, reporting on the results of the meeting. When you do this, it is advisable to include something about the development of things and what you hope to do in the future, thus enabling you to convey your feelings of gratitude.

2. When writing to someone you know on a personal basis, it is better to write in a friendly manner, rather than using formal language.

5-1と5-2のフローと文例

5-1「面談相手に礼状を書く」のフロー

謹啓　青葉も日増しに緑を増す頃となりました。ますますご清適のことと存じます。

さて、先日御社に参上しました折りには、ご多忙中にもかかわらず貴重な時間を割いてお打ち合わせ頂き、誠にありがとうございました。 ― ①労をとってくれたことに対して礼を述べる

おかげさまで、私どものカーペットを日本市場で販売するにあたっての問題点や御社との提携の可能性について、率直なご意見をお伺いすることができました。 ― ②得られた成果を述べる

心から感謝申し上げます。 ― ③感謝の気持ちを述べる

何分、日本市場には不慣れな私どもではございますが、今後ともよろしくご指導、お引立てのほどお願い申し上げます。 ― ④今後の支援、指導を依頼する

まずは、略儀ながら書中をもって御礼申し上げます。

敬具

5-2「紹介者に礼状を書く」のフロー

拝啓　不順な天候が続きますが、お変わりございませんか。

先日は昔の誼を頼りに勝手なお願いを申し上げましたところ、さっそくお聞き届けいただき、吉田物産株式会社へのご紹介の労を執ってくださいまして、本当にありがとうございました。日本に来てまだ日の浅い私にとりまして、こんなに暖かく心強いご支援はございません。 ― ①労をとってくれたことに対して礼を述べる

心から厚く御礼申し上げます。 ― ③感謝の気持ちを述べる

ご紹介いただきました吉田物産へは、本日お伺いし鈴木常務を始めとする皆様と提携の件について親しく懇談させていただきました。前向きに検討していただけるとのことで、誠にうれしく存じております。 ― ②得られた成果を述べる

結果についてはまた改めてご報告いたしますが、とりあえずお礼かたがた途中経過をご一報申し上げます。

時節柄どうぞくれぐれもご自愛ください。

敬具

（下線の部分は自分の状況に合わせて書いてください。）

①労をとってくれたことに対して礼を述べる

Extending thanks for taking the trouble to . . .

＊先日御社に参上しました折りには、ご多忙中にもかかわらず貴重な時間を割いてお打ち合わせ頂き、誠にありがとうございました。(5-1)

I would like to express my deep appreciation for your taking time out of your busy schedule the other day to meet with us when we visited your company.

＊先日は勝手なお願いを申し上げましたところ、さっそくお聞き届けいただき、吉田物産株式会社へのご紹介の労を執ってくださいまして、本当にありがとうございました。(5-2)

I really want to thank you for your immediate response the other day when I made a selfish request, and for going to the trouble of writing an introduction to Yoshida Trading, Incorporated, for me.

＊先日はさっそく弊社商品のプレゼンテーションの機会をいただき、ありがとうございました。

I want to thank you for giving us the chance so soon to make a presentation of our product the other day.

②得られた成果を述べる

Informing of results obtained

＊おかげさまで、私どものカーペットを日本市場で販売するにあたっての問題点や御社との提携の可能性について、率直なご意見をお伺いすることができました。(5-1)

Thanks to you, we learned much from your frank opinions about possible problems we may incur when selling our carpets in the Japanese market and about the possibilities of a business tie-up with you.

＊おかげさまで、弊社製品の日本市場進出について意を強くいたしました。

Thanks to you, our company's desire to advance into the Japanese market has become even stronger.

＊おかげさまで、製品の特長などをご説明申し上げることができ、また、貴重なご意見も頂戴して、認識を新たにすることができました。

Thanks to you, we were able to explain the merits of our products and also to get your valuable opinion and see everything in a new light.

③感謝の気持ちを述べる

Extending feelings of gratitude

＊心から感謝申し上げます。(5-1)

We are deeply grateful.

＊心から厚く御礼申し上げます。(5-2)

I extend to you my heartfelt thanks.

＊ご厚情のほどありがたく感謝申し上げております。

I am deeply grateful for your kindness/favor/support/etc.

④今後の支援（しえん）、指導を依頼する

Requesting continued support and guidance

＊今後ともよろしくご指導、お引立（ひきた）てのほどお願い申し上げます。(5-1)

We ask for your continued guidance and support in the future.

＊なにとぞ今後とも貴社のご高庇賜（こうひたまわ）りますよう改（あらた）めてお願い申し上げます。

I ask again that your company please give us your kind favor.

＊何卒（なにとぞ）よろしくご指導ご鞭撻（べんたつ）お願い申し上げます。

I ask you to please give us your support and encouragement.

5-3 面談の結果をまとめた報告を書く

Compiling a report of the results of the meeting

S&A社の営業課員は、こちらが販売提携を希望している吉田物産を訪問して打ち合わせた内容について、社内報告会を開き内容を報告書にまとめます。

The sales department employees of S&A Corporation hold an in-house meeting to report on the meeting with Yoshida Trading, with whom they are hoping for a business tie-up, and to draw up a formal report.

平成○年○月○日

吉田物産(株)　訪問報告

日　時：　平成○年○月○日(水)　午後2時～4時

場　所：　吉田物産(株)　本社3階会議室

出席者：	吉田物産	鈴木　弘	常務取締役（営業担当）
		山田　栄三	営業部長
		伊藤　明	営業課長
		森　達夫	営業課
	当　社	H. G. スミス	支社長
		山本　良雄	営業部長
		中野　次郎	営業一課長
		加藤　勇人	営業一課

会談内容：吉田物産より要望のあった追加資料、商品見本などは（詳細は添付2参照）早急に先方へ届けることが必要となった他、当日の打ち合わせ内容次の通り。

1．当社より本日の打合せ会実現について謝意を述べた後､以下について説明：
①S&A社の日本における営業概況。(「会社案内」配布)
②主力商品デュクロンの特性。(「製品カタログ」と商品見本配布)
③提携の申し入れ。

2．吉田側より営業概況の説明。(詳細は添付1参照)

3．質疑応答に入り、吉田側より提携の条件、メリットなどについて突っ込んだ質問あり。

4．吉田側は当社との提携につき社内で検討し、結論が出次第当社に伝えると約束。

以上

添付（1&2）

加藤記

常務取締役：managing director　要望がある：request　追加資料：additional materials　詳細：details　添付：attachment　参照：see; refer　謝意を述べる：express gratitude　概況：general overview　配布：handing out　主力商品：main product　提携の申し入れ：proposal for a tie-up　質疑応答に入る：enter question-and-answer period　突っ込んだ質問：penetrating questions　～次第：as soon as～

Date (year, month, day)

Report of visit to Yoshida Trading, Inc.

Date, time: Year, month, day (Wednesday) 2:00-4:00 P.M.
Place: Yoshida Trading, Inc., Headquarters, third-floor conference room
Those in attendance:
Yoshida Trading: Suzuki Hiroshi, Managing Director (Sales)
Yamada Eizo, Sales Department Manager
Ito Akira, Sales Section Chief
Mori Tatsuo, Sales Section
Our Company: H. G. Smith, Office Manager
Yamamoto Yoshio, Sales Department Manager
Nakano Jiro, Sales First Section Chief
Kato Hayato, Sales First Section

Contents of meeting: In addition to the fact that it became necessary to send additional materials and product samples requested by Yoshida Trading (see Attachment #2 for details) to the other party immediately, the results of our discussion are as follows:

1. After expressing our company's gratitude for holding the meeting, we explained the following:
(1) Gave a general overview of our company's sales in Japan (passed out company profile)
(2) Explained the special characteristics of our main product Dukelon (passed out product catalog and product sample)
(3) Proposed tie-up

2. Yoshida representatives gave a general outline of their sales (see Attachment #1 for details)

3. Entered question-and-answer period. Yoshida reps asked penetrating questions about conditions for a tie-up and the possible merits for their company.

4. Yoshida reps said they would consider our proposal for a tie-up within their company and inform us of their decision as soon as possible.

(the end)

Attachments (1&2)

Kato, Secretary

留意事項

1) 社内報告は、5W1Hを基本に内容をわかりやすく簡潔(かんけつ)にまとめます。

2) 社内用の文書では、「内容(は)次の通り(です)」「約束(した)」の(　)部のように、書かなくても理解できる範囲(はんい)で「は」「で」「を」などの助詞や「～する」などを省(はぶ)いた表現がよく用いられます。

1. An in-house report basically uses the pattern "5Ws, 1H" (when, what, where, who, why, and how), and brings the contents together in an easy-to-understand, concise form.

2. In a document for in-house use, particles like は, で, and を and verb endings like ～する are often omitted. For example, in the phrases 内容は次の通りです, or 約束した, the underlined words may be omitted.

5-4 歳暮の送り状を書く

Writing a message to announce a year-end gift

日ごろお世話になっている相手や重要取引先に、季節の習慣的な贈り物である歳暮や中元を贈ると同時に、相手先に送り状（「送りました」という案内状）を出します。

It is customary in Japan to give seasonal gifts to parties to whom you are indebted, including important customers and business associates. When you send one, also send a notification to the other party that you have sent it.

平成○年○月○日

小 川　　正 様

S&Aコーポレーション
日本支社長　H. G. スミス

拝啓　師走に入り何かとご多忙のことと存じます。

私どもも、
お陰をもちまして、所期の業績を挙げることができました。これも一重に皆様の格別のご愛顧の賜物と、厚く御礼申し上げます。

つきましては、感謝の印として本日別便にて心ばかりの品を送らせて頂きました。ご笑納願えれば幸に存じます。

今後とも、よろしくお引立てのほど、お願い申し上げます。

末筆ながら、皆様のご健康、ご発展とよきご迎年をお祈り申し上げます。

敬具

お陰をもちまして：thanks to your support　所期の業績を挙げる：achieve expected performance　格別のご愛顧の賜物：your gift of special encouragement　感謝の印：symbol of gratitude　別便にて：by separate delivery　心ばかりの品：small gift　ご笑納願う：please accept it　よき迎年：a good new year

---

Date (year, month, day)

Ogawa Tadashi (Mr.)

S&A Corporation
Japan Office Manager H. G. Smith

Salutations: I imagine you are extremely busy now at the end of the year.

We, too,
thanks to your support, have been able to achieve our expectations. Let me express my deep appreciation for your special encouragement.

In this regard, I have taken the liberty of sending you a small present today by separate delivery as a symbol of our gratitude. It would please me if you would accept it.

I would be grateful for your continued support in the future.

In closing, I pray for health, growth, and a good new year for all of you.

Sincerely yours

留意事項

1) 日本では、何かあったときの贈り物以外に、一年に二回時季の贈り物をして平素のお礼と季節のあいさつをする習慣があります。12月初めころの贈り物は「歳暮」、7月半ばころの贈物は「中元」といいます。(時期がずれた時は、「暑中お見舞」「暑中お伺い」、「残暑お見舞」「寒中お見舞」「寒中お伺い」などの表現を用います。)

2) 品物を送ると同時に、送り状を送付します。送り状は、物を送る際の案内状です。誰がどんな目的で何を送ったかを相手に知らせます。受け取る側でも、案内状で品物の到着をあらかじめ知っていれば、安心して受け取ることができますし、腐りやすいものや品物が到着しないときにはその対策も早急に手配できます。

3) 事務的な物品を送るのとは違い、季節の贈り物や何かあった時どきの贈り物は贈る理由があってのことですから、ふだん世話になっていることへの礼や、相手が特別に厚意を示してくれたことに対する礼を述べます。

4) 今後の支援を願い、相手の繁栄を祈る定型のあいさつを簡潔に書くのが通例です。

5) その人の具体的な援助のあるなしにかかわらず、「お陰を持ちまして」とか「お陰様で」などといった感謝の表現を書いておきます。

6) 贈り物の内容は、具体的に書かずに「心ばかりのもの」「粗品」「些少ですが」などといった謙遜した表現を用いるのが普通です。

7) 「私」とか「弊社」などの自分たちを表すことばは、行の末尾か行の中に来るように書きます。

1. In Japan, in addition to gifts given when something special happens, it is customary to send seasonal gifts (two times a year) to express thanks for continuing support in the day-to-day operations and as a seasonal greeting. The gift given in early December is called 歳暮(せいぼ) (year-end gift) and the one given in mid-July is called 中元(ちゅうげん) (midyear gift). When you deviate from this schedule, you may use such phrases as 暑中(しょちゅう)お見舞(みまい)/暑中お伺(うかが)い (midsummer greeting), 残暑(ざんしょ)お見舞 (late-summer greeting) or 寒中(かんちゅう)お見舞/寒中お伺い (midwinter greeting).

2. Whenever you send a gift, send a message announcing that you have sent something. The message is sent at the same time as the gift, telling the recipient who it is from, what it is, and why it is being sent. It will be good for the recipient to know to expect the arrival of a gift because they can receive it without concern, and if the gift doesn't arrive promptly (especially if it is something that might spoil), they can take appropriate action.

3. Unlike sending business items, there is always a reason behind the sending of gifts. It may be a thank you for the constant support given by the recipient, or it may be a thank you given for a special favor. In any case, you should acknowledge it with a thank you.

4. It is normal to conclude your letter with a concise formal greeting.

5. Regardless of whether or not you are the recipient of that party's concrete support, phrases such as お陰をもちまして or お陰様で ("I am grateful for your support," or "I am indebted to you") are often used.

6. In Japan, you usually do not indicate the exact contents of the gift. Instead, you write something like 心ばかりのもの, 粗品(そしな), 些少(さしょう)ですが ("it's a small gift" or "a small token of my gratitude").

7. Do not begin a line with 私 (I) or 弊社(へいしゃ) (our company). If you use these words, they should come at the end of the line or somewhere in the middle.

5-5 出張報告を書く

Writing a report of a business trip

展示(てんじ)会参加の準備打ち合わせに出張した営業課員が、その内容と対策試案(しあん)を記(しる)した出張報告を上司に提出します。

An employee of the sales department writes a report to his supervisor on the briefing session for an exhibition he attended. He explains what happened at the session and the tentative plans for the exhibition.

出 張 報 告 書

199○年○月○日

営業部長殿

営業一課　加藤勇人(はやと)（印）

下記の通り出張しましたので、ご報告いたします。

記

1．月　日：199○年○月○日（金）　午後1時～7時
2．出張先：幕張(まくはり)メッセ
3．目　的：「春のインテリア・フェスティバル」現地説明会への出席
4．成　果：①説明会の次第は、添付(てんぷ)Ⅰ参照
②説明役は、協会理事の三浦　忠(ただし)氏ほか
③説明の要点は、以下の通り
フェスティバルの会場は、「幕張メッセ第三会場」
同会場のレイアウトは、添付Ⅱの通り
各社へのブース割当(わりあ)ては、クジ引き抽選(ちゅうせん)による
会場運営は、前日午後5時から打合せ
④ブース抽選の結果、当社は「C-5」（添付Ⅱの赤印）で、中央部に近く好位置といえる
⑤現地を見ての加藤のディスプレイ試案は、添付Ⅲの通り

以　上

（添付資料）
Ⅰ．説明会案内
Ⅱ．フェスティバル会場レイアウト
Ⅲ．ディスプレイ加藤試案

～先：place of ～　成果：results　次第：order　添付(てんぷ)：attachment　参照：see; refer　～役：(persons) in charge of ～　協会理事：association trustee　要点：main points　ブース割当(わりあ)て：booth allotment　クジ引き抽選(ちゅうせん)による：(decided) by drawing lots　会場運営：management of auditorium　好位置：favorable location　試案：tentative plan

Report of Business Trip

Date (year, month, day)

The Honorable Sales Department Manager

Sales Department First Section Kato Hayato (seal)

Below is a report of my business trip.

Details

1. Date, time: Year, month, day (Friday) 1:00–7:00 P.M.
2. Place: Makuhari Messe
3. Purpose: Attend the on-site briefing for the "Spring Home Furnishings Fair"
4. Results: (1)Order of business for briefing (see Attachment # I)
(2)Persons in charge of briefing: Miura Tadashi (Association Trustee), and others
(3)Main points of briefing were as follows:
Place of fair—Makuhari Messe, Third Auditorium.
Layout of this auditorium is shown in Attachment #II.
Booths for each company were assigned by drawing lots.
As for the management of the auditorium, we will meet beginning at 5:00 P.M. on the day prior to the event.
(4)As a result of the drawing, our company will have Booth C-5 (marked in red on Attachment #II), a good location near the middle.
(5)Kato's tentative plan for the display, after viewing the actual site, is seen in Attachment #III

(the end)

(Attachments)
I. Order of business for briefing
II. Layout of festival auditorium
III. Kato's display plan

留意事項

1) 出張報告は、5W1Hを基本に出張の月日時間、出張先、目的、見聞(けんぶん)や打ち合わせ内容、所見または対策などを記(しる)します。
2) 文章は簡潔(かんけつ)な表現で記します。「参照(ください)」「打ち合わせ(を行う)」「～の通り(です)」などの(　)部を省略(しょうりゃく)した文体が多用されます。
3) 関係資料があれば添付(てんぷ)します。

1. Reports of business trips basically follow the 5Ws and 1H pattern and include the date of the trip, where you went, the purpose, what you saw, heard, and discussed, your views, and possible steps to be taken.
2. Use concise sentences. Omit the underlined parts of the following: 参照ください, 打ち合わせを行う, ～の通りです.
3. Related materials should accompany the report.

第6課

会議を終えて議事録を書く

Writing the minutes of meetings

会議が行われたとき、議題、経過、決定内容などを日時、場所、出席者名を含めて記録したものを議事録といいます。議事録は、

⑴記録を残す

⑵会議出席者には議事内容を確認させる

⑶出席しなかった上司や関係者へは会議の内容を報告したり周知したりする

ためにも使われます。

議事録には、次のような内容を記載します。

⑴会議の目的、開催日時、場所、出席者名と会議内容を書きます。

⑵会議の内容は、議題と結論を主体にその理由、議事の経過、決定事項、合意事項や以前からの懸案事項、今回の保留事項と今後の展望などを箇条書きにして、簡潔にまとめます。また、会議の招集者名、記録担当者名を書いておきます。（普通、招集者側が記録も担当します。）

議事録(ぎじろく), or minute-taking, is a record made when a meeting is held, and includes such matters as the subject of discussion, progress, decisions reached, as well as the time, date, and place, and those who attended.

Recording an agenda:

1. keeps a record;
2. lets those present have a record of the proceedings and content of the meeting;
3. can also be used for informing those in higher positions and other related persons who did not attend of the content of the meeting.

The following points should be included:

1. The objective of the meeting, the date, time and place of occurrence, those present, and the content of the meeting.
2. The content of the meeting includes the subject of discussion and conclusion as well as the progress made, decided matters, mutually consented issues or long-pending problems, undecided matters in the meeting, and future prospects, etc. These should be written concisely in an itemized statement. Also, the names of those who organized the meeting and the minutes-taker should be included. (Usually, the meeting organizers will also be taking minutes.)

6-1 提携先検討会議の議事録を書く

Writing the minutes of a meeting to consider an affiliation partner

S&A社では、支社長以下関連する部課のメンバーを集めて、販売提携先をどこにするかを話し合うための全体会議が開かれ、その内容について議事録を作ります。

At S&A Corporation, the office manager and members of related departments come together for a general meeting to discuss which company they want an affiliation with, and the minutes of the meeting are written.

199○年○月○日

提携先検討会議議事録

日時： 199○年○月○日（月） 09:00～11:00

場所： 第5会議室

出席： スミス支社長

（営業部） 山本営業部長、（営業企画課）井上課長

（営業一課） 中野課長、加藤（記録）

（営業二課） 橋本課長、峰

（戸田工場） 田山工場長

（経理部） 丸山経理部長、斎藤経理課長

（総務部） 青山総務部長、秋山総務課長代理

議題： 提携先検討の件

議事：

山本営業部長から、日本における販売促進のためかねてから販売提携先の選定を行ってきたが、この程候補の3社を得たので、この内の1社を選ぶことにしたいと発言があった。

現在までに得られた情報をもとに検討。

多くのメーカーを抱えている社よりも、当社の意向を汲んで小回りの利く方がよい、製品の引取りなどの面から財務的に資産内容のよい社を選ぶ、全国的に販売網を持つところがよいなどいろいろ意見が出た。

候補企業の財務内容、販売網などは経理課が業者を利用して信用調査を行い確認し、既提携先の有無や提携条件については営業企画課が窓口になって打診を行い、最終候補を絞ることとなった。

なお、打診の順番は、

①株式会社インテックス

②高島インテリア株式会社

③吉田物産株式会社

とする。

以上

加藤記

課長代理：representative/acting chief (of a section)　議題：topic　販売促進：sales promotion　選定を行う：undertake selection　候補：candidate　抱える：carry; deal with　当社の意向を汲む：respond to our intentions　小回りが利く：can maneuver more effectively　製品の引取り：trading of products; taking over of products　財務的に資産内容がよい：assets are financially sound　全国的に販売網を持つ：have a nationwide sales network　業者を利用する：hire a company in the trade　既提携先の有無：whether or not tie-ups are already formed (with other companies)　〜条件：conditions of 〜　窓口になる：become the contact　打診を行う：sound out　最終候補を絞る：narrow it down to a final candidate　〜記：record

Date (year, month, day)

Minutes of meeting to consider tie-up partner

Date, time: Year, month, day (Monday) 9:00–11:00 A.M.
Place: Conference room # 5
Those in attendance: Office Manager Smith
(Sales Department) Manager Yamamoto
(Sales Planning Section) Chief Inoue
(Sales Section One) Chief Nakano, Kato (Secretary)
(Sales Section Two) Chief Hashimoto, Mine
(Toda Factory) Manager Tayama
(Accounting Department) Manager Maruyama, Accounting Section Chief Saito
(General Affairs Department) Manager Aoyama, Section Representative Chief Akiyama
Topic: RE: Considering a tie-up partner
Business:

Sales Department Manager Yamamoto made the following statement. We have already begun work on selecting a tie-up partner to promote our sales in Japan, and three companies have emerged as candidates. I think we should choose one of these three. The three were considered using information already on hand.

A number of opinions emerged. For example, rather than choosing a company that deals with many different manufacturers, it would be better to choose a smaller, more versatile company that can respond to our intentions, or to choose a company that is financially sound from the trading standpoint, or to focus on a company with a nationwide sales network.

To narrow down the field to a final choice, for financial stability and networking, it was decided that the accounting section would hire an investigation agency to conduct a credit check on the candidate companies; the sales planning section will become the contact to sound out whether the candidates have already formed tied-ups with other companies and the conditions of these tie-ups.

Furthermore, they will be sounded out in the following order:
(1) Intex, Incorporated
(2) Takashima Interior, Incorporated
(3) Yoshida Trading, Incorporated

(the end)
Recorded by Kato

留意事項

1) 重要な発言には、発言者の氏名を記録することがあります。
2) 社内への周知には、議事録の写しやその抜き書きしたものを用います。
3) 記書きや議事の箇条書きの結語には「以上」と記して、その記載事項の終わりであることを示します。

1. There are times when the name of the presenter is included when important points of discussion are noted.
2. Copies of minutes and extracts are used in order to inform all within the company of the contents of a meeting.
3. After a short description of the meeting and a listing of all the items of business, write 以上 (the end) to show that this is where the contents stop.

6-2 カタログ作成打ち合わせ会議の議事録を書く

Writing the minutes of a meeting to discuss the production of a catalog

S&A社では、総合カタログの作成に関する社内会議が開かれます。そこで、予算や作成部数などについての方針が決められ、議事録を作ります。

An in-house meeting is held at S&A Corporation to discuss the production of a general catalog. The policy concerning the budget and number of copies to be printed is decided, and minutes are written.

カタログ作成につき社内打合せ会議の

議　事　録

1）日　時：　○月○日（金曜日）　午前10時～正午

2）場　所：　本社会議室

3）出席者：　総務部　青山部長、中山総務課長、渡辺秘書室長

経理部　丸山部長

営業部　山本部長、中野営業一課長、橋本営業二課長、井上営業企画課長、山口営業企画課員

戸田工場　田山工場長

4）議　題：「デュクロン」の総合カタログ作成の件

5）議　事：　まず山本営業部長からカタログ作成の趣旨(しゅし)が述(の)べられ、議題の各事項について、井上営業企画課長から細部の説明があった。各部課長から、質問、発言があり、最終的に次の通り決定、山本部長が各事項の確認を行った。

①予算：　400万円

②用紙：　A4版サイズとし、表紙は厚紙のミラーコート紙、本文はコート紙とする。

③レイアウト：コート紙を三つ折りにして、中央のページに商品サンプルを貼(は)り付ける。

文案、デザイン、写真などのレイアウト全般(ぜんぱん)は、指定デザイナーと打合す。

④作成部数：　4,000部

⑤発注先(はっちゅうさき)：　MAP社

⑥納期(のうき)：　　　平成○年○月○日

以上

平成○年○月○日

記録　山口（営業企画課）

押印欄(おういんらん)								

議題：topic　趣旨(しゅし)：purpose　各事項：particulars　ミラーコート紙：glossy paper　三つ折りにする：folded into thirds　貼(は)り付ける：attach　文案：draft　～全般(ぜんぱん)：overall ～　指定デザイナー：appointed designer　発注先(はっちゅうさき)：company to which (you) place an order　納期(のうき)：delivery date　記録：record

Minutes of meeting to discuss the production of a catalog

1. Date, time: Month, day (Friday) 10-12 noon

2. Place: Main office conference room

3. Those in attendance: (General Affairs Department) Manager Aoyama, General Affairs Section Chief Nakayama, Secretary Office Chief Watanabe
(Accounting Department) Manager Maruyama
(Sales Department) Manager Yamamoto, Sales Section One Chief Nakano, Sales Section Two Chief Hashimoto, Sales Planning Section Chief Inoue, Sales Planning Section Yamaguchi
(Toda Factory) Manager Tayama

4. Topic: Production of a general catalog for Dukelon

5. Business: First, Sales Department Manager Yamamoto explained the purpose of producing a catalog, and then Sales Planning Section Chief Inoue gave a detailed explanation of the particulars. Section chiefs asked questions and expressed opinions, with the following decisions coming out of the discussion. Manager Yamamoto confirmed the content with all present.
(1) Budget: 4 million yen
(2) Size: A-4; use heavy glossy paper for the cover and coated paper for the inside.
(3) Layout: Fold the coated paper in thirds, attaching a product sample to the middle section. Consult with an appointed designer about the overall layout—draft, design, and pictures.
(4) Number of copies to print: 4,000
(5) Order to: MAP Company
(6) Deadline for delivery: Year, month, day

(the end)

Date (year, month, day)

Recorded by Yamaguchi (Sales Planning Section)

Seals								

留意事項

1) 重要な決定が行われたときは、作成した議事録の内容に間違いのないことを確認するため、議事録原本に出席者の印を押してもらうことがあります。

2) 記書きや議事の箇条書きの結語には「以上」と記して、その記載事項の終わりであることを示します。

3) 記録の責任を示すため、記録者の名前を記すことがあります。

1\. When important decisions are made, those in attendance are asked to affix their seal to the original minutes, thus affirming that it contains no mistakes.

2\. After a short description of the meeting and a listing of all the items of business, write 以上 (the end) to show that this is where the contents stop.

3\. At times, the name of the secretary is noted, showing who is responsible for writing the minutes.

6-1と6-2のフローと文例

6-1「提携先検討会議の議事録を書く」のフロー

199○年○月○日 ・記録日

提携先検討会議議事録

日時：　199○年○月○日（月）09:00～11:00 ・日　時

場所：　第5会議室 ・場　所

出席：　スミス支社長 ・出席者

（営業部）　山本営業部長、（営業企画課）井上課長

（営業一課）　中野課長、加藤（記録）

（営業二課）　橋本課長、峰

（戸田工場）　田山工場長

（経理部）　丸山経理部長、斎藤経理課長

（総務部）　青山総務部長、秋山総務課長代理

議題：　提携先検討の件 ・議　題

議事： ・議　事

山本営業部長から、日本における販売促進のためかねてから販売提携先の選定を行ってきたが、この程候補の3社を得たので、この内の1社を選ぶことにしたいと発言があった。（後略）

以上

加藤記 ・記録者

6-2「カタログ作成打ち合わせ会議の議事録を書く」のフロー

カタログ作成につき社内打合せ会議の

議　事　録

1）日　時：　○月○日（金曜日）　午前10時～正午 ・日　時

2）場　所：　本社会議室 ・場　所

3）出席者：　総務部　青山部長、中山総務課長、渡辺秘書室長 ・出席者

経理部　丸山部長

営業部　山本部長、中野営業一課長、橋本営業二課長、井上営業企画課長、山口営業企画課員

戸田工場　田山工場長

4）議　題：「デュクロン」の総合カタログ作成の件 ・議　題

5）議　事：　まず山本営業部長からカタログ作成の趣旨が述べられ、議題の各事項について、井上営業企画課長から細部の説明があった。各部課長から、質問、発言があり、最終的に次の通り決定、山本部長が各事項の確認を行った。（後略） ・議　事

以上

平成○年○月○日 ・記録日

記録　山口（営業企画課） ・記録者

押印欄								

・押印欄

「議事録」 Minutes of a meeting

- 日　時　date
- 場　所　place
- 出席者　those present
- 議　題　subject
- 議　事　agenda

　議事の概要（がいよう）（議事の経緯（けいい）、発言の内容、発言者の氏名など）

　outline of agenda (circumstances of agenda, contents of address, name of addresser, etc.)

　決定事項　issues decided

“以上”　end

- 記録日　date recorded
- 記録者　minute-taker
- 押印欄（おういんらん）　stamp seal

〈議事の経緯（けいい）の書き方〉

How to write the circumstances of the agenda

＊山本営業部長から、…………ことにしたい**と発言があった**。(6-1)

Sales Department Manager Yamamoto made the following statement . . . .

＊…………**などいろいろな意見が出た**。(6-1)

A number of opinions emerged. For example, . . .

＊議題の各事項**について**、井上営業企画課長**から**細部の**説明があった**。(6-2)

Sales Planning Section Chief Inoue gave a detailed explanation of the particulars.

＊最終的に次の通り決定、山本部長**が**各事項の**確認を行った**。(6-2)

The following decisions came out of the discussion, and Manager Yamamoto confirmed the content with all present.

〈決定事項の書き方〉

How to write the issues decided

＊既提携先（きていけい）の有無（うむ）や提携条件**については**、営業企画課**が**窓口になって打診（だしん）を行い、最終候補（こうほ）を絞る（しぼ）**こととなった**。(6-1)

To narrow down the field for the final choice, the sales planning section will become the contact to sound out whether the candidates have already formed tied-ups with other companies and the conditions of these tie-ups.

＊打診（だしん）の順番**は**、……**とする**。(6-1)

They will be sounded out in the following order.

＊用紙**は**A４版サイズ**とし**、表紙**は**ミラーコート紙、本文**は**コート紙**とする**。(6-2)

A-4 size, heavy glossy paper will be used for the cover and coated paper for the inside.

6-3 カタログ作成のための追加予算の申請をする
Applying for additional funding for the production of a catalog

営業企画課長は、会議の決定に基づいて、不足分のカタログ作成予算の追加申請書を書きます。
Based on the decision made at a meeting, the chief of the planning section of the sales department writes an application for additional funds needed to produce a catalog.

199○年○月○日

写 営業部長、経理課長

総 務 課 長 殿

営 業 企 画 課 長（印）

<u>カタログ作成追加予算の件（申請）</u>

当上期においては、カタログ作成費として300万円を予算に計上願っておりますが、その後の検討の結果、当初予定の3,000部を4,000部に増加することになりましたので、作成費として100万円を追加し、合計400万円として修正計上願いたく、申請します。

以 上

添付書類：カタログ作成社内打合せ会議の議事録（写）

上期：the first half of the year　～費：～ budget/funds　計上する：set aside (a budget)　当初予定：originally planned　増加：increase　修正計上：revised budget　添付書類：attached documents

Date (year, month, day)

Copies: Sales Department Manager, Accounting Section Chief

The Honorable General Affairs Section Chief

Sales Planning Section Chief (seal)

<u>Additional funding for production of a catalog (request)</u>

For the first half of the current year, we requested a budget of 3 million yen to produce the catalog, but after consideration, we decided to increase the originally planned number to be produced from 3,000 to 4,000. For this reason, we wish to request a revised budget, an increase in the budget of 1 million yen, giving a grand total of 4 million yen.

(the end)

Attached document: Minutes of the meeting to discuss the production of a catalog (copy)

留意事項

1)上司の許可を求める書類には「稟議書」がありますが、例のように「申請書」という形式もあります。申請書は、あまり重要ではない案件や出張・休暇などの許可・認可を、その権限のある部署や人に求めるときに使います。対等の立場などにある相手に何かを依頼するときは「依頼状」の形をとります。

2)上の例は、すでに決済を受けている案件の金額の増額の例です。すでに決められている予算額があればそのことを記し、新しい申請内容を書きます。

3)必要ならば、追加の根拠となった会議の議事録を添付します。

4)決定事項の実施期日や数量的な条件などの付帯条件があれば、それも付け加えます。

1. When requesting the permission of a superior, 稟議書(りんぎしょ) (circular letters) are often used, but as in the example, the request can also take the form of an application (申請書(しんせいしょ)). This form is used for less important matters, or for seeking the permission or approval of the section or person responsible for such matters as going away on business or taking a vacation. When requesting something from someone who is your equal, use the 依頼状 (request) form.

2. This example deals with an increase in the monetary amount for an item already approved. If a budget figure has already been decided on, first note that amount, and then write the contents of the new request.

3. If necessary, attach the minutes of the meeting at which the decision to make the additional request was made.

4. Add other incidental conditions, such as the date for implementation, or conditions relating to the number of copies, etc., if any.

6-4 会議の結論により取り引きを打診する

Sounding out intentions to do business as a result of decisions made at a meeting

S&A社は、社内会議の決定方針に従って、提携候補の吉田物産宛に提携の意思があるかないかを打診する文書を書きます。

S&A Corporation, in accordance with the policy decided on at an in-house meeting, writes a letter to Yoshida Trading, their candidate for a tie-up, to sound out whether or not Yoshida is interested in becoming linked up.

平成○年○月○日

〒150-0000　東京都渋谷区青山6-1-2
吉田物産株式会社
　営業部長　山田栄三殿

〒100-0004　東京都千代田区大手町1-2-1
平成ビル８階　#801号
S&Aコーポレーション
日本支社長　（サイン）
H. G. スミス

謹啓　貴社益々ご隆盛のこととお慶び申し上げます。

さて、

誠に突然ですが、弊社とのお取引をお願い申し上げたく、本状を差し上げました。

弊社は、

アメリカのニューヨークに本社を持つ家具、インテリアの製造販売会社で、５年前に日本に進出、ユニークな商品を提供する会社としてさらに日本市場での売上を伸ばすべく努力中であります。

　この度、デューク社が開発した特殊カーペット「デュクロン」の東アジア地区での独占販売権を得ましたのを機会に、この商品の全国的な規模での販路拡張を展開することになりました。

　つきましては、かねてから広くインテリアを手掛けて実績を上げておられます御社と、ぜひお取引をお願いいたしたく存じます。近日中にご都合を伺って改めて参上のうえお打ち合わせ申し上げたく存じておりますが、本日はとりあえず書中をもって貴意を得たく申し上げます。

　なお、貴検討のご参考までに弊社の会社案内と営業案内を同封させて頂きました。また、弊社の信用状況などにつきましては「うめ銀行浜松町支店」にご照会を賜れば幸いに存じます。

　突然のお願いにて誠に恐縮に存じますが、まずは要用のみ申し上げます。　敬具

同封書類：　会社案内、営業案内書　各１通　以上

提供する：offer; supply　～べく：should　特殊（とくしゅ）：specialty　東アジア地区での独占販売権を得る：have exclusive sales rights in East Asia　～を機会に：using the opportunity of ～　全国的な規模（きぼ）：nationwide scale　販路拡張（はんろかくちょう）を展開する：expand a market　手掛（てが）ける：deal (with)　実績を上げる：show fine performance　近日中：in the near future　参上のうえ打ち合わせる：visit (you) and have a meeting　貴意（きい）を得る：get your opinion　検討の参考までに：for help in your deliberations/considerations　同封する：include　照会（しょうかい）：inquiry

---

Date (year, month, day)

150-0000 Tokyo-to, Shibuya-ku, Aoyama 6-1-2
Yoshida Trading, Incorporated
Sales Department Manager Yamada Eizo (Mr.)

100-0004 Tokyo-to, Chiyoda-ku, Otemachi 1-2-1
Heisei Bldg. 8th fl., Room #801
S&A Corporation
Japan Office Manager (signature)
H. G. Smith

Salutations: I rejoice at your increasing prosperity and well-being.

Now, this is sudden, but I am sending this letter to request that you form a tie-up with our company.

Our company has its headquarters in New York City, and we manufacture and supply home furnishings. Five years ago we entered Japan, offering unique products, and we are presently exerting efforts to increase our sales in the Japanese market.

We have now received the exclusive rights to sell a specialty carpet called Dukelon, first developed by the Duke Company in East Asia. Using this opportunity, we have decided to expand our market for this product to a nationwide scale.

In this regard, we would like very much to affiliate with your company, as one that has dealt widely with home furnishings and shown very fine performance. In the near future, we would like to contact you for an appointment, and visit you for a meeting to consider this proposal. Today, I am writing to you because I would like to know of your wishes.

Furthermore, I have included a profile of our company and a guide to our sales to help in your deliberations. For information on our company's credit standing, we would be happy if you would inquire at Ume Bank, Hamamatsu-cho Branch.

I sincerely apologize for the suddenness of this request, and have just mentioned only the main concerns.

Sincerely yours

Enclosed documents: 1 company guide, 1 business guide

(the end)

留意事項

1) 過去に取り引きのない会社に出すので、先方の検討資料として、自社の概要(がいよう)や商品の説明などを書いた資料を同封します。

2) 提携(ていけい)など企業に大きな影響をおよぼす案件の場合、そしてこちらがまだ知名度(ちめいど)の低い企業のときは、自社の信用状況の確認・裏付(うらづ)けのためにどこに確かめたらよいのか、その照会(しょうかい)先を示すことがあります。その時は、照会先にあらかじめそのような措置(そち)をとったことを知らせておくことが必要です。

3) ビジネス文書では「貴意(きい)を得たく(存じ以上のごとく)申し上げます」の(　　)部を省略(しょうりゃく)した簡略(かんりゃく)な表現が多用されます。

1. As this letter is sent to a company you have not dealt with before, include a profile of your company and an explanation of products with your letter for their reference.

2. When items that will have a major impact on the business (such as a tie-up) are involved, or when you are not yet well-known, you sometimes provide references for the other party so that they can confirm your company's trustworthiness, etc. When you do this, you must inform your references that you have given out their name.

3. In business letters, the following underlined words are often omitted: 貴意(きい)を得たく<u>存じ以上のごとく</u>申し上げます (I would like to know of your wishes).

第7課

取り決めなどの内容を確認する
Confirming the contents of agreements

面談や電話などの口頭でなされた約束事や打ち合わせは、誤解や聞き違いなどのトラブルを避けるため、またこちらの理解や措置を相手に間違いなく伝えるために、文書で内容をお互いに確認しておくことが大切です。

内容が微妙で重大なときほど、確認の文書は大切な意味を持ちます。確認文を出すときは、不明確な部分は社内の関係者に確かめ、用いる語句・表現は必要に応じて弁護士の見解を求める慎重さが必要です。

また、確認文を受け取ったときは、こちらの理解と相違はないかを確かめ、万一行き違いがあればその訂正を求めなければなりません。

When appointments have been made verbally (by telephone, and so on), in order to ensure no misunderstandings took place, or to ensure that you have been fully understood, it is also advisable to make a written confirmation outlining the contents of the conversation for the benefit of both parties.

When the issue is delicate and important, it is necessary to write a confirmation letter. When sending out letters of confirmation, check any unclear points with the relevant parties. Care should be taken in the use of words and expressions, and, in this respect, it may be necessary to ask the opinion of a lawyer.

When you receive a letter of confirmation, check that there has been no misunderstandings. If there are any, they must be communicated to the other party.

7-1 訪問の日時を確認する
Confirming the date and time of an appointment

吉田物産の山田部長がスミス日本支社長の訪問の申し入れを承諾(しょうだく)したので、スミスは、お礼とともに訪問の日時の確認の書状を書きます。

Mr. Yamada, manager of Yoshida Trading, has accepted Japan Office Manager Smith's desire to pay them a visit, so Mr. Smith writes to express his thanks and also to reconfirm the date and time for the visit.

199○年○月○日

吉田物産株式会社

営業部長　山田　栄三　殿

S&Aコーポレーション

日本支社長　H. G. スミス（印）

貴社ご訪問の件

拝啓(はいけい)　時下(じか)益々(ますます)ご清祥(せいしょう)のこととお慶(よろこ)び申し上げます。

さて、先日お願い致(いた)しました貴社にお伺(うかが)いする件につき、早速(さっそく)ご承引賜(しょういんたまわ)りまして、誠(まこと)にありがとうございました。つきましては、ご指定通り、

○月○日（火）　午後２時

弊(へい)営業部員ともども参上させて頂(いただ)きますので、何卒(なにとぞ)よろしくお願い申し上げます。

当日は鈴木常務取締役(じょうむとりしまりやく)殿にもご紹介頂けるとのことで、誠に幸(さいわ)いに存じます。

まずは取り急ぎ、参上日時確認かたがた御礼(おんれい)申し上げます。

敬具

承引(しょういん)：consent　ご指定通り：as appointed　参上する：visit　常務取締役(じょうむとりしまりやく)：managing director

Date (year, month, day)

Yoshida Trading, Incorporated
Sales Department Manager Yamada Eizo (Mr.)

S&A Corporation
Japan Office Manager H. G. Smith (seal)

RE: Paying a visit to your company

Salutations: Allow me to congratulate you on your good health and well-being at this time.

Now, concerning my recent request to pay a visit to your company, thank you very much for consenting to my proposal so quickly. In this regard, I would like to confirm that members of our sales department and I will visit your company on the appointed date of

(Month, day), (Tuesday) at 2:00 P.M.

We are extremely pleased to hear that we will be able to meet Managing Director Suzuki on that day, too.

I hasten to write to confirm our appointment to visit your company and also to thank you for this opportunity.

Sincerely yours

留意事項

1) 重要な約束や取り決めをしたときは、すぐあとに文書で内容を確認し、思い違いや解釈（かいしゃく）の相違（そうい）がないようにします。

2) 相手とのやり取りで不明確な部分について、社内の関係者の理解を確かめて文書を作ります。

3) 受け取った側で確認文書の内容に誤（あやま）りや表現に事実と違う点を見つけた場合は、すぐに先方に連絡して訂正（ていせい）を求めます。訂正しなければならない所があるのに、そのまま放置（ほうち）しておくと、確認文を認めたものと取られることがあります。

4) 確認が目的の文書は、客観的、具体的に、必要事項を簡潔（かんけつ）に書きます。

5) この例のように相手先訪問などで同位職以上の人も同席するような特別な処遇（しょぐう）を受けたときは、確認文の中でそれに対する感謝の気持ちも表します。

6) 文書の目的である部分（7-1では訪問日時）をはっきり示すため、行を変えて独立表示としたり、上下に1行ずつのスペースをあけて書くことがあります。

1. When an important appointment or agreement has been made, you should write to confirm the contents immediately, in order to avoid any misunderstandings or differences in interpretation.

2. When there is anything unclear in the communications with the other party, check with the other people concerned within the company before writing the document.

3. When you discover a mistake in the contents of the confirmation letter, you should contact the sender immediately to request a correction. If you do not respond, the sender will assume you approve of it as it is.

4. When a letter is written for confirmation purposes, the essential points should be written concisely, objectively, and clearly.

5. As in this example, when you are going to receive special treatment, such as being introduced to a higher-ranking official than yourself, you should express your appreciation for this in the confirmation letter.

6. To clearly show the purpose of your letter (in this example, the objective is to confirm the date and time of an appointment), change lines so that the specific information you want to confirm is on a new line. Sometimes you may want to double space both above and below that information.

7-2 企業研修の参加申し込みを確認する
Confirming an application to participate in business training

S&A社の山本部長は、電話で部下のセミナー参加を申し込みましたが、間違いのないように文書で内容を確認します。

Manager Yamamoto of S&A Corporation writes a letter to confirm the application to a seminar he has made by phone for his subordinates.

199○年○月○日

(社)企業研修センター
所長　土井　浩二　殿

S&Aコーポレーション　日本支社
営業部長　山本　良雄（印）

<u>リーダーシップ開発セミナー参加申込の件</u>

前略　先日はお電話で相変わらずお元気そうなお声に接し、大変お懐かしゅうございました。

その節お話ししました通り、私自身が昨年貴センターのセミナーに参加させていただき、土井所長はじめ皆様に連日ご指導いただきました経験は誠に貴重なもので、その後の私の大きな自信の源となっております。

この意義あるセミナーをぜひ若手社員にも経験させたいと考えていましたところ、幸い今年も同じカリキュラムで開かれるとのこと、お電話でお伝えした下記営業部員2名を予定通り参加申込させていただきます。

どうかよろしくご指導のほどお願い申し上げます。

まずは確認かたがたご連絡申し上げます。

草々

記

第5回（○月○日開催）リーダーシップ開発セミナー参加希望者：

営業一課所属　加藤　勇人　23歳

営業二課所属　峰　龍吉　28歳

以上

（社）：corporate juridical person（＝社団法人）　企業研修センター：business training center　リーダーシップ開発セミナー：leadership development seminar　お声に接する：hear (your) voice　お懐かしゅう：bring back fond memories　～始め：～ and　連日：day after day　自信の源：source of confidence　意義ある：meaningful　若手：young employees　幸い：happily; luckily　～希望者：registrations (for ～)　～所属：belonging to ～

Date (year, month, day)

Business Training Center, Inc.
Manager Doi Koji (Mr.)

S&A Corporation, Japan Office
Sales Department Manager Yamamoto Yoshio (seal)

RE: Leadership Development Seminar Registration

I hasten to write that it brought back fond memories when I spoke with you on the phone the other day and heard your always cheerful voice once again.

As I mentioned at that time, I myself participated in a seminar at your center last year, and the experience of receiving the guidance of you and your staff day after day was extremely valuable. Since then, that experience has given me a strong source of self-confidence.

When I was considering providing some of our young employees with the experience of such a meaningful seminar, I heard that luckily a seminar with the same curriculum as last year will be held. We are planning to have the following two employees of our sales department participate, as I mentioned over the phone.

I would appreciate your advice.

I first wanted to contact you for confirmation.

Sincerely yours

Details

Registrations for the Fifth Leadership Training Seminar (to be held [month, day])

Sales Section One Employee　Kato Hayato, age 23
Sales Section Two Employee　Mine Ryukichi, age 28

(the end)

留意事項

1) リストにしたほうがわかりやすいものは、記書きにして別表示にします。そのほうが、文の流れも中断されずにすみます。

2) 文書中の氏名で読みが難しいとみられるもの、特殊な読み方をするものについては、ふりがなをつけることがあります。

3) 宛先の企業名などは、省略せずに書くのが正式です。しかし、親しい間柄や当方が客の立場のとき、または

1.　When items are more easily understood in list form, write these items separately from the rest of the letter. In this way, the flow will not be interrupted.

2.　When including names that the recipient may have difficulty reading, or when they are to be read in a special way, include *furigana* with the name to show proper pronunciation.

3.　The name of the company being contacted should not be abbreviated. However,

簡単な内容の文書のときなどは、簡略化することがあります。

上の例の(社)は「社団法人」の略です。このほか略記としては、

株式会社 → (株)
有限会社 → (有)
財団法人 → (財)

などがあります。

4) 旧知の間柄やこちらが顧客の立場にあるときは、慶賀のあいさつを省略することがあります。

5) この種の参加申し込みなどは、所定の用紙があってそれに記入して提出すればよいことが多いのですが、上の例は所定様式ではない形で文書を書く例です。

when you either know the other party well, or you are a customer, or the contents of the letter are simple, you may simplify the company name by using abbreviations. The (社) in the Japanese text refers to 社団法人 (a corporate juridical person). Other common abbreviations include:

(株) = 株式会社(かぶしきがいしゃ)
—joint-stock company
(有) = 有限会社(ゆうげんがいしゃ)
—limited (liability) company
(財) = 財団法人(ざいだんほうじん)
—a foundation

4. When you have known the other party for a long time or you are a customer, you may omit the congratulatory greeting.

5. Prescribed forms are often available for this type of application, but this example illustrates how to write a letter when no set form is provided.

7-1と7-2のフローと文例

7-1「訪問の日時を確認する」のフロー

貴社ご訪問の件

拝啓　時下益々ご清祥のこととお慶び申し上げます。

さて、先日お願い致しました貴社にお伺いする件につき、早速ご承引賜りまして、誠にありがとうございました。つきましては、ご指定通り、

①承諾してくれたことに対して礼を述べる

○月○日(火)　午後2時

弊営業部員ともども参上させて頂きますので、何卒よろしくお願い申し上げます。

②決定事項を確認する

当日は鈴木常務取締役殿にもご紹介頂けるとのことで、誠に幸いに存じます。

③相手の配慮に対して礼を述べる

まずは取り急ぎ、参上日時確認かたがた御礼申し上げます。

敬具

7-2「企業研修の参加申し込みを確認する」のフロー

リーダーシップ開発セミナー参加申込の件

前略　先日はお電話で相変わらずお元気そうなお声に接し、大変お懐かしゅうございました。

その節お話ししました通り、私自身が昨年貴センターのセミナーに参加させていただき、土井所長はじめ皆様に連日ご指導いただきました経験は誠に貴重なもので、その後の私の大きな自信の源となっております。

この意義あるセミナーをぜひ若手社員にも経験させたいと考えていましたところ、幸い今年も同じカリキュラムで開かれるとのこと、お電話でお伝えした下記営業部員2名を予定通り参加申込させていただきます。

②決定事項を確認する

どうかよろしくご指導のほどお願い申し上げます。

まずは確認かたがたご連絡申し上げます。

草々

記

第5回（○月○日開催）リーダーシップ開発セミナー参加希望者：

営業一課所属　加藤　勇人　23歳

営業二課所属　峰　龍吉　28歳

④記――決定事項

以上

（下線の部分は自分の状況に合わせて書いてください。）

①承諾してくれたことに対して礼を述べる

Extending thanks for consent given

＊先日お願い致しました貴社にお伺いする件につき、早速ご承引賜りまして、誠にありがとうございました。 (7-1)

Concerning my recent request to pay a visit to your company, thank you very much for consenting to my proposal so quickly.

＊貴社ご訪問の件、ご快諾下さいましてありがとうございました。

As to the matter of visiting your company, thank you for agreeing so readily.

＊この度貴社ご主催の展示会に当社の出展をご承認頂き、誠にありがとうございました。

Thank you very much for your approval of our application for the exhibition you will present.

②決定事項を確認する

Confirming the issues decided

＊ご指定通り、○月○日（火）午後２時　弊営業部員ともども参上させて頂きますので、何卒よろしくお願い申し上げます。 (7-1)

I would like to confirm that members of our sales department and I will visit your company on the appointed date of (month, day), (Tuesday) at 2:00 P.M.

＊お電話でお伝えした下記営業部員２名を予定通り参加申込させていただきます。どうかよろしくご指導のほどお願い申し上げます。 (7-2)

We are planning to have the following two employees of our sales department participate, as I mentioned over the phone. I would appreciate your advice.

＊ご指定の○月○日に搬入作業をさせて頂きますので、どうぞよろしくお願いいたします。

I would like to confirm that I will make the delivery as of the set date of (month, day).

③相手の配慮に対して礼を述べる

Extending thanks for unexpected consideration

＊当日は鈴木常務取締役にもご紹介頂けるとのことで、誠に幸いに存じます。 (7-1)

We are extremely pleased to hear that we will be able to meet Managing Director Suzuki on that day, too.

＊当日はご担当の方々にもお引合わせいただける由、ご高配厚くお礼申し上げます。

I am deeply grateful for your kindness in introducing us that day to the various persons in charge.

＊また、開会式にもご招待頂き、ありがとうございました。ご配慮に厚く感謝申し上げます。

Thank you very much for inviting us to the opening ceremony also. I am deeply grateful for your consideration.

④記――決定事項（日時、参加者など）

Description—issues decided (date, participants, etc.)

社外 通知する〈送り状〉 giving notice

7-3 資料やサンプルを送り、その内容を確認する

Confirming that materials and samples have been sent

S&A社の山本部長は、吉田物産から求められた資料を送り、その送り状を書きます。

Manager Yamamoto of S&A Corporation sends materials requested by Yoshida Trading and writes a letter to confirm that they have been sent.

199○年○月○日

吉田物産株式会社

営業部長　山田　栄三　殿

S&Aコーポレーション　日本支社

営業部長　山本　良雄（印）

追加資料、商品見本送付の件

拝啓　時下益々ご清栄のこととお慶び申し上げます。

先日は私共のために貴重なお時間を割いていただき、誠にありがとうございました。鈴木常務殿をはじめ御一同様に私どもの説明をお聞き取りいただき、提携の件を前向きにご検討いただけるとのこと、心より感謝申し上げます。

当日ご要望のありました、下記追加資料および商品見本を同封の上お送り申し上げます。さらに追加のご要望等がありましたら、どうぞ何なりとお申し付け下さい。

まずは取り急ぎお礼かたがた用件まで。

敬具

記

1．デュクロン紹介ビデオテープ　3本
2．デュクロンほか商品標準価格表　3部
3．カーペットのリニューアル、メンテナンスの事業紹介　3部
4．デュクロンほか商品見本　3セット

以上

追加資料：additional materials　送付：sending　時間を割く：take time　常務：managing director　～をはじめ：～ and　一同：(all) others; everyone　お聞き取りいただく：listen to (our talk)　提携の件：the matter of a tie-up　前向きに検討する：give favorable consideration　要望がある：have a request　同封の上：

after including　何なりと：anything; whatever　標準価格表：standard price list
リニューアル：renewal　メンテナンス：maintenance

Date (year, month, day)

Yoshida Trading, Incorporated
Sales Department Manager Yamada Eizo (Mr.)

S&A Corporation, Japan Office
Sales Department Manager Yamamoto Yoshio (seal)

RE: The sending of additional materials and product samples

Salutations: I rejoice that you are increasingly well and prospering at this time.

Thank you very much for taking time the other day to meet with us. Allow me to express my deepest appreciation for the way in which Managing Director Suzuki and the others listened to our explanation and for the favorable consideration you gave to our proposal for a tie-up.

I have included here the additional materials and a sample of the product that you requested at the time of the meeting. If you would like us to send anything else, please feel free to request it.

I hasten to write to thank you again and to give you this information.

Sincerely yours

Details

1. Video tape introducing Dukelon—3 copies
2. Standard price list for Dukelon, etc.—3 copies
3. Introduction of carpet renewal and maintenance business—3 copies
4. Product samples of Dukelon, etc.—3 sets

(the end)

留意事項

1) 送付物の発送を相手先に通知する文書を「送り状」といいます。
2) 特別に依頼されたものや重要な物品を送る際は、送った、受け取らないなどの行き違いを避けるために、発送日や送付物の内容、数量を書いた送り状を作ります。木箱入りなどの荷姿や書留速達便などの送付の手段を書くこともあります。
3) 送り状には通例のあいさつを記しますが、この手紙では相手先の常務の同席など特記すべきことがあったので、それも記して謝意を表しています。

1. The letter sent to confirm the sending of materials to the recipient is called 送り状(おくりじょう).
2. When sending something that has been requested specifically or something important, to avoid anything going wrong, such as the other party not receiving it, send a letter stating such information as the date of sending, contents of the package, and number of items included. You may also include information on how it is packed (e.g., 木箱(きばこ)入り—packed in wooden container) or how it is sent (e.g., 書留速達(かきとめそくたつ)—special delivery registered mail).
3. Include a general greeting with this contents of delivery. In this letter, a word of thanks is also expressed because there is a special need to mention the presence of a managing director at the recent meeting.

第8課

相手先に対して回答を催促(さいそく)する

Pressing the other party for a reply

こちら側が待っている回答や返答が遅れているときは、先方に返事を催促(さいそく)することは大切な手続きです。

そのような手続きをする際は、ビジネスの社会ではいつまた協力関係を持つかわかりませんから、仮(かり)に相手に非がある場合でもなるべく友好関係を維持(いじ)できるような語句・表現を用いて文章を書きます。

When an answer or reply is slow in coming, it is important for the requesting party to press for a reply.

Even when the other party is at fault, when writing this kind of letter it is important to maintain friendly relations with the company, because in this business world you don't know whether or not you may be engaged in a cooperative relationship with that company again. Therefore, be careful to use words and phrases aimed at maintaining friendly relations.

8-1 販売提携の申し入れに対する回答を催促する

Pressing for a reply to a proposal for an affiliation

S&A社は吉田物産に販売提携についての申し入れをしましたが、返事が来ないので催促の文書を書きます。

S&A Corporation proposed that Yoshida Trading link up with them, but having not yet received a reply, they send a letter pressing for a reply.

199○年○月○日

吉田物産株式会社
　営業部長　山　田　栄　三　殿

S&Aコーポレーション　日本支社
営業部長　山　本　良　雄（印）

<u>デュクロン販売提携の件</u>

謹啓　時下初夏の候、貴社益々ご清祥の段お慶び申し上げます。

さて、

先日はご多用中のところお時間を割いて頂き、弊社S&Aの「デュクロン」の販売提携につきまして、ご懇談の機会を得ましたこと、ありがとうございました。

その後、御社内のご検討も進まれた頃かと存じますが、結果はいかがでございましたでしょうか。

何かご検討に追加資料など必要ではないかと考え、誠にぶしつけとは存じますが、ご連絡させて頂きました。あしからずご了承の上、貴社のご意向などを伺えれば幸せに存じます。

末筆ながら、ご自愛専一にお過ごしのほどお祈り申し上げます。

敬白

時間を割く：take time　懇談の機会を得る：get the chance to talk　追加資料：additional materials　ぶしつけと存ずる：I know it's impolite　了承の上：after understanding/acknowledging　意向：intentions　ご自愛専一にお過ごしのほど：devoting yourself to taking care of your health

Date (year, month, day)

Yoshida Trading, Incorporated
Sales Department Manager Yamada Eizo (Mr.)

S&A Corporation, Japan Office
Sales Department Manager Yamamoto Yoshio (seal)

RE: Dukelon tie-up

Salutations: Here at the beginning of summer, allow me to congratulate your company on its increasing health and well-being.

Now, thank you very much for taking time out of your extremely busy schedule and giving us the chance to talk about the possibility of linking up with S&A Corporation to sell our product Dukelon.

Since that time, we have been wondering how your in-house review of the matter is progressing and whether or not you have reached a decision yet.

I have also wondered if perhaps you need more materials for your deliberations, so, though I know it is impolite, I am contacting you at this time. I hope you will understand our situation, and I look forward to hearing your intentions.

In closing, it is my prayer that you devote yourself fully to taking care of your health.

Sincerely yours

留意事項

1) 返事が遅れているときの催促は、仮に先方に非がある場合でも「誠にぶしつけとは存じますが」などとていねいな表現で書き、なるべく友好関係を維持するように配慮します。ただし、こちらの言い分ははっきり述べます。

2) 文書の末尾の相手個人の「健康を祈る」「自愛を祈る」という記述は、個人的に親しい場合や親愛の情を表すときなどに書きますが、必ず書かなければならないものではありません。事務的な文では省略するのが普通です。

1. When exerting pressure because a reply is slow in coming, even when the fault is with the other party, be considerate and maintain friendly relations by using polite phrases like "I know this is extremely impolite, but . . ." However, convey your message clearly.

2. If you want to express personal friendship or closeness, add phrases like "I pray for your health" or "take care of yourself" at the end of your letter; it is not necessary, however, to include these words at all. They are usually omitted in business letters.

8-2 販売提携の申し入れに対する回答を強く催促する
Demanding a reply to a proposal for an affiliation

S&A社は吉田物産に先日の販売提携の申し入れにつき、回答次第では今後会社の方針を変更しなければならないこともあり得るので早急に返事がほしいと、回答期限を決めてやや強い調子で催促します。

With regard to S&A Corporation's request to Yoshida Trading for a sales tie-up, it may become necessary for S&A Corporation to change aspects of its company policy, depending on Yoshida Trading's answer, and therefore the company wants a response promptly. They decide on a deadline for the answer and send a rather strong demand for a reply.

平成○年○月○日

〒150-0000
東京都渋谷区青山 6-1-2
吉田物産株式会社
営業部長
　山　田　栄　三　殿

〒100-0004
東京都千代田区大手町 1-2-1
S&Aコーポレーション　日本支社
　支社長　（サイン）
　H. G. スミス

販売提携に関すること

謹啓　秋冷の候、ますますご清適の段慶賀に存じます。
　先日は弊社の特殊カーペット「デュクロン」のプレゼンテーションの機会を作って頂きましたこと、誠にありがとうございました。

　さて、「デュクロン」の販売代理店の件はご検討頂けましたでしょうか。私どもとしましても、御社のように信用も厚く手広くご商売をなさっているところと、ぜひお取り引き願いたいものと考えております。
　しかしながら、最近他社からの引き合いもあり、弊社といたしましても本件につき近く結論を出さなければならない状況になってきております。

　つきましては、お忙しいところ恐縮ですが、本件につき今月末までに御社のご意向をお聞かせ願えれば幸甚に存じます。何分宜しくお願いいたします。
　もしご回答済みのときは非礼の段何卒ご容赦ください。

敬具

特殊（とくしゅ）：specialty　プレゼンテーションの機会を作る：create an opportunity to make a presentation　販売代理店の件：the matter of (becoming) a sales agent　信用が厚い：trustworthy　手広く商売をする：do business widely　他社からの引き合いがある：receive inquiries from other companies　意向：intentions　幸甚（こうじん）に存じます：I would be very glad/obliged　回答済（ず）み：already sent reply　非礼の段：the impoliteness　容赦（ようしゃ）：excuse; pardon

Date (year, month, day)

150-0000 Tokyo-to, Shibuya-ku, Aoyama 6-1-2
Yoshida Trading, Incorporated
Sales Department Manager Yamada Eizo (Mr.)

100-0004 Tokyo-to, Chiyoda-ku, Otemachi 1-2-1
S&A Corporation, Japan Office
Office Manager (signature)
H. G. Smith

RE: Sales tie-up

Salutations: As the autumn chill comes on, I rejoice at your continued good health.
Thank you very much for creating an opportunity for us to make a presentation to you the other day on our specialty carpet Dukelon.

Now, have you given consideration to becoming a sales agent for Dukelon? We as a company would very much like to do business with your company, because you are trustworthy and do business on a wide level.
However, we have recently received inquiries from other companies, and it has become necessary for us to make a final decision on this matter soon.

For this reason, I hesitate to ask, knowing how busy you are, but I would be obliged if you could let us know your intentions on this matter by the end of this month. We appreciate your consideration.
If you have already sent your decision to us, please excuse the impoliteness of this inquiry.

Sincerely yours

留意事項

1)「強い調子」で催促（さいそく）する場合にも、ことば遣（づか）いはていねいにします。上位職の名で相手の上位職宛（あて）に催促状を書くのも効果があります。

2) 先方が回答を急がなければならないと思うような理由を加えます。

3) 万一先方が回答済（ず）みであった場合を考えて、念のため文書の末尾に、「もし行き違いで回答済みのときは、非礼の段なにとぞお許しください」などと書き添（そ）えるほうが礼をわきまえた文になります。

1. Even when sending a letter expressing strong demand, use polite language. It is sometimes effective to send the letter from a high-ranking person in the company to a top official in the other company.

2. Add an explanation that will make the other party feel they must reply promptly.

3. In case the other party has already sent their reply, add a sentence at the end of your letter saying, “If this letter crosses paths with your reply, please forgive my impoliteness.” That will make your courteous intentions clear.

4) 通常の催促は単に「返事をいただきたい」などと記(しる)しますが、強い催促文では、回答の期限を設けるとか回答遅延(ちえん)の理由をただす、あるいは期限が来れば回答の有無(うむ)にかかわらず当方では結論を出さなければならない事情があるなどと、表現はソフトでも先方が返事を出さざるを得ないような表現を用います。

4. In a normal letter asking for a reply, you simply write "I would like to receive your answer," but when making a strong demand, you may want to set a deadline by which the other party must reply or ask why their answer has been delayed, or you may explain that whether they answer by the deadline or not, your situation is such that you must reach a final conclusion by the date of the deadline. The expressions you use should be gentle, while also demanding a response.

8-1と8-2のフローと文例

8-1「販売提携の申し入れに対する回答を催促する」のフロー

デュクロン販売提携の件

謹啓　時下初夏の候、貴社益々ご清祥の段お慶び申し上げます。

さて、

先日はご多用中のところお時間を割いて頂き、弊社S&Aの「デュクロン」の販売提携につきまして、ご懇談の機会を得ましたこと、ありがとうございました。　（①これまでの労に対して礼を述べる）

その後、御社内のご検討も進まれた頃かと存じますが、結果はいかがでございましたでしょうか。　（②経過を照会する）

何かご検討に追加資料など必要ではないかと考え、誠にぶしつけとは存じますが、ご連絡させて頂きました。あしからずご了承の上、貴社のご意向などを伺えれば幸せに存じます。　（③回答を催促する）

末筆ながら、ご自愛専一にお過ごしのほどお祈り申し上げます。

敬白

8-2「販売提携の申し入れに対する回答を強く催促する」のフロー

販売提携に関すること

謹啓　秋冷の候、ますますご清適の段慶賀に存じます。

先日は弊社の特殊カーペット「デュクロン」のプレゼンテーションの機会を作って頂きましたこと、誠にありがとうございました。　（①これまでの労に対して礼を述べる）

さて、「デュクロン」の販売代理店の件はご検討頂けましたでしょうか。　（②経過を照会する）私どもとしましても、御社のように信用も厚く手広くご商売をなさっているところと、ぜひお取り引き願いたいものと考えております。

しかしながら、最近他社からの引き合いもあり、弊社といたしましても本件につき近く結論を出さなければならない状況になってきております。

つきましては、お忙しいところ恐縮ですが、本件につき今月末までに御社のご意向をお聞かせ願えれば幸甚に存じます。何分宜しくお願いいたします。　（③回答を催促する）

もしご回答済みのときは非礼の段何卒ご容赦ください。

敬具

（下線の部分は自分の状況に合わせて書いてください。）

①これまでの労に対して礼を述べる

Extending thanks for services so far

＊先日はご多用中のところお時間を割いて頂き、弊社S&Aの「デュクロン」の販売提携につきまして、ご懇談の機会を得ましたこと、ありがとうございました。(8-1)

Thank you very much for taking time out of your extremely busy schedule and giving us the chance to talk about the possibility of linking up with S&A Corporation to sell our product Dukelon.

＊先日は弊社の特殊カーペット「デュクロン」のプレゼンテーションの機会を作って頂きましたこと、誠にありがとうございました。(8-2)

Thank you very much for creating an opportunity for us to make a presentation to you the other day on our specialty carpet Dukelon.

＊○月○日付貴社発注書をもって弊社商品のご注文をいただきまして、ありがとうございました。

Thank you very much for ordering our product by your company's order form dated (month, day).

②経過を照会する

Inquiring into progress

＊その後、御社内のご検討も進まれた頃かと存じますが、結果はいかがでございましたでしょうか。(8-1)

Since that time, we have been wondering how your in-house review of the matter is progressing and whether or not you have reached a decision yet.

＊「デュクロン」の販売代理店の件はご検討頂けましたでしょうか。(8-2)

Have you given consideration to becoming a sales agent for Dukelon?

＊○月○日付請求書にてご送金ご依頼申し上げました弊社商品代金の件、いかが相成っておりますでしょうか。

Regarding the matter of the bill dated (month, day) for our goods, we are wondering whether payment has been completed or not.

③回答を催促する

Pressing for a reply

＊何かご検討に追加資料など必要ではないかと考え、誠にぶしつけとは存じますが、ご連絡させて頂きました。あしからずご了承の上、貴社のご意向などを伺えれば幸せに存じます。

(8-1)

I have wondered if perhaps you need more materials for your deliberations, so, though I know it is impolite, I am contacting you at this time. I hope you will understand our situation, and I look forward to hearing your intentions.

＊最近他社からの引き合いもあり、弊社といたしましても本件につき近く結論を出さなければならない状況になってきております。つきましては、お忙しいところ恐縮ですが、本件につき今月末までに御社のご意向をお聞かせ願えれば幸甚に存じます。(8-2)

We have recently received inquiries from other companies, and it has become necessary for us to make a final decision on this matter soon. For this reason, I hesitate to ask, knowing how busy you are, but I would be obliged if you could let us know your intentions on this matter by the end of this month.

*業務ご繁忙(はんぼう)のため、おとりまぎれになっているのではと存じますが、事情ご賢察(けんさつ)のうえ至急(しきゅう)お返事をお聞かせ願えれば幸(さいわ)いです。

I know that you must be preoccupied with the pressure of business, but after considering the conditions I would be happy if you would let me have your reply immediately.

8-3 回答に必要な補足資料の送付を求める
Requesting that additional materials necessary to make a reply be sent

吉田物産は販売提携の申し入れに対する回答が遅れ、S&A社から催促を受けましたが、回答の遅れている事情を述べ、追加資料を請求する手紙を出します。

Yoshida Trading receives a letter pressing for an answer to the sales tie-up proposal, and responds by explaining their reason for the delay and asking for additional materials.

199○年○月○日

S&Aコーポレーション　日本支社
　営業部長　山　本　良　雄　殿

吉田物産株式会社
　営業部長　山　田　栄　三（印）

プレゼンテーション補足資料の件

拝啓　盛夏の候となりました。益々ご清栄のこととお慶び申し上げます。

先日は貴社業務および製品に関し懇切なプレゼンテーションをして頂き、誠に有り難うございました。

また、早速追加資料と商品見本をお送り頂き、重ねて御礼申し上げます。

さて、頂きました情報・資料を社内で検討している段階で、「デュクロンのアメリカにおける販売実績を知りたい」との要望が出て参りました。誠に恐縮ですが、資料がありましたらお送り頂ければ幸いです。できましたら、発売当初から「年次別、品番別」に頂ければなお好都合です。

勝手ばかり申して恐れ入りますが、何卒よろしくお願い申し上げます。

取り急ぎ用件のみにて失礼いたします。

敬具

懇切な：cordial　追加資料：additional materials　検討している段階：be in the process of examining　販売実績：sales performance　要望が出る：a request emerges　発売当初から：from the beginning of sales　年次別：by yearly (sales)　品番別：by product number　なお好都合：it is more convenient　勝手ばかり：a lot of selfish requests

Date (year, month, day)

S&A Corporation, Japan Office
Sales Department Manager Yamamoto Yoshio (Mr.)

Yoshida Trading, Incorporated
Sales Department Manager Yamada Eizo (seal)

RE: More materials on your presentation

Salutations: The middle of summer has come. May I congratulate you on your increasing health and prosperity.

Thank you very much for the cordial presentation you made on the work of your company and products recently.
Also, allow me to express appreciation for the prompt manner in which you sent us the additional materials and product samples.

We are now in the process of examining the information and materials here within the company, and the following request has emerged: "We would like to know the performance of Dukelon sales in the United States." If you have such information, we would appreciate your sending it to us. If possible, it would be more convenient for us to have the results from the beginning of sales activities, both yearly and by product number.

I apologize for these selfish requests, but ask for your kind assistance.
Forgive me for hastily writing only these items of business.

Sincerely yours

留意事項

1) 回答が遅れることがあらかじめわかっているときは、事前にそのことを連絡しておくのが礼儀(れいぎ)です。
2) やむを得ず遅れて回答の猶予(ゆうよ)を求めるときは、検討の遅れた理由をはっきり示して先方の了解(りょうかい)を求めます。上の例では、資料の追加(ついか)を求めていますが、「社内で検討を進めているが、資料不足でまだ結論を得ることができない。資料の補充(ほじゅう)があれば検討結果も出る」という検討の遅れの理由を柔らかく述(の)べています。

1. When you know that your answer is going to be late, it is polite to let the other party know this beforehand.
2. When asking to put off a reply for an unavoidable reason, you should clearly explain the reason for being late and ask for the other party's understanding. In the above example, additional materials are requested, and a reason for the delay in the examination is tactfully extended, as in the following: "Our investigation is in progress, but due to insufficient materials we are unable to present a conclusion. If you have supplementary materials for investigation, a result will soon be reached."

8-4 回答の催促を受けて中間連絡をする
Making an interim reply in response to a request

吉田物産は、S&A社との提携問題についての回答催促に対して、前向きに検討していることを示しながらも、もうしばらく猶予がほしいと回答します。
In response to S&A Corporation's request for a reply on the tie-up issue, Yoshida Trading explains that while giving it favorable consideration, they still need a little more time.

199○年○月○日

S&Aコーポレーション　日本支社
　営業部長　山本　良雄　殿

吉田物産株式会社
営業部長　山田　栄三（印）

デュクロン販売提携の件

拝復　○月○日付の貴簡拝受しました。
　貴社との提携について弊社側の結論がなかなか出ず、大変お待たせしていて申し訳ありません。否定的要素があるというようなことでは決してなく、単に社内での検討に時間がかかっているというのが実情です。

　一日も早く結論に達するように目下打ち合わせを重ねておりますので、いましばらくご猶予下さるようお願い申し上げます。

　誠に簡単ですが、取り急ぎ現況をお知らせ申し上げます。
　スミス支社長ならびに関係部署の方々にも、何卒、あしからずお伝え願います。

草々

販売提携：sales tie-up　貴簡：your letter　拝受する：receive　結論が出る：a decision is made　なかなか～ない：not easily/readily ～　否定的要素がある：there are negative elements　決して～ない：absolutely not ～　単に：simply　実情：actual situation　結論に達する：reach a decision　目下：currently　いましばらく：for a short while　猶予：postponement　現況：present situation　関係部署の方々：the staff in the related sections

Date (year, month, day)

S&A Corporation, Japan Office
Sales Department Manager Yamamoto Yoshio (Mr.)

Yoshida Trading, Incorporated
Sales Department Manager Yamada Eizo (seal)

RE: Dukelon tie-up

Salutations: I received your letter of (month, day). I sincerely apologize for being so slow in giving you our decision with regard to a tie-up with your company, which is not easily reached.
This is absolutely not because of any negative elements in your proposal; but actually it is simply because it is taking us considerable time within the company to give it consideration.

We are currently consulting in order to come to a decision as soon as possible and ask now for a short postponement in our answer.

This is extremely simple, but I hasten to inform you of our present situation.
Please kindly pass this information on to Manager Smith and the staff in the related sections.

Sincerely yours

留意事項

1)回答が遅れていることについては、その理由を示す必要があります。肯定的な結論が出そうなときは、その状況を伝えるような表現を用いることで相手の納得(なっとく)を求めます。

2)回答が遅れるときなど、関係先の理解を求めるため、先方の上司以外の関係者にもこちらの文書の趣旨(しゅし)を伝えてもらいたい旨(むね)を付け加えることがあります。

1. In regard to the lateness of a response, you must explain the reason for the delay. When you will probably be giving an affirmative response, use phrases to explain these conditions and ask for the other party's understanding.

2. When your response is late, you might make an addition to the letter to gain the understanding of the other party, asking that the purport of this letter be conveyed to other related persons, except section heads in the company.

第9課

申し入れを断る
Refusing proposals

先方からの依頼・申し出・要求に対して、同意できない場合は断りの文書を書かなければなりません。

断りの文書では、その理由に事実をすべて述べる必要はありません。また、相手方の欠陥や短所などを指摘する表現は避けて、相手方が断られたことに納得するような理由を述べることが大切です。

断る文書もビジネス交渉の一つの締め括りを表す文書なので、こちらの誠意を示すよう全般の語句や表現に注意し、相手の信頼と今後の友好関係を失わないように留意します。

In cases where requests or proposals from another company cannot be met, a letter of refusal should be sent.

In such a letter it is not necessary to include all of the reasons for your refusal. Also, avoid expressions pointing out any of the company's defects or shortcomings. However, giving a satisfactory reason for the refusal is important.

Since the letter is essentially a way of putting an end to business negotiations, in order to express yourself sincerely, care should be taken not to use words and expressions that would cause a loss of trust or damage future relations.

社外 断る refusal

9-1 販売提携(ていけい)の申し入れを断る

Refusing a proposal for a sales affiliation

インテックス社は、S&A社から販売代理店を引き受けてほしいとの申し入れを受けましたが、従来から同種商品を扱っているのでそれとの競合(きょうごう)を避けたいという理由で、提携(ていけい)を断る文書を書きます。

Intex, Inc., received a proposal from S&A Corporation to become a sales agent, but as they already handle a similar product, they write a letter of refusal to avoid competition between the two products.

平成○年○月○日

〒100-0004　東京都千代田区大手町1-2-1

平成ビル　#801号

S&Aコーポレーション　日本支社

支社長　H. G. スミス　殿

〒176-0003　東京都練馬区羽沢5-5-8

(株)インテックス

営業部長　高　橋　吉　男（印）

<u>デュクロン販売提携(ていけい)見送りの件</u>

拝復(はいふく)　時下(じか)ますますご清祥(せいしょう)の段お慶(よろこ)び申し上げます。

さて、○月○日付け貴信にてお申し越しの「デュクロン」の販売代理店の件、早速弊社(さっそくへいしゃ)内部で検討させて頂(いただ)きました。その結果、せっかくのお申し越しながら、今回は貴意(きい)に添(そ)いかねるとの結論に達しましたので、書中をもってご連絡申し上げます。

従来からの取引先との関係で、弊社では既(すで)にカーペットも取扱いの商品の一つに入っているためであります。

何卒(なにとぞ)事情ご賢察(けんさつ)の上、あしからずご了承(りょうしょう)下さいますようお願い申し上げます。

まずは、ご返書まで申し上げます。

敬具

見送り：shelve; decline; pass up (the opportunity)　販売代理店：sales agent　せっかく：with much trouble; kindly　貴意に添いかねる：not be able to go along with your intentions　結論に達する：reach a conclusion　従来からの取引先：a company with which business is already being done　事情賢察の上：with an understanding of the situation　了承：acknowledgment

Date (year, month, day)

100-0004 Tokyo-to, Chiyoda-ku, Otemachi 1-2-1
Heisei Bldg., Room #801
S&A Corporation, Japan Office
Manager H. G. Smith (Mr.)

176-0003 Tokyo-to, Nerima-ku, Hanezawa 5-5-8
Intex, Inc.
Sales Manager Takahashi Yoshio (seal)

RE: Shelving the Dukelon sales affiliation

Salutations: Allow me to congratulate you on your increasing good health and well-being at this time.

Now, regarding your letter of (month, day) requesting that we become a sales agent for Dukelon, we gave prompt consideration to the possibility within our company. We appreciate your kind proposal but have reached the conclusion that at this time we are not able to go along with your intentions, and take this opportunity to relay this to you in writing.

This is because of a relationship we have had with another dealer from before, so that carpets are already included among the products we handle.
I'm afraid I must ask for your understanding of this situation.

I am sending you this written reply forthwith.

Sincerely yours

留意事項

1)「考えておきます」とか「検討します」などのどちらとも取れるような表現は避けます。
2)将来取り引きの可能性があるかもしれませんから、そのようなことを考えてていねいな表現でこちらの意思を伝えます。

1. Avoid using phrases like "I will think about it" or "I will consider it," which can be understood either positively or negatively.
2. Think about the fact that the possibility may arise to work with the other company in the future, and use polite language to convey your message.

9-2 支払い条件の緩和を求める申し出を断る
Refusing a request to ease terms for payment

S&A社は、取引先の山田家具から支払い条件の緩和を申し入れられていました。しかし、特定の会社だけを例外扱いはできないと、その申し出を断る文書を書きます。

S&A Corporation receives a request from Yamada Furniture asking that the terms for payment be eased. They write a letter refusing this request, because they cannot make an exception for any one specific company.

199○年○月○日

有限会社　山田家具
　社長　山田　栄作　殿

S&Aコーポレーション　日本支社
営業部長　山本　良雄（印）

支払条件変更ご要望の件

拝啓　日頃は弊社の製品販売につき格別のご高配を頂き、有り難く御礼申し上げます。

さて、この度弊社に対するお支払条件につき、現行の月末締め当日起算30日約束手形払いを同60日払いに変更してほしい旨のお申し出を頂きました。

いろいろご事情があってのご要望とは存じますが、弊社はすべてのお取引先に対して同一条件でのお取引をお願いしており、誠に申し訳ございませんが、貴社だけを例外とするわけには参りません。

何卒弊社の方針をご賢察下さいまして、現行通りのご決済をご継続下さいますよう、お願い申し上げます。貴意に添いかねます段、あしからずご容赦下さい。

まずは取り急ぎご回答申し上げます。

敬具

要望：wish; desire　日頃：always; recently　格別の高配：special attention/consideration　～に対する支払条件につき：with relation to the matter of payment terms　現行の：present; existing　月末締め：month-end settlement　当日起算：calculated from that day　30日約束手形払い：30-day promissory note of payment; 30-day payment of note　変更する：change　申し出：request　事情がある：have conditions/reasons　同一条件での取引：the same business terms　方針：policy　賢察：understanding　決済：settlement　継続する：continue　貴意に添いかねます段：not being able to go along with your intentions/wishes　容赦する：forgive

Date (year, month, day)

Yamada Furniture, Ltd.
President Yamada Eisaku (Mr.)

S&A Corporation, Japan Office
Sales Department Manager Yamamoto Yoshio (seal)

RE: Your wish to change the conditions of payment

Salutations: Allow me to express our appreciation for the special attention you always give the sale of our company's products.

Now, with relation to the issue of payment terms, we received your request to change our present policy from payments settled with a 30-day promissory note at the end of each month to 60-day terms.

We realize there are a number of conditions that make this desirable for you, but our company requests that all of our dealers (agents) conform to the same business terms. Therefore, I am sorry to say that there is no way we can make an exception for your company alone.

We ask that you kindly understand our company's policy and request that you continue to settle accounts according to the present terms. Please forgive us for not being able to go along with your wishes.

I hasten to send this answer at this time.

Sincerely yours

留意事項

1) こちらが先方の希望を理解した上で断っていること示すため、先方の申し出の内容を繰(く)り返して確認します。
2) なぜ断るか、その理由をはっきり述(の)べます。

1. To show that you understand the request of the other party when you make a refusal, repeat the contents of their request for confirmation.
2. Explain clearly why you are refusing.

9-1と9-2のフローと文例

9-1「販売提携の申し入れを断る」のフロー

デュクロン販売提携見送りの件

拝復　時下ますますご清祥の段お慶び申し上げます。

さて、○月○日付け貴信にてお申し越しの「デュクロン」の販売代理店の件、早速弊社内部で検討させて頂きました。その結果、せっかくのお申し越しながら、今回は貴意に添いかねるとの結論に達しましたので、書中をもってご連絡申し上げます。

従来からの取引先との関係で、弊社では既にカーペットも取扱いの商品の一つに入っているためであります。

何卒事情ご賢察の上、あしからずご了承下さいますようお願い申し上げます。

まずは、ご返書まで申し上げます。

敬具

①用件を確認する

②理由を述べて断る

③理解と了承を求める

9-2「支払い条件の緩和を求める申し出を断る」のフロー

支払条件変更ご要望の件

拝啓　日頃は弊社の製品販売につき格別のご高配を頂き、有り難く御礼申し上げます。

さて、この度弊社に対するお支払条件につき、現行の月末締め当日起算30日約束手形払いを同60日払いに変更してほしい旨のお申し出を頂きました。

いろいろご事情があってのご要望とは存じますが、弊社はすべてのお取引先に対して同一条件でのお取引をお願いしており、誠に申し訳ございませんが、貴社だけを例外とするわけには参りません。

何卒弊社の方針をご賢察下さいまして、現行通りのご決済をご継続下さいますよう、お願い申し上げます。貴意に添いかねます段、あしからずご容赦下さい。

まずは取り急ぎご回答申し上げます。

敬具

①用件を確認する

②理由を述べて断る

③理解と了承を求める

（下線の部分は自分の状況に合わせて書いてください。）

①用件を確認する

Confirming business matters

＊○月○日付け貴信にてお申し越しの「デュクロン」の販売代理店の件、早速弊社内部で検討させて頂きました。(9-1)

Regarding your letter of (month, day) requesting that we become a sales agent for Dukelon, we gave prompt consideration to the possibility within our company.

＊この度弊社に対するお支払条件につき、現行の月末締め当日起算 30 日約束手形払いを同 60 日払いに変更してほしい旨のお申し出を頂きました。(9-2)

With relation to the issue of payment terms, we received your request to change our present policy from payments settled with a 30-day promissory note at the end of each month to 60-day terms.

＊○月○日付題記貴信をもってお申し越しの件、確かに承りました。

We have definitely received the above-mentioned proposal which you wrote in your letter of (month, day).

②理由を述べて断る

Sending a refusal and giving reasons

＊せっかくのお申し越しながら、今回は貴意に添いかねるとの結論に達しましたので、書中をもってご連絡申し上げます。従来からの取引先との関係で、弊社では既にカーペットも取扱いの商品の一つに入っているためであります。(9-1)

We appreciate your kind proposal but have reached the conclusion that at this time we are not able to go along with your intentions, and take this opportunity to relay this to you in writing. This is because of a relationship we have had with another dealer from before, so that carpets are already included among the products we handle.

＊いろいろご事情があってのご要望とは存じますが、弊社はすべてのお取引先に対して同一条件でのお取引きをお願いしており、誠に申し訳ございませんが、貴社だけを例外とするわけには参りません。(9-2)

We realize there are a number of conditions that make this desirable for you, but our company requests that all of our dealers (agents) conform to the same business terms. Therefore, I am sorry to say that there is no way we can make an exception for your company alone.

＊弊社では、家電関係の取扱業務について縮少しておりますので、残念ながらお申し出に添いかねる次第です。

Since we are reducing our business in home appliances, I am sorry to say it is not possible to go along with your proposal.

③理解と了承を求める

Asking for understanding and acknowledgment

＊何卒事情ご賢察の上、あしからずご了承下さいますようお願い申し上げます。(9-1)

I'm afraid I must ask for your understanding of this situation.

＊何卒弊社の方針をご賢察下さいまして、現行通りのご決済をご継続下さいますよう、お願い申し上げます。貴意に添いかねます段、あしからずご容赦下さい。(9-2)

We ask that you kindly understand our company's policy and request that you continue to settle accounts according to the present terms. Please forgive us for not being able to go along with your wishes.

＊せっかくのお申し越しに、心苦しく存じますが、申し上げましたような事情により、どうかお許し下さるようお願いいたします。

I feel very sorry for rejecting your kind request, but please forgive us for doing so by taking into consideration the circumstances I mentioned above.

9-3 交渉条件が合わないので、提携の申し入れを取り止める
Withdrawing a proposal for an affiliation because negotiating terms are unacceptable

S&A社は、高島インテリア社に対して、販売提携の交渉条件が合わないため、提携の申し入れを取り止める文書を送ります。

Because S&A Corporation cannot accept the conditions for an affiliation put forth by Takashima Interior, the company sends a letter withdrawing its proposal for the tie-up.

営第　○○○　号
199○年○月○日

高島インテリア株式会社
営業部長　森　田　稔　殿

S&Aコーポレーション日本支社
支社長　H. G. スミス（サイン）

「デュクロン」販売提携の件

拝復　時下ますますご清祥のことと大慶に存じ上げます。

さて、かねてよりお話し合いを重ねて参りました弊社製品「デュクロン」の販売提携の件につき、このたび貴社より最終的条件のご提示をいただき、ありがとうございました。

その後、社内において鋭意検討を続けてまいりましたが、お申し越しの関東地区専売権は、ほかの販売提携先との関係もあり、どうしてもお受けするわけにはまいりません。

この件について、貴社としては、ご再考の余地はない由を承り、誠に残念ではございますが、今回の販売提携にはご縁がなかったものと諦めざるを得ないかと存じます。いろいろとお手数をお掛けしましたが、事情ご賢察のうえ、なにとぞ悪しからずご了承のほどお願い申し上げます。

今後とも、ますます貴社のご発展を祈念いたしますとともに、近い将来にはビジネスでのご縁がありますよう心から期待いたしております。

敬　具

販売提携：sales tie-up　最終的条件の提示：presentation of final terms　鋭意検討を続ける：continue examining carefully　関東地区専売権：exclusive sales rights in the Kanto area　再考の余地がない：have no room to reconsider　縁がない：no connection; no relationship　～ざるを得ない：have no choice but to ～　手数を掛ける：cause you trouble　事情賢察のうえ：with an understanding of our situation　了承のほど：acknowledging; approving of　ますます：continued; more and more　発展を祈念する：pray for growth

Sales Document # ______
Date (year, month, day)

Takashima Interior, Incorporated
Sales Department Manager Morita Minoru (Mr.)

S&A Corporation, Japan Office
Manager H. G. Smith (signature)

RE: Dukelon sales tie-up

Salutations: Allow me to congratulate you on your increasing health and well-being at this time.

Now, with relation to the proposal being discussed for quite some time that you link up with us for the sale of Dukelon, I want to thank you for giving us a presentation of your company's final terms.

Since receiving it, we have continued examining it carefully within our company and must say that we cannot accept your request for exclusive sales rights in the Kanto area, because of our relationships with other distributors (sales associates).

It is regrettable, but as we understand your company has no room for reconsideration of this point, we have no choice but to withdraw this sales tie-up proposal. We apologize for causing so much trouble, but ask that you kindly understand our position.

We sincerely hope that in the near future we may have the opportunity to do business with you and are praying for the continuing growth of your company.

Sincerely yours

留意事項

1)交渉成立・不成立のどちらの場合でも、当方の意思は必ず文書で伝えます。
2)断る文書は、なるべく早く発送するように注意します。何も意思表示をしないまま時間が経過すると、条件に同意をしたものと解釈される場合もありえます。
3)断る場合であっても、まず交渉への協力に感謝するとともに、断ることとなった事情をよく説明して相手に納得してもらえるようにします。
4)最後に改めて将来の取り引きの機会を期待する旨を記して、友好関係を保持する形で文書を終えるように配慮します。

1. Whether negotiations end in success or failure, always inform the other party in writing of your position.
2. Be careful to send a letter of refusal as soon as possible. If you do nothing to make your position known, the other party may interpret this to mean that you are in agreement with their conditions.
3. Even though you are refusing, first thank the other party for their cooperation in the negotiations and fully explain why you have refused in order to enable them to understand your position.
4. At the end of your letter, express your hope that sometime in the future you will have the opportunity to do business with them in order to end the negotiations amicably.

第10課

取引条件の交渉をする

Negotiating terms for doing business

取引条件を交渉するときは、こちらの考えや条件を明確な形で先方に示すことが必要です。

交渉が一回の提案で決まることは、あまりありません。最初の提案に反対提案があり、その反対提案に再提案がなされるというように意見のやり取りや提案内容の変更が何回も行われ、それにともなって文書のやり取りが何度も行われます。

特に価格の提示にあたっては、どのような条件のもとでその価格が提示されているのか、その条件の明示が大切です。

交渉の結果によっては、仕事に影響を受ける社内の部署や関係先に対しても、交渉の進行や妥結などについて、必要に応じた周知策や処置を取らなければならないことがしばしば起こります。

When negotiating terms for doing business, it is important to clearly express your thoughts and business conditions on the matter to the other party.

There is no guarantee that a proposal will be settled the first go-around. Exchanging proposals may go back and forth many times. First proposals are met with counterproposals, which are then followed by a second proposal.

This is especially true when presenting a price for a product, and it is important to state clearly the basis for presenting such a figure.

It is often necessary to give information about how the negotiations are progressing, or have been settled, to any parties within and outside the company who are affected by the result of the negotiations, and then take the appropriate action.

10-1 商品の価格と取引条件を提示する 1

Presenting prices of merchandise and business terms (1)

S&A社は、販売提携を結んだ吉田物産に特殊カーペット「デュクロン」の納入価格と付帯条件を提案する文書を作ります。

S&A Corporation writes a letter to Yoshida Trading, with whom they have entered into a sales tie-up, proposing the delivery price and accompanying conditions for the specialty carpet Dukelon.

平成○年○月○日

〒150-0000　東京都渋谷区青山 6-1-2
　吉田物産株式会社
　　営業部長　山田　栄三　殿

〒100-0004　東京都千代田区大手町 1-2-1
平成ビル 8 階　801号室
S&Aコーポレーション日本支社
支社長　H. G. スミス（サイン）

<u>「デュクロン」納入価格お見積りの件</u>

拝啓　盛夏の候、貴社ますますご清栄の段、お喜び申し上げます。

　さて、先日は弊社の特殊カーペット「デュクロン」について懇談の機会を設けていただき、誠にありがとうございました。私どもの商品と取引の基本構想については、すでにご説明させていただいておりますので、本日は下記の通り、価格条件を提示させていただきます。

　なお、本価格は御社との関係を考慮した価格であることを申し添えます。

　よろしくご検討のほど、お願い申し上げます。

敬具

記

1．取引価格　　（標準品）1 m²当り　10,000円（ただし、貴社倉庫渡し）
　　　　　　　　　＊特別仕上げ品は標準品の20%増し
2．運賃諸掛　　弊社負担
3．支払条件　　月末締め、当日起算30日約束手形払

以上

納入価格見積り：delivery price estimate　特殊：specialty　懇談の機会を設ける：create an opportunity to talk　基本構想：basic plan/idea　御社との関係を考慮する：take into account the relationship with your company　申し添える：add　検討のほど：examining　標準品：standard product　～当り：per ～　倉庫渡し：delivery to a warehouse　～%増し：～% increase/more　運賃諸掛：freight expenses　～負担：bear (costs); paid by ～　支払条件：payment terms　月末締め：month-end settlement　当日起算：calculated from that day　30日約束手形払：30-day promissory note of payment; 30-day payment by note

Date (year, month, day)

150-0000 Tokyo-to, Shibuya-ku, Aoyama 6-1-2
Yoshida Trading, Incorporated
Sales Department Manager Yamada Eizo (Mr.)

100-0004 Tokyo-to, Chiyoda-ku, Otemachi 1-2-1
Heisei Bldg. 8th fl., Room #801
S&A Corporation, Japan Office
Manager H. G. Smith (signature)

RE: Delivery price estimate for Dukelon

Salutations: At the height of the summer, I rejoice at your increasing health and prosperity.

Now, I want to thank you for the recent opportunity you gave us to hold a discussion about our company's specialty carpet Dukelon. We have already been allowed to give an explanation of our products and a basic plan for doing business, so today I would simply like to present our pricing terms as noted below.

In addition, allow me to add that we decided these prices taking into account the relationship between our two companies.

I ask that you examine them carefully.

Sincerely Yours

Details

1. Market price (standard product): 10,000 yen per square meter (delivery to your warehouse)
   *Special-order products are priced 20% above the standard price.
2. Freight expenses: paid by our company
3. Payment terms: accounts will be settled at the end of the month with a 30-day promissory note

(the end)

留意事項

1) 交渉は双方の利益のぶつかり合いですから、時には厳しいやり取りがなされます。しかし経営上、取り引きが１回限りでなく長く続くことを重視しますから、厳しいやり取りの内容の文書であってもその表現はあくまでも礼儀と節度を保って友好関係のうちに交渉が進むような配慮が必要です。

1. As negotiations involve exchanges between two parties, each working for their own profit, there are times when the exchanges become intense. Doing business, however, attaches much more importance to long-term dealings than to a one-time-only event. This means that even though the contents of a letter may involve intense

2) 取引条件に関する文書では、商品の内容や受け渡し場所と時期、代金の支払い方法などを明確に書きます。価格は付帯条件によって大きく変わりますから、どのような条件でその価格が提示されているのかを明示します。

3)「終わりのあいさつ」は書かないこともあります。特に、同じ用件で何度も文書のやり取りをするときは、省略したほうがすっきりします。また、「時候のあいさつ」「慶賀のあいさつ」(先方が健康で発展していることを祝うあいさつ)も略して頭語と結語のみにすることもあります。

exchanges, the language used must maintain a sense of courtesy and moderation. Consideration must be shown so that negotiations can move forward on friendly terms.

2. In a letter related to terms of doing business, information such as the contents of the merchandise, place and time of delivery, and method of payment must be stated clearly. As the price will vary greatly, depending on accompanying conditions, it is especially important to explain the conditions related to the quoted price.

3. Sometimes you do not write a closing greeting. Especially when you exchange a number of letters related to the same subject, eliminating that greeting seems much more appropriate. Sometimes you also leave out seasonal and congratulatory greetings, and write only a salutation and a complimentary close.

10-2 商品の価格と取引条件を提示する 2

Presenting prices of merchandise and business terms (2)

東京システム販売は、S&A社に導入をはかっているOA機器の新システムについて提案書をまとめ、リースと買い取りの双方(そうほう)についての価格見積書(みつもりしょ)を作ります。

Tokyo System Sales is attempting to put together a proposal for a new system of OA equipment for S&A Corporation, providing a written estimate for both lease and purchase arrangements.

199○年○月○日

S&Aコーポレーション日本支社
営業部長 山 本 良 雄 殿

東京システム販売株式会社
営業部長 代 々 木 進(印)

貴社OA機器新システムにつきご提案配送のこと

拝啓(はいけい) 貴社ますますご清祥(せいしょう)のこととお慶(よろこ)び申し上げます。

さて、

このたび貴社コンピュータとその関連OA機器の新替(しんがえ)につき見積(みつもり)/新システムの提案を提出するようお申付けを頂戴致(ちょうだいいた)しましたこと誠(まこと)に有(あ)り難(がた)く厚く御礼(おんれい)申し上げます。

このほどお申付けの貴社OA機器の新システムについての弊(へい)提案書ができましたので、ご要望(ようぼう)の買取/リース双方(そうほう)につき別冊貴覧(きらん)に供(きょう)します。

なお、同書中にも記載(きさい)致しておりますが、
リース金額:月間 金弐(に)百弐拾(じゅう)万円也(なり) (ソフト使用料とも)
お買取金額:金壱(いち)億壱千万円也 ただし、現金払い。(分割支払いなどのご希望の場合は、別途(べっと)お打合せ申し上げたく)
お見積書の有効期限:本日より二週間

リース/買取金額ともかなり勉強申し上げておりますので、何分のご検討のほどお願い申し上げます。

まずは、ご提案書拝送(はいそう)のご案内まで申し上げます。

敬具

(添付(てんぷ)書類)
S&Aコーポレーション日本支社殿
新OAシステムご提案書(お見積書とも) 正副各1部 同封

以上

提案：proposal　配送：delivery　新替につき：as for the renewal in the system　見積：estimate　提出する：hand in　申付けを頂戴する：receive an order　要望：request　買取：purchase　リース：lease　双方：both　別冊：separate sheets　貴覧に供する：offer for your reference; show　同書中：in the above-mentioned documents　記載する：write　月間：per month　弐：two　拾：ten　也：(used after price figures)　ソフト使用料とも：charge for software use included　買取金額：purchase price　壱億：one hundred million　分割支払い：paying in installments　～希望の場合：in the case that you wish ～　別途打合せする：have a special/separate discussion　有効期限：term of validity　かなり勉強する：considerably reduce　拝送：send　～のご案内まで：we will announce that ～　添付書類：attached documents

---

Date (year, month, day)

S&A Corporation, Japan Office
Sales Department Manager Yamamoto Yoshio (Mr.)

Tokyo System Sales, Incorporated
Sales Department Manager Yoyogi Susumu (seal)

RE: Delivering a proposal for a new system of OA equipment for your company

Salutations: Allow me to congratulate you on your good health and well-being.

Now, allow me to express my deep gratitude for your instructions to hand in an estimate/proposal for a new system of computers and related OA equipment for your company.

We have now completed the proposal, as instructed, for a new system of OA equipment for your company, and on separate sheets will include terms for both purchase and lease for your reference.

Please note that the following are written elsewhere in the separate sheets.

Lease price: 2.2 million yen per month (software use included)
Purchase price: 110 million yen (terms: cash, paid in full) (If you wish to pay in installments, please contact us for the details.)
Term of validity: two weeks from today

We have reduced the price considerably for both lease and purchase, so we ask that you kindly give this your consideration.

First of all, we will forward the proposal.

Sincerely yours

(Attached documents)
The Honorable S&A Corporation, Japan Office
new OA system proposal (including estimates) in duplicate—1 copy each

(the end)

留意事項

1)代金の支払い条件は価格を構成する重要な基準ですから、提案文の中に条件としてはっきり書きます。

2)提案書、見積書は、別紙として添付するときがあります。価格や金額とその条件などは、見積書のほかに本文の中にも重複して書いておいたほうが確実です。

3)価格の見積提案には外部環境の変化も考慮して、見積もりの有効期限を付けるのが通例です。期限を設けたときはそれを明示します。

4)金額など重要な数字は、手書き文字などで読み間違えたり第三者に書きかえられたりする恐れのあるときは、漢数字(例:壱・弐・参など)で書くか漢数字とアラビア数字を併記することがあります。タイプで印字したときやチェックライターで印字したときは、併記することはありません。

5)「時候のあいさつ」は、必ず書かなければならないものではありません。省略することもあります。

1. As payment terms are extremely important criteria in the setting of prices, note these terms clearly in the proposal.

2. Sometimes you attach a proposal or estimate as a separate sheet. When doing this, it is safer to note the price or value and terms in the general letter as well as on the estimate sheet.

3. In a proposal of estimated price, you must take into consideration changes in the external environment, and therefore it is customary to attach a time period for when this price will be valid. When you specify a time period, note it clearly on your proposal.

4. When the letter is handwritten and includes important figures in the price, either write them using the numbers in kanji characters alone (壱, 弐, 参 "one, two, three," and so on) or both kanji characters and Arabic numerals. This avoids both mistakes in reading the figures or in having them be rewritten by a third party. When the figures are typed or imprinted with a check writer, however, this is not necessary.

5. Seasonal greetings do not always have to be written. They are often omitted.

10-1 と 10-2 のフローと文例

10-1「商品の価格と取引条件を提示する 1」のフロー

「デュクロン」納入価格お見積りの件

拝啓　盛夏の候、貴社ますますご清栄の段、お喜び申し上げます。

さて、先日は弊社の特殊カーペット「デュクロン」について懇談の機会を設けていただき、誠にありがとうございました。（①交渉の段階を確認する）私どもの商品と取引の基本構想については、すでにご説明させていただいておりますので、本日は下記の通り、価格条件を提示させていただきます。（②条件を提示する）

なお、本価格は御社との関係を考慮した価格であることを申し添えます。
よろしくご検討のほど、お願い申し上げます。（③提示した条件について説明する＋検討を依頼する）

敬具

記

1．取引価格　　（標準品）１㎡当り　10,000円（ただし、貴社倉庫渡し）
　　　　　　　　＊特別仕上げ品は標準品の20%増し
2．運賃諸掛　　弊社負担
3．支払条件　　月末締め、当日起算30日約束手形払

（④記――提示条件の内容）

以上

10-2「商品の価格と取引条件を提示する 2」のフロー

貴社ＯＡ機器新システムにつきご提案配送のこと

拝啓　貴社ますますご清祥のこととお慶び申し上げます。

さて、
このたび貴社コンピュータとその関連ＯＡ機器の新替につき見積／新システムの提案を提出するようお申付けを頂戴致しましたこと誠に有り難く厚く御礼申し上げます。（①交渉の段階を確認する）

このほどお申付けの貴社ＯＡ機器の新システムについての弊提案書ができましたので、ご要望の買取／リース双方につき別冊貴覧に供します。（②条件を提示する）

なお、同書中にも記載致しておりますが、
　リース金額：月間　金弐百弐拾万円也　（ソフト使用料とも）
　お買取金額：金壱億壱千万円也　ただし、現金払い。（分割支払いなどのご希望の場合は、別途お打合せ申し上げたく）
　お見積書の有効期限：本日より二週間

（③提示した条件について説明する＋検討を依頼する）

リース／買取金額ともかなり勉強申し上げておりますので、何分のご検討のほどお願い申し上げます。

まずは、ご提案書拝送のご案内まで申し上げます。

敬具

（添付書類）

S＆Aコーポレーション日本支社殿

新OAシステムご提案書（お見積書とも）　正副各１部　同封

以上

（下線の部分は自分の状況に合わせて書いてください。）

①交渉の段階を確認する

Confirming the conditions of negotiations

＊先日は弊社の特殊カーペット「デュクロン」について懇談の機会を設けさせていただき、誠にありがとうございました。(10-1)

I want to thank you for the recent opportunity you gave us to hold a discussion about our company's specialty carpet Dukelon.

＊○月○日付貴信にて「デュクロン」のお見積をいただき、ありがとうございました。(10-3)

Thank you for your letter of (month, day), giving estimated prices and business terms for Dukelon.

＊このたび、貴社の新製品に関する広告計画について提案の機会をいただきまして、誠にありがとうございました。

Thank you very much for giving us the opportunity to propose an advertising plan for your new product.

②条件を提示する

Presenting conditions

＊本日は下記の通り、価格条件を提示させていただきます。(10-1)

Today I would simply like to present our pricing terms as noted below.

＊○月○日付貴営総第○○○号見積ご依頼について、同封別紙のとおりお見積申し上げます。

Regarding the request for an estimate in your letter # ______ from your sales department dated (month, day), I am enclosing an estimate on a separate sheet.

＊ここに貴社製品の広告宣伝計画を下記の通りご提案いたします。

Please find below the proposed advertising plan for your company's product.

③提示した条件について説明する ＋ 検討を依頼する

Explaining conditions presented and requesting an examination

＊本価格は御社との関係を考慮した価格であることを申し添えます。よろしくご検討のほど、お願い申し上げます。(10-1)

Allow me to add that we decided these prices taking into account the relationship between our two companies. I ask that you examine them carefully.

＊リース／買取金額ともかなり勉強申し上げておりますので、何分のご検討のほどお願い申し上げます。(10-2)

We have reduced the price considerably for both lease and purchase, so we ask that you kindly give this your consideration.

＊本提案は市場における綿密な調査に基づいたものであり、貴社の販売目標達成に貢献しうるものと確信いたします。ご検討のほど、よろしくお願いいたします。

The proposal is based on a detailed investigation of the market, and we believe it will contribute to your achieving your sales goal. Please examine it carefully.

④記――提示条件の内容

Description—contents of conditions presented

10-3 提示された価格の値引きを要求する
Requesting a lowering of prices as presented

吉田物産は、S＆A社からの価格提案に対して値引きを求める文書を書きます。
Yoshida Trading writes S&A Corporation requesting a lowering of the prices suggested in S&A's proposal.

199〇年〇月〇日

S＆Aコーポレーション日本支社
　支社長　H.G.スミス　殿

吉田物産株式会社
営業部長　山田　栄三（印）

「デュクロン」納入（のうにゅう）価格の件

拝啓（はいけい）　時下（じか）ますますご清栄（せいえい）のこととお慶（よろこ）び申し上げます。

さて、〇月〇日付貴信にて「デュクロン」のお見積（みつもり）をいただき、ありがとうございました。さっそく社内で検討いたしましたが、もう少しご考慮（こうりょ）いただかないと当社が扱うメリットが出ないとの結論に達しました。御社（おんしゃ）にもいろいろご事情はおありとは存じますが、値引き率に問題が残っておりますので、何卒（なにとぞ）再検討下さいますようお願い申し上げます。ご賢察（けんさつ）の上、ご提示価格の15％以上の値引きをご考慮いただければ幸（さいわ）いに存じます。

なお、勝手ながらご返事は遅くとも今月末までにお願いいたします。

上記ご検討のほどよろしくお願い申し上げます。

敬具

納入（のうにゅう）価格：delivery price　見積（みつもり）：estimate　考慮（こうりょ）いただく：give some consideration　メリットが出ない：there would be no value　結論に達する：come to a conclusion　事情がある：have reasons　～率：percentage/rate of ～　問題が残る：the problem remains　賢察（けんさつ）の上：with an understanding　提示価格：list price　遅くとも：at the latest

Date (year, month, day)

S&A Corporation, Japan Office
Manager H.G. Smith (Mr.)

Yoshida Trading, Incorporated
Sales Department Manager Yamada Eizo (seal)

RE: Dukelon delivery price

Salutations: I rejoice at your increasing health and prosperity at this time.

Now, thank you for your letter of (month, day), giving estimated prices and business terms for Dukelon. We immediately studied your proposal within the company, but came to the conclusion that unless our company was given a little more reduction there would be no value in our carrying your product. I realize that you have many things to consider, but we still have a problem with our discount percentage and ask that you kindly reconsider your position. With an understanding of our position, we would be pleased if you would consider a discount of some 15 percent off the list price.

And, though I realize this is a selfish request, could you possibly give us a reply by the end of the month.

We ask for your consideration on the above matters.

Sincerely yours

留意事項

1) 相手先の提案を断れば商談は終わりですが、商談の内容にまだ興味があるときや条件が改定できれば考慮の余地があるときは、相手が提案を修正する可能性があるどうかを確かめ、カウンターオファー（反対申し込み。相手からある条件を示された時に、逆にこちらから別の条件を提案すること）をします。

2) どうして提案または見積もりに不満足で反対提案するのか、その理由を明らかにすると、ただ値引きを求めるよりも説得力があります。

3) 通常の返事よりも早い回答がほしいときは、その旨を書きます。

1. If you refuse the other party's proposal, business discussions are finished. But if you are still interested in the contents of the discussions, or if you might be able to continue the discussion on the condition that the proposal were changed, you should ask the other party if they have room to bargain and then make a counterproposal.

2. Clearly explaining why you find the proposal or estimate unsatisfactory is much more convincing than simply requesting a lowering of the price.

3. When you want a quick answer, note this in your letter.

社外 再提案する counterproposal

10-4 値引き要求に対して、価格条件を再提示する

Presenting a new price list in response to the request

Ｓ＆Ａ社は吉田物産からの値引き要求に対して、可能な限りの価格再検討をして、再提案の見積もりを作ります。

In response to Yoshida Trading's request for lower prices, S&A Corporation reconsiders their prices to see how low they can possibly go and then puts together a new estimate proposal.

199○年○月○日

吉田物産株式会社
　営業部長　　山　田　栄　三　殿

Ｓ＆Ａコーポレーション日本支社
営業部長　　山　本　良　雄（印）

<u>デュクロン納入価格の件</u>

拝復　本件に関する○月○日付貴状、拝受致しました。

　弊社見積のデュクロン納入価格「１㎡当り　￥10,000」をさらに15％以上値引きするように、とのお申し出は、弊社にとって原価割れとなりますので、どうしてもお受けするわけにはまいりません。しかしながら、たってのご要望でもあり、社内でさらに検討を重ねた結果、最大限の譲歩として、下記の通り８％以上の値引きを承諾させていただきます。弊社の採算上きわめて厳しい数字ではございますが、貴社との提携成立に対する謝意を込めての出精でございますので、事情ご賢察のうえ、ぜひご承諾下さいますようお願い申し上げます。

　まずは取り急ぎご回答申し上げます。

敬具

記

<u>再提示価格条件</u>

　月間最低取引量を40,000㎡とし、

30,000㎡まで　　１㎡当り　￥9,200
30,000㎡超の分　１㎡当り　￥9,000
（取引単位 1,000㎡、貴社指定倉庫渡し）

　お支払い条件等については、前状の通り。

　ただし、本価格は３カ月毎に見直すものとする。また、何らかの大きな環境変化があった場合は、互いに誠意をもって協議に応ずるものとする。

以上

納入価格：delivery price　拝受する：accept; receive　見積：estimate　～当り：per ～　申し出：proposal　原価割れ：(sell) below cost　～わけにはいかない：cannot ～　たっての要望：earnest wish　最大限の譲歩：maximum concession　承諾する：accept　採算上：in terms of the profitability　きわめて厳しい数字：very severe reduction　提携成立：establishment of a tie-up　謝意を込める：express gratitude　出精：manage to do; do one's best　事情賢察の上：with an understanding of our situation　回答：answer　～超の分：portion over ～　取引単位：unit of business　指定倉庫渡し：delivery to the designated warehouse　支払条件等：terms of payment, etc.　～毎：every ～　見直す：reexamine　環境変化がある：experience environmental change　互いに誠意をもって協議に応ずる：have a discussion together in good faith

---

Date (year, month, day)

Yoshida Trading, Incorporated
Sales Department Manager Yamada Eizo (Mr.)

S&A Corporation, Japan Office
Sales Department Manager Yamamoto Yoshio (seal)

RE: Dukelon delivery price

Salutations: I received your letter of (month, day) on the above subject.

Your request that we discount our company's delivery estimate of ¥10,000 per square meter of Dukelon an additional 15 percent or more is something we cannot do, as it would mean we had to sell below cost. Because this is your earnest wish, however, we have studied the matter further and, as a result, have decided that around 8 percent is the most we could possibly reduce our price, as set out below. This figure will cut greatly into our profits, but we will do it as an expression of gratitude for your diligence in the establishment of a tie-up with our company. Therefore, we ask for your kind understanding of our situation and sincerely hope that you will accept our offer.

I hasten to give you this answer.

Sincerely yours

Details

Revised presentation of prices

Assuming a minimum total of 40,000 square meters per month,
up to 30,000 square meters—9,200 yen per square meter
Portion over 30,000 square meters—9,000 yen per square meter
(Unit of business—1,000 square meters, delivered to your designated warehouse)

Terms for payment, etc., are as specified in a previous document.

We reserve the right to reexamine the basic price every three months. If some kind of major environmental change occurs, we will have a discussion together in good faith.

(the end)

留意事項

1)商談をなんとかまとめたいときは、相手のカウンターオファーに対しさらにこちらの検討結果を提案します。

2)前回の提案になかった付帯(ふたい)条件や提案内容の見直し条件があれば、付け加えて書きます。

3)付帯条件が前回と同様のときは、変化のないことを書きます。

1. When you want somehow or other to conclude business discussions successfully, present the results of your investigation of the other party's counterproposal back to them.

2. If there are accompanying conditions or content changes not in the final proposal or areas you have changed upon reconsideration, add them to your new proposal.

3. When accompanying conditions are the same as before, note that they were not changed.

10-5 交渉内容の情報コントロールについて社内に周知させる
Announcing controls on in-house reporting of negotiations

S＆A社のスミス日本支社長は、進行中の吉田物産との販売提携問題は業界への影響が大きいので各部門長に情報をコントロールする旨、社内周知させます。

Seeing that the sales tie-up issue in the talks now underway between S&A Corporation and Yoshida Trading could have a great effect on the business world, S&A Corporation's Japan Office Manager Smith issues an in-house memo to all section chiefs telling them to control information within the company.

199○年○月○日

各部長

支社長　（サイン）

吉田物産に関する機密保持と情報一本化

ご承知の通り、当社は現在吉田物産(株)との間で提携についての交渉を行っております。各位におかれても、それぞれの分野で本プロジェクトの推進に携わって頂いていることと思います。

吉田物産は家具、カーペット市場の大手取扱商社ですから、吉田と当社の提携問題は業界に大きな衝撃を与えることになります。

その意味で、この提携交渉についての情報は別途指示するまで、絶対に外部に漏れないようにしなければなりません。

ついては、今後、次の事項を各部徹底願いたく、宜しくご手配下さい。

①吉田物産との話は、文書、口頭を問わず、最高機密扱いとすること。

②対外窓口は山本営業部長と営業一課のラインに一本化し、社外からの本件についての問い合わせがあった場合は、すべてこの窓口に絞ること。

以上

機密保持：maintaining confidentiality　情報一本化：unifying information　承知のとおり：as you know　提携：tie-up　交渉を行う：undertake negotiations　各位におかれても：each of you　それぞれの分野：each field/area　推進に携わる：take part in promoting　～市場：～ market　大手取扱商社：major distributing company　業界に衝撃を与える：have a great impact on the business world　別途指示する：give special/separate instructions　外部に漏れる：leak outside (the company)　事項：items　徹底：thorough　手配する：arrange　口頭：verbal　～を問わず：regardless of ～　最高機密扱い：handle as highly confidential　対外窓口：contact with outside　～のラインに一本化する：serve as only line　～に絞る：direct/limit to ～

Date (year, month, day)

To each Department Manager

Manager (signature)

Maintaining confidentiality and unifying information regarding Yoshida Trading

As you all know, our company is now involved in negotiations with Yoshida Trading (Inc.) about a tie-up. Each of you is involved in the promotion of this project with relation to your own area.

As Yoshida Trading is a major distributor in the furniture and carpet market, a tie-up between it and our company will have a great impact on the business world.
Because of this, until you receive special instructions to do so, you must not allow any information concerning this tie-up to leak outside the company.

In this regard, from now on please arrange to have your department thoroughly comply with the following items:

(1) All discussions with Yoshida Trading, regardless of whether they are written or oral, are to be handled as highly confidential.

(2) Sales Department Manager Yamamoto and the sales department first section will serve as the only contacts with the outside; any questions from the outside regarding this issue should be directed to them.

(the end)

留意事項

1) 会社の経営の根幹に関わる問題や外部への影響の大きい案件、まだ決着がついていない事案などは、「秘」扱いにしたり情報窓口を決めて事情を知った者だけが統一された内容・表現で外部に説明することが非常に大切です。事情を知らないで、誤った対応で誤解を与え

1. Problems related to a company's basic management policies, items that could have a real effect on the outside, and items that have not yet been resolved should either be treated as confidential or you should limit the number of people who are aware of the information by setting up one spokesperson through whom all information passes, ensur-

たり、外部から不利益となる干渉を受けたりしないようにするためです。

2) 社内全体が責任者の意図を十分に理解して協力できるように、守秘の理由と方針、そしてその期限を明らかに示します。

3) 部門の最高責任者から、部門役職者への文書の宛先は、企業によって表現は異なりますが、「部長各位」「各部長」(部長宛の例)とするのが普通です。またそれらに「殿」をつけた「部長殿各位」「各部長殿」といった形もよく用いられます。

ing a unified stance. It is extremely important that a unified stance be presented to the outside. This is to avoid having mistaken information given out by someone who doesn't know what is really going on, something that might be detrimental to the negotiations.

2. To enable everyone in the company to fully understand the intentions of the responsible person, you must clearly explain the reasons and plans for maintaining confidentiality and also note the period of time it will be in effect.

3. Different companies have different customs, but usually letters from the highest ranking official in a department are addressed to the people next in control in the following way: 部長各位 or 各部長 (to each department manager). The honorific 殿 (Mr., Mrs., Ms.) is often added to these, as in 部長殿各位 or 各部長殿.

第11課

決裁を求めて稟議書・申立書を書く

Writing circular letters/statements to secure approval

日本の企業では、日常の案件処理のために「ボトム・アップ」による意思決定が行われることが多く、その文書として一般に稟議書を回します。会社によっては、稟議書のことを申立書ということもあります。

稟議書は、定型書式がある場合と特に書式を定めていない場合とがあります。決裁者は、関係部門の意見を確認して決裁し、必要があれば実施の条件を付けます。

なお、最近、先進企業の間では、電子稟議システムを採用する動きがあります。

In the business world, it is customary for decisions to be made from the "bottom up" and the 稟議(りんぎ)書 (circular letter) is generally used for this purpose. Some companies call these circular letters 申立(もうしたて)書 (statements).

There are times when a specified form is used for the circular letter, and other times when it is handwritten. The persons among whom the letter is circulated give their approval, after discussing the content with the personnel in their department, and if necessary attach conditions for putting the matter into effect.

Recently, some enterprises are moving to adopt the circular letter system by e-mail.

11-1 契約条件の承認を求める 1

Seeking the approval of contract terms (1)

S&A社の山本営業部長は、吉田物産との契約条件について稟議を起案し、社内の検討・協議を経て、支社長の決裁を求めます。

S&A Corporation's Sales Department Manager Yamamoto composes a circular letter concerning the contract terms with Yoshida Trading, and after having them studied and discussed in-house, he seeks the approval of the office manager.

協議	資材部長	経理部長	工場長

営本第○○○号

平成○年○月○日

日本支社長殿

営業部長　山本良雄（印）

稟　議　書

吉田物産(株)との契約条件の件

下記のとおり申し立てるので、ご承認願いたい。

記

1．契約条件　吉田物産(株)と交渉中の「デュクロン」の価格など契約条件は次のとおりとし、最終妥結を図りたい。

(1)価格（m²当り）

月間30,000m²まで　　9,200円（８％引き）

月間30,000m²超の分　9,000円（10％引き）

ただし、取引単位1,000m²、毎月最低取引量40,000m²及び吉田物産指定倉庫渡しとする

(2)決済条件

月末締め、当日起算の30日約束手形払い

(3)その他

ア．売買基本契約及び代理店契約はS&Aフォームによる

イ．注文、配送、代金回収、クレーム処理などの具体的方法は別途打ち合わせ、文書化する

2．理　　由　数回の担当者段階での打合せを経て、吉田物産の担当役員鈴木常務との最終交渉を行なった結果、上記の線で妥結することが適当と思われる。

3．添付資料　収支計画案

以　上

上記の申立てどおり承認する

承認第〇〇号

平成〇年〇月〇日

支社長（サイン）

協議：discussion; consultation　申し立てる：raise　交渉中：in negotiations　最終妥結を図る：try for a final agreement　～当り：per ～　～%引き：～% discount　～超の分：portion over ～　取引単位：unit of business　指定倉庫渡し：delivery to the designated warehouse　決済条件：settlement terms　月末締め：month-end settlement　当日起算：calculated from that day　30日約束手形払い：30-day promissory note of payment; 30-day payment by note　売買基本契約：basic sales contract　代理店契約：dealership contract　配送：delivery　代金回収：collection of payment　クレーム処理：dealing with a complaint　別途打ち合わせる：have a special/separate discussion　文書化する：put into writing　担当者段階：at the level of the staffers in charge　～を経る：going through ～　常務：managing director　上記の線：above line　添付資料：attached materials　収支計画案：plan for income and expenditures

Discussed—Materials Department Manager,
Accounting Department Manager,
Factory Manager

Sales Document # __________
Date (year, month, day)

The Honorable Japan Office Manager

Sales Department Manager Yamamoto Yoshio (seal)

Circular Letter

RE: Contract terms with Yoshida Trading (Inc.)

I raise the following items and ask for your approval:

Detail

1. Contract terms: I would like to set the following pricing and other terms in our current Dukelon-related negotiations with Yoshida Trading (Inc.) and try for a final agreement.

(1) Price (per square meter)
The first 30,000 square meters per month—9,200 yen (8% discount)
Portion over 30,000 square meters per month—9,000 yen (10% discount)
Unit of business—1,000 square meters, minimum order per month of 40,000 square meters, delivered to Yoshida Trading's designated warehouse

(2) Settlement terms

Settle accounts at the end of the month with a 30-day promissory note

(3) Other

a. S&A's form will be used for both the basic sales contract and the dealership contract.

b. Special discussions will be held to deal with procedures for ordering, delivery, collection of payment, and complaints, and these will be put in writing.

2. Rationale: after passing through a number of discussions among the staffers in charge, which followed final negotiations with Managing Director Suzuki, the official responsible for Yoshida Trading, I feel that the line I have indicated above is an appropriate place for compromise.

3. Attached materials: plan for income and expenditures

(the end)

I approve of the above statement.

Approval document # ________

Date (year, month, day)

Office Manager (signature)

留意事項

1) 稟議書（りんぎしょ）は、担当の起案（きあん）者が書いて、上司・関係部署の承認（しょうにん）・合意などを示す押印（おういん）・コメントをもらってから、最終決定者に提出します。

2) 稟議の案件は、最終決定してから実施（じっし）に移されます。

3) 稟議書には、案件の件名、内容、理由を明記します。社内文書も社外文書も、一般に記書（きが）きは「以上」でしめくくります。ただ、社内文書では「以上」が結語（けつご）にもなります。

4) 必要に応じて、関係のある数字その他の説明資料を添付（てんぷ）します。

5) 社内文書ですから、儀礼（ぎれい）は最小限にとどめ、簡潔（かんけつ）で事務的な表現を用います。

1. A circular letter is written by the person in charge and circulated among superiors and chiefs of related departments for their approval and mutual agreement. After receiving their seals of approval and comments, it is presented to the person who holds the final decision-making power.

2. Items on the circular letter are instituted after receiving final approval.

3. Spell out the topic, description, and reason for the circular letter. The "記書(きが)き" section is generally concluded with 以上 (the end) in both in-house and out-going letters, but writing 以上 in in-house letters would also signify a conclusion.

4. Related figures and other explanatory documents are attached as necessary.

5. As this is an in-house communication, courteous language is kept to a minimum, and concise, businesslike expressions are used.

11-2 契約条件の承認を求める 2

Seeking the approval of contract terms (2)

S&A社の営業部は、コンピュータ・ターミナルを社内へ導入することについて、支社長の決裁を得るため稟議書を提出します。

The sales department of S&A Corporation presents a circular letter for the purpose of gaining the office manager's approval, regarding the introduction of a computer terminal into the company.

稟議書

S&Aコーポレーション日本支社

起案 平成○年○月○日 稟議書番号 第○○○号	起案部署名	担当役員	部長	課長	起案者
	営業部	丸山	山本	中野 小川	加藤
[決裁] 決裁日 平成○年○月○日 決裁者 H.G. Smith 承認 否認	協議部署名	承認	否認	理由・条件	
	有田常務 内野常務	有田 内野		ソフト検品を充分に行うこと	

[件名] YMN社コンピュータ・ターミナル導入の件

本年10月をもって、YMN社製コンピュータ・ターミナル導入のことといたしたい。

1. 理由と効果： 受注・生産・発送・納入並びに代金請求・入金管理の合理化と省力化
2. 所要経費： 6,500万円
3. 導入機器と台数： 添付別紙のとおり
4. 設置期日： 本年10月1日、同日運用開始予定
5. 設置場所： 営業部・経理部・工場/倉庫 各1台 計3台
6. その他： 関連ソフトは納入時までに完成 テストの後、納入。

(注) YMN社の社歴書ほか、別添。

起案：drafting a plan　部署名：section name　担当役員：official in charge　決裁：approval　否認：denied　協議：discussion　常務：managing director　ソフト検品を行う：carry out an inspection of software　件名：subject　コンピューター・ターミナル導入：installation of computer terminal　受注：accepting an order　発送：dispatch　納入：delivery　代金請求：invoicing; demanding payment　入金管理：management of (process of) receiving payments　省力化：power saving　所要経費：cost　添付別紙のとおり：as per attached documents　設置期日：date of installation　運用開始予定：plan to start operation　社歴書：company history

Circular letter

S&A Corporation, Japan Office

Date created (year, month, day); Circular letter # ＿＿＿＿＿

Created by Sales Department; Responsible official—Maruyama (seal); Department manager—Yamamoto (seal); Section chief—Nakano (seal), Ogawa (seal); Document author—Kato (seal)

Approval: Date approved—year, month, day
Approved by H. G. Smith (signature); Approved (circled)/Denied (crossed out)

Discussed by Managing Director Arita, Managing Director Uchino; Approved—Arita (seal), Uchino (seal); Denied; Reason/Conditions—To carry out a full inspection of software

Subject: RE: Installation of computer terminal made by YMN Company

Would like to install a computer terminal made by YMN Company in October of this year.
1. Reason and results: for power saving and simplifying the processes involved in accepting orders, production, dispatch, delivery, invoicing, and the management of receiving payments
2. Cost: 65 million yen
3. Equipment and numbers: see attached document
4. Date of installation: October 1, this year—plan to begin using the same day
5. Place to be installed: 3 machines, one installed in each of the following departments: sales, accounting, factory/warehouse
6. Other: related software will be completed by the day of installation; begin using after tests are completed

Please note: Attachments include a company history of YMN Company.

留意事項

1) 会社所定の書式による一般的な稟議書の例です。
2) 案件の目的・実施された場合の効果、費用、実施期日などについて、具体的に簡潔に書きます。

1. This is one example of a company-prescribed form for a circular letter.
2. The purpose of the item, what will result if it is made operational, expense, and date of implementation should be specifically and concisely spelled out.

11-1 のフローと文例

11-1「契約条件の承認を求める1」のフロー

稟議書

吉田物産(株)との契約条件の件 ——●件　名

下記のとおり申し立てるので、ご承認願いたい。——●決裁・承認を申請する

記

1．契約条件　吉田物産(株)と交渉中の「デュクロン」の価格など契約条件は次のとおりとし、最終妥結を図りたい。

(1)価格（m²当り）

月間30,000 m²まで　　9,200円（8％引き）

月間30,000 m²超の分　9,000円（10％引き）

ただし、取引単位1,000m²、毎月最低取引量40,000m²及び吉田物産指定倉庫渡しとする

(2)決済条件

月末締め、当日起算の30日約束手形払い

(3)その他

ア．売買基本契約及び代理店契約はS&Aフォームによる

イ．注文、配送、代金回収、クレーム処理などの具体的方法は別途打ち合わせ、文書化する

2．理　由　数回の担当者段階での打合せを経て、吉田物産の担当役員鈴木常務との最終交渉を行なった結果、上記の線で妥結することが適当と思われる。

3．添付資料　収支計画案

以　上

——●決裁・承認事項

「稟議書」　Letter of approval

- 件　名　Subject of letter
- 決裁・承認を申請する　Apply for decision/approval
- 決裁・承認申請事項（目的、条件、理由など）

  Matters to be considered for decision/approval
  (aim, conditions, reasons, etc.)

以上　end

●決裁・承認を申請する

Apply for decision/approval

＊下記のとおり申し立てるので、ご承認願いたい。(11-1)

I raise the following items and ask for your approval.

＊下記のとおり取扱いたく、申し立てます。

I would like to deal with the following items and request your approval.

＊下記により実施いたしたいので、ご承認願います。

I would like to put into effect the following items and request your approval.

〈決裁・承認事項の書き方〉

How to write matters regarding decision/approval

＊契約条件は次のとおりとし、最終妥結**を図りたい**。(11-1)

I would like to set the terms as follows, and try for a final agreement.

＊本年10月をもって、YMN社製コンピュータ・ターミナルを導入**のこととといたしたい**。(11-2)

Would like to install a computer terminal made by YMN Company in October of this year.

〈条件の書き方〉

How to write conditions

＊取引単位1,000 m²、毎月最低取引量40,000 m²及び吉田物産指定倉庫渡し**とする** (11-1)

The unit of business is 1,000 square meters, with a minimum order per month of 40,000 square meters, and delivery to a Yoshida Trading's designated warehouse.

＊売買基本契約及び代理店契約**は**S&Aフォーム**による** (11-1)

S&A's form will be used for both the basic sales contract and the dealership contract.

11-3 社内取引価格について申し立てる
Making a statement concerning in-house delivery prices

スミス日本支社長は、本社営業本部長に対して、支社と本社との間の商品受け渡し(わた)の価格条件について申し立てします。

Japan Office Manager Smith prepares a statement addressed to the sales department manager at headquarters regarding terms for delivery pricing between the Japan Office and headquarters.

東京　199○年○月○日

本社　営業本部長殿
　　　(営業一課)

日本支社長（サイン）

デュクロンC. I. F. 価格と日本向け品揃え(ぞろ)の件（申立て）

日本国内での営業活動強化に伴い(ともな)、日本総代理店を「吉田物産」に絞って(しぼ)交渉中(こうしょう)のことはご高承(こうしょう)のとおりですが、このほど「デュクロン」の納入(のうにゅう)価格について、日本の不況もあり厳しい(きび)要求が出ました。有力な販売網(もう)を持ち、売上数量も大きな相手先ですので、なんとか商談をまとめたく存じます。

ついては「デュクロン」の東京C. I. F. 価格を1㎡U. S. ＄40.00、数量は月間供給量(きょうきゅう)40,000㎡を最低限とすることを条件としてご裁可(さいか)のうえ、製造部門にもご連絡方(かた)よろしくお取り計らい(はか)願います。

以　上

（写(うつし)）本社　製造本部長（製造二課）

～向け：for ～; aimed at ～　品揃え(ぞろ)：stocking (of goods)　営業活動強化：strengthening of sales activities　総代理店：general distributor; exclusive agency　～に絞る(しぼ)：choose; select　交渉中(こうしょう)：in negotiations　高承(こうしょう)のとおり：as you know　納入(のうにゅう)価格：delivery price　厳しい(きび)要求が出る：strong demand emerges　有力な販売網(もう)を持つ：hold influential sales network　売上数量：amount of sales　なんとか～たい：want somehow to ～　商談をまとめる：bring business talks to a successful conclusion　月間供給量(きょうきゅう)：monthly supply　裁可(さいか)：approval　～部門：～ department　取り計らい(はか)：deal with; take care of

Tokyo, Date (year, month, day)

The Honorable Sales Department Manager,
Headquarters Sales Section One

(signature), Japan Office Manager

RE: Statement on Dukelon CIF price and stocking for Japan

In line with the strengthening of our sales activities in Japan, as you know, we are presently negotiating only with Yoshida Trading to become our exclusive agency. Partly because of the recession in Japan, they recently presented us with a strong demand concerning the delivery price for Dukelon. Because they have an influential sales network with a great many sales, we want, if at all possible, to bring these business negotiations to a successful settlement.

Therefore we will propose the Tokyo CIF price as US $40.00 for 1 squre meter, with the condition that the minimum amount of monthly supply be 40,000 square meters.

We seek your approval and ask that you also inform the manufacturing division of our plan.

(the end)

(copies) Headquarters, Manufacturing Division Manager (Manufacturing Section Two)

留意事項

1) 製造とともに販売を行っている会社では、社内取り引きとして、工場で生産された製品を支店や営業部門に渡す際の受渡価格を決めているのが普通です。

2) 「申し立てる」とは、業務上の案件の処理について、担当部署から上司に提案して承認を仰ぐことをいいます。

3) 支社と本社間の申立書の場合も、社内文書として頭語や結語などは省いて簡潔に書きます。

4) 社内への周知と案件の円滑な実施を図るため、必要に応じて写しを関係部署に送ります。写しの送り先は、文書の左末尾か文書の始めの左上に書き、その前に「写」と注記します。

1. In a company that both manufactures and sells its merchandise, it is usually the manufacturing division, whose job it is to send merchandise to branch offices and sales departments, that sets delivery prices for in-house sales.

2. 申し立てる (making a statement) refers to a business procedure whereby the person responsible for a certain department makes a proposal to a superior asking for his or her approval.

3. Statements between branch offices and the headquarters are considered in-house communications, and therefore should be written concisely, without headings or closings.

4. To facilitate information flow and the smooth activation of plans within the company, copies should be sent to related departments as needed. The places where copies are to be sent should be noted either in the lower left or upper left corner of the document, preceded by the word 写(うつし) (copy).

11-4 検討資料として、稟議書に取引先の会社経歴書を添付する

Attaching a business partner's company history to a circular letter for reference

S&A社は、社内で提携先について検討を行いましたが、その際、次の例のような会社経歴書が添付されました。

S&A Corporation conducted an in-house investigation into candidates for a tie-up. On that occasion, a company history like the one in the following example was attached for reference.

会　社　経　歴　書

1．会　社　名　　株式会社インテックス

2．設立年月日　　昭和35年３月１日

3．代表者名　　鈴木武雄

4．所　在　地　　東京都練馬区羽沢 5-5-8

5．事業の目的　　カーテン、カーペットその他家具・インテリア商品の販売

6．資　本　金　　払込済資本金5,000万円（平成○年２月28日現在）

7．株　　　主　　鈴木武雄、鈴木美智子、鈴木健次、鈴木　操

8．会社の沿革
- 昭和24年４月10日　鈴木家具店として発足
- 昭和35年３月１日　鈴木家具株式会社に改組
資本金を50万円とする
- 昭和43年３月１日　株式会社インテックスと改称
- 昭和48年10月１日　資本金500万円に増資
カーテン、カーペット部門拡大
- 昭和63年10月１日　資本金5,000万円に増資

9．役　　　員
- 代表取締役社長　鈴木武雄
- 専務取締役　山川　弘
- 常務取締役　鈴木健次
- 取締役総務部長　斉藤　繁
- 取締役営業部長　高橋吉男
- 監査役　佐藤幸男
- 監査役　山田一幸

10.	営業品目	カーテン、カーペット、床材、布製壁紙ほかインテリア・装飾関係商品全般
11.	主要取引銀行	うめ銀行練馬支店、松竹銀行池袋支店、大地銀行新宿支店
12.	主要取引先	東京繊維紡績株式会社、東洋絨毯株式会社、京都染色株式会社、大和家具株式会社、山手インテリア株式会社ほか
13.	従　業　員	80名
14.	年　　商	12億円（平成○年度）

以　上

株式会社：joint-stock company　設立：foundation　所在地：address　払込済資本金：paid-up capital　～現在：as of ～ (date)　株主：stockholders　沿革：history　発足：begin　改組：reorganize　改称：change (company) name　増資：increase capital investment　～部門拡大：expand ～ division　役員：officials　代表取締役社長：representative director, president　専務取締役：executive director　常務取締役：managing director　監査役：auditor　営業品目：merchandise; sales items　床材：flooring　布製壁紙：cloth wallpaper　装飾関係商品：furnishing-related goods　～全般：general　主要取引銀行：major banks　繊維：textiles　紡績：spinning (cloth/etc.)　絨毯：carpet　染色：dyeing　年商：annual sales　～年度：～ fiscal year

Company History

1. Name of company: Intex, Inc.
2. Founded: March 1, 1960
3. Name of representative: Suzuki Takeo
4. Address: Tokyo-to, Nerima-ku, Hanezawa 5-5-8
5. Business: sale of curtains, carpets, other home furnishings, furniture and interior goods
6. Capitalization: 50 million yen (paid up capital) (as of current year, February 28)
7. Stockholders: Suzuki Takeo, Suzuki Michiko, Suzuki Kenji, Suzuki Misao
8. History: April 10, 1949, begun as Suzuki Furniture Store;
   March 1, 1960, reorganized as Suzuki Furniture, Inc., with capital investment of 500,000 yen;
   March 1, 1968, changed name to Intex, Inc.;
   October 1, 1973, increased capital investment to 5 million yen, and added curtain and carpet divisions;
   October 1, 1988, increased capital investment to 50 million yen
9. Officers: Representative Director, President—Suzuki Takeo
   Executive Director—Yamakawa Hiroshi
   Managing Director—Suzuki Kenji

Director, Manager of General Affairs Department—Saito Shigeru
Director, Manager of Sales Department—Takahashi Yoshio
Auditor—Sato Sachio
Auditor—Yamada Kazuyuki

10. Merchandise: curtains, carpet, flooring, cloth wallpaper, and other general home furnishings and accessories
11. Major banks: Ume Bank, Nerima Branch; Shochiku Bank, Ikebukuro Branch; Daichi Bank, Shinjuku Branch
12. Major dealers: Tokyo Textile Spinning, Inc., Toyo Rug, Inc., Kyoto Dyeing, Inc., Yamato Furniture, Inc., Yamate Interior Inc., etc.
13. Employees: 80
14. Annual sales: 1,200 million yen (for the fiscal year ______)

(the end)

留意事項

1) 会社経歴書は、取引先内容の判断資料として、打ち合わせ会議の文書や決裁(けっさい)書類などに添付(てんぷ)されます。
2) 会社経歴書には、社名、設立(せつりつ)年月日、所在地、代表者名、役員、事業内容、会社の沿革(えんかく)、株主、取引金融(きんゆう)機関名、主要取引先、従業員数、年商などが記載(きさい)されています。
3) 稟議(りんぎ)のための資料として、本文のような会社経歴書のほかに、「会社案内」なども利用されます。

1. The company history is attached to documents for discussion or approval, as a part of the study materials related to a candidate for a tie-up.
2. A company history should include: company name, date of founding, address, name of representative, officers, business description, company development, stockholders, financial institutions it deals with, major dealers, number of employees, annual sales, etc.
3. In addition to the company history, a company profile is often attached to a circular letter.

第12課

申し入れを承諾する

Accepting a proposal

相手の申し入れを承諾する場合には、文書で意思表示をします。その際には、こちらの感謝の気持ちを表すとともに、その条件を確認することが大切です。また、交渉不成立の場合には断り文を出しますが、今後の取引の可能性への配慮が必要です。

この文書は、ビジネス交渉の一つのしめくくりを示すものなので、こちらの誠意を表すよう語句・表現に注意します。また、一般に、発信の前後には電話や面談を通じてこちらの意思を伝えておきます。

When accepting a proposal made by another party, it is important to put your thoughts into writing. While expressing your appreciation for the proposal, it is also important to confirm its terms at the same time. When negotiations end in failure, you send a letter of rejection, but remember to give consideration to the possibility of future business dealings with that company.

As this communication is one way to end business negotiations, be careful to use words and phrases that express your sincerity. Also, it is general practice to also inform the other party by telephone or personal visit, either before or after sending this communication.

12-1 販売提携の申し入れを承諾する

Accepting a proposal for an affiliation

吉田物産は、S&A社からの販売提携の申し入れを承諾し、契約条件などについて確認します。

Yoshida Trading accepts the proposal for a sales tie-up from S&A Corporation and confirms the contract terms, etc.

営本第○○○号
199○年○月○日

S&Aコーポレーション日本支社
　支社長　ハワード　G. スミス　殿

吉田物産株式会社
常務取締役　鈴木　弘（印）

「デュクロン」販売提携の件

拝啓　時下ますますご清栄のこととお慶び申し上げます。

さて、かねてよりお申し越しの貴社商品「デュクロン」の販売提携の件につきましては、種々ご高配賜り誠にありがとうございます。先日は、また、わざわざご来社いただきまして、お手数をお掛けいたしました。

つきましては、本件に関し、その後社内において慎重に検討を重ねました結果、「デュクロン」が持つカーペット材としての特色を高く評価し、下記の条件により、弊社が取り扱わせていただくことと決定いたしました。

契約書調印その他の段取りにつきましては、弊社の営業部長山田との間でお打合せのうえ、取り進めていただきたく存じます。

今後とも「デュクロン」販売のいよいよの発展を祈念しつつ、取りあえず書中ご通知まで申し上げます。

敬　具

記

[契約条件]

1．価　　格　　デュクロン100%織りカーペット「ニューヨーク」印
　　　月間30,000m²まで　　9,200円／m²
　　　月間30,000m²超の分　　9,000円／m²
　　ただし、毎月最低40,000m²引取を条件とする。

2．決済条件　　毎月月末締め、当日起算の30日約束手形払い

3．その他　　⑴売買基本契約書及び代理店契約書は、S&Aフォームによる。
　　⑵注文、配送、クレーム処理などの具体的な取扱いについては、別途打合せのうえ、文書化する。

以　上

常務取締役(じょうむとりしまりやく)：managing director　種々：various　高配賜る(こうはいたまわる)：receive (your) kind support　わざわざ：take the trouble to ～　手数を掛(か)ける：cause trouble　慎重(しんちょう)に検討を重ねた結果：based on careful examinations　～材：～ materials　高く評価する：highly rate　契約書調印(けいやくしょちょういん)：signing of the contract　段取り(だんどり)：arrangements　取り進める：move on　いよいよの発展を祈念(きねん)しつつ：with a prayer for the continued development　～織(お)り：woven ～　～印：～ brand　～超(ちょう)の分：portion over ～　～を条件とする：must be on the condition that ～　決済(けっさい)：payment　月末締(じ)め：month-end settlement　当日起算(きさん)：calculated from that day　30日約束手形払い：30-day promissory note of payment; 30-day payment by note　売買基本契約(けいやく)書：basic sales contract　代理店：dealer　配送：delivery　クレーム処理(しょり)：dealing with a complaint　別途(べっと)：separately　文書化する：put in writing

---

Sales Document # __________
Date (year, month, day)

S&A Corporation, Japan Office
Office Manager Howard G. Smith (Mr.)

Yoshida Trading, Incorporated
Managing Director Suzuki Hiroshi (seal)

RE: Dukelon sales tie-up

Salutations: Allow me to congratulate you on your good health and well-being at this time.

Now, with relation to the message you conveyed to us earlier regarding a sales tie-up for your company's product Dukelon, I want to express my deep appreciation for your support. Also, thank you for taking the trouble to visit us the other day.

In this regard, as a result of careful examinations regarding this matter within the company, we concluded that because we rate very highly the special characteristics of the materials that go into making Dukelon, our company agrees to handle that carpet under the terms listed below.

Would you please consult with our Sales Department Manager Yamada and move on to specific plans for the actual signing of the contract and other arrangements.

With a prayer for the continued development of Dukelon sales in the future, we write simply to inform you of our decision.

Sincerely yours

Details

[Contract terms]

1. Cost: Dukelon 100% woven carpet, "New York" brand
   The first 30,000 square meters per month—9,200 yen per square meter
   Portion over 30,000 square meters per month—9,000 yen per square meter
   Minimum order per month must be at least 40,000 square meters
2. Terms of payment: accounts will be settled at the end of the month with a 30-day promissory note
3. Other
   (1) S&A's form will be used for both the basic sales contract and the dealership contract.
   (2) Special discussions will be held to deal with procedures for ordering, delivery, complaints, etc., and these will be put in writing.

(the end)

留意事項

1) 重要な申し入れなどを承諾する場合は、儀礼的な意味だけでなく、ビジネスの段階を確認する意味で、必ず文書でやり取りするようにします。
2) まず相手の協力に対して感謝の気持ちを述べたうえで、契約条件を漏れのないように箇条書きで列挙し、内容を確認します。未決定の事項がある場合は、その旨を明記します。
3) 今後の段取りについては、担当者などを示し、細部は改めて打ち合わせることとします。
4) 取り引きのこれからの成功と発展を期待して本文を終わります。

1. When approving an important proposal, you must always put it in writing, not only out of courtesy but also to confirm the status of the business relationship.
2. After expressing appreciation for the other party's cooperation, outline the contents of the contract terms for confirmation as a guard against omissions. Clearly outline any matters not yet decided upon.
3. Regarding future procedures, indicate the person responsible and decide on a time to discuss the details further.
4. End the body of the letter by expressing hopes for to the success and growth of your dealings together in the future.

社外　承諾する・確認する　agreement/confirmation

12-2 OA機器の納入条件を承諾する

Accepting payment terms for OA equipment

S&A社は、OA機器を社内に導入するにあたり、かねてから交渉中の東京システム販売に対して提示の条件を承諾する旨の文書を出します。

S&A Corporation has been planning to install OA equipment in their company for some time and has been negotiating with Tokyo System Sales in this regard. They send a letter to the company accepting their terms.

営第○○○号
平成○年○月○日

東京システム販売株式会社
代表取締役　赤坂　透　殿

S&Aコーポレーション日本支社
営業部長　山本良雄（印）

コンピュータ・ターミナル導入の件

前略　かねてよりお打合わせ中の題記の件につき、貴社ご提示の条件を下記のとおり確認し、承諾のこととといたしますので、よろしくお取り計らいください。

記

1)機器種類：　YMN 社製 PO-9901型コンピュータ・ターミナル　3台
2)設置場所：　当支社営業部、経理部及び戸田工場　各1台
3)設置期日：　本年10月1日から使用開始として、それに合わせて設置する（工程は、貴社スケジュールどおりとする）
4)関連ソフト：上の期日に合うように、テストランも含めて貴社スケジュールどおりとする
5)代金決済：　貴社の標準契約書による

なお、上記により改めて契約書を作成のこととしたいので、ご手配願います。

以　上

代表取締役：representative director　コンピュータ・ターミナル導入：installation of computer terminal　題記の件：the above-mentioned subject　提示：present　～のこととする：decide to ～　取り計らい：dealing with　機器種類：type of equipment　～型：～ model/type　設置：installment　～に合わせて：so as to ～; to coincide with ～　工程：process　期日に合う：conform to the date decided　テストラン：test run　代金決済：payment of costs　標準契約書：standard contract form　手配：preparation; arrangement

---

Sales Document # __________
Date (year, month, day)

Tokyo System Sales, Incorporated
Representative Director Akasaka Toru (Mr.)

S&A Corporation, Japan Office
Sales Department Manager Yamamoto Yoshio (seal)

RE: Installation of computer terminal

Regarding our ongoing talks on the above-mentioned subject, I hasten to inform you that we confirm and approve of the terms you presented, as noted below, and ask that you now deal with the matter.

Details

1. Type of equipment: Model PO 9901 computer terminal made by YMN Company (3 terminals)
2. Place to be installed: our company's sales department, accounting department, and Toda Factory (1 terminal each)
3. Date of installation: install so as to begin use on October 1, this year (the process will follow your company's schedule)
4. Related software: conforming to the date decided, we will follow your company's schedule, including the time set for a test run of the software
5. Payment: per your company's standard contract form

In addition, we would like to ask you to prepare a new contract according to the above terms.

(the end)

留意事項

1) 上の例は社外文書ですが、S&A社は相手の東京システム販売に対して発注する立場なので、あまりていねいな表現をする必要はなく、事務的な文書で十分です。そのため、初めと終わりのあいさつ的な表現は省いています。

2) 内容を確認するため、契約条件などをもう一度列挙します。

1. This example is an out-going the company letter, but as S&A Corporation is placing an order with Tokyo System Sales, you need not use extremely polite language. Business-type expressions are adequate. For this reason, you may omit the opening and closing greetings.

2. To confirm the contents, list the contract terms one more time.

12-1と12-2のフローと文例

12-1「販売提携の申し入れを承諾する」のフロー

「デュクロン」販売提携の件

拝啓　時下ますますご清栄のこととお慶び申し上げます。

さて、かねてよりお申し越しの貴社商品「デュクロン」の販売提携の件につきましては、種々ご高配賜り誠にありがとうございます。先日は、また、わざわざご来社いただきまして、お手数をお掛けいたしました。

つきましては、本件に関し、その後社内において慎重に検討を重ねました結果、「デュクロン」が持つカーペット材としての特色を高く評価し、下記の条件により、弊社が取り扱わせていただくことと決定いたしました。

①用件を確認する＋承諾する

契約書調印その他の段取りにつきましては、弊社の営業部長山田との間でお打合せのうえ、取り進めていただきたく存じます。

②今後の段取りを知らせる

今後とも「デュクロン」販売のいよいよの発展を祈念しつつ、取りあえず書中ご通知まで申し上げます。

③成功と発展を願う

敬　具

記

［契約条件］

1．価　　格　デュクロン100％織りカーペット「ニューヨーク」印

月間30,000 m²まで　9,200円／m²

月間30,000 m²超の分　9,000円／m²

ただし、毎月最低40,000 m²引取を条件とする。

2．決済条件　毎月月末締め、当日起算の30日約束手形払い

3．その他　(1)売買基本契約書及び代理店契約書は、S&Aフォームによる。

(2)注文、配送、クレーム処理などの具体的な取扱いについては、別途打合せのうえ、文書化する。

④記――承諾条件の内容

以　上

12-2「OA機器の納入条件を承諾する」のフロー

コンピュータ・ターミナル導入の件

前略　かねてよりお打合わせ中の題記の件につき、貴社ご提示の条件を下記のとおり確認し、承諾のこといたしますので、よろしくお取り計らいください。

①用件を確認する＋承諾する

記

1)機器種類：　YMN社製PO-9901型コンピュータ・ターミナル　3台

2)設置場所：　当支社営業部、経理部及び戸田工場　各1台

3)設置期日：　本年10月1日から使用開始として、それに合わせて設置する(工程は、貴社スケジュールどおりとする)

4)関連ソフト：上の期日に合うように、テストランも含めて貴社スケジュールどおりとする

④記――承諾条件の内容

5)代金決済：　貴社の標準契約書による

なお、上記により改めて契約書を作成のこととしたいので、ご手配願います。——②今後の段取りを知らせる

以　上

（下線の部分は自分の状況に合わせて書いてください。）

①用件を確認する＋承諾する

Confirming business and giving consent

＊本件に関し、社内において慎重に検討を重ねました結果、下記の条件により、弊社が取り扱わせていただくことと決定いたしました。(12-1)

As a result of careful examinations regarding this matter within the company, we concluded that our company agrees to handle (that carpet) under the terms listed below.

＊かねてよりお打合わせ中の題記の件につき、貴社ご提示の条件を下記のとおり確認し、承諾のことといたしますので、よろしくお取り計らいください。(12-2)

Regarding our ongoing talks on the above-mentioned subject, I hasten to inform you that we confirm and approve of the terms you presented, as noted below, and ask that you now deal with the matter.

＊○月○日のお手紙にてお申し越しのありました協賛依頼の件、当方といたしましても、願ってもないことと、喜んで請けさせて頂きます。

Regarding the matter of your unexpected request for sponsorship written in your letter dated (month, day), we will happily undertake it.

②今後の段取りを知らせる（担当者氏名など）

Notifying of future plans (name of person in charge, etc.)

＊契約書調印その他の段取りにつきましては、弊社の営業部長山田との間でお打合わせのうえ、取り進めていただきたく存じます。(12-1)

Would you please consult with our Sales Department Manager Yamada and move on to specific plans for the actual signing of the contract and other arrangements.

＊上記により改めて契約書を作成のこととしたいので、ご手配願います。(12-2)

We would like to ask you to prepare a new contract according to the above terms.

＊詳細につきましては、早急に検討の上、ご連絡申し上げますので、その節はよろしくお願いいたします。

As for the details, I/we will contact you after an urgent examination. Thank you for your cooperation in advance.

③成功と発展を願う

Praying for success and development

＊今後とも「デュクロン」販売のいよいよの発展を祈念しつつ、取りあえず書中ご通知まで申し上げます。(12-1)

With a prayer for the continued development of Dukelon sales in the future, we write simply to inform you (of our decision).

＊今後とも貴社との提携業務がますます進展することを祈念しております。

We pray that our business tie-up with your company will continue to develop in the future as well.

＊今回の新システム導入により貴社の業務合理化が一層進展することをお祈り申し上げます。

We pray that the installation of the new system this time will add to the development of your business rationale.

④記——承諾条件の内容

Description—contents of conditions approved

〈条件の書き方〉

How to write conditions

＊毎月最低40,000 m² 引取**を**条件**とする**。(12-1)

Minimum order per month must be at least 40,000 square meters.

＊売買基本契約書及び代理店契約書**は**、S＆Aフォーム**による** (12-1)

S&A's form will be used for both the basic sales contract and the dealership contract.

＊貴社の標準契約書**による** (12-2)

Per your company's standard contract form.

＊工程**は**、貴社スケジュールどおり**とする** (12-2)

The process will follow your company's schedule.

12-3 相手先に交渉成立の礼状を書く

Thanking the other party for concluding negotiations

S&A社は、吉田物産に対し販売提携成立のお礼を述べ、今後の取り引きへの協力を依頼します。

S&A Corporation expresses gratitude to Yoshida Trading for establishing a sales tie-up and requests cooperation with business dealings in the future.

営本第〇〇〇号
平成〇年〇月〇日

吉田物産株式会社
常務取締役 鈴木 弘 殿

S&Aコーポレーション日本支社
支社長 (英字サイン)
(ハワード G. スミス)

「デュクロン」販売提携の件

拝復 酷暑の候 ますますご隆昌のこととお喜び申し上げます。

さて、〇月〇日付貴信をもってお申し越しのありました題記取引ご決定の趣有り難く拝承いたしました。このたびの販売提携実現によりまして、貴社の永年にわたる販売網と弊社の商品開発力とが一体となり、「デュクロン」の日本における販売展開が飛躍的に拡大するものと確信いたします。

なにとぞ、今後とも末永くご支援、ご厚誼を賜りますよう、改めてお願い申し上げる次第でございます。

取引条件の細部や契約書調印そのほか関係事項の処理につきましては、追ってお打ち合わせのうえ、早急に段取りを進めることといたしたく、よろしくお願い申し上げます。

まずは取りあえず書中をもちまして御礼かたがたごあいさつ申し上げます

敬 具

常務取締役：managing director　販売提携：sales tie-up　題記取引決定の趣：information on a decision made concerning the above business　拝承する：receive　永年にわたる：covering many years　販売網：sales network　商品開発力：ability to develop new products　一体となる：become one (body)　販売展開：sales operation　飛躍的に拡大する：expand rapidly　確信する：be certain; really believe　末永く：unending　支援：support　厚誼を賜る：receive (your) kindness　～次第である：such being the case; in brief ～　取引条件の細部：details of the business terms　契約書調印：signing of the contract　関係事項の処理：dealing with related issues　早急に段取りを進める：quickly proceed with arrangements　～ことといたしたく：I/we would like to ～

Sales document # ________
Date (year, month, day)

Yoshida Trading, Incorporated
Managing Director Suzuki Hiroshi (Mr.)

S&A Corporation, Japan Office
Office Manager (Signed in English)
Howard G. Smith

RE: Dukelon sales tie-up

Salutations: May I congratulate you on your continuing prosperity at this time of sweltering heat.

Now, I appreciate your letter of (month, day) informing me of your decision concerning the above topic. The actualization of our sales tie-up brings together your sales network, which has been built up over many years, and the ability of our company to develop new products, and we are certain this will lead to the rapid sales expansion of Dukelon in its new market in Japan.

At this time, I once again express our hope for your unending support and kindness now and in the future.

Let us soon discuss the details of our tie-up, the signing of the contract, and the handling of other related items, so that we can quickly proceed with arrangements. We ask your cooperation.

In the meantime, I am writing this letter in part to express my thanks to you.

Sincerely yours

留意事項

1) 販売提携の交渉が成立した場合、契約書調印、細部打ち合わせなどに先立ち、まず正式に感謝の気持ちを表明する文書を送ります。礼状ですから、語句・表現はていねいなものにします。このような文書には、単に礼を言うだけではなく、今後の両者の友好的な提携関係を確認するという意味もあります。

2) この種の礼状の場合は、お礼を述べたり今後の愛顧をお願いするのに、「今後とも末永くご支援、ご厚誼を賜りますよう、お願い申し上げます」など定型的な表現が一般に用いられます。

1. When negotiations for a sales tie-up are concluded successfully, the first thing you do is to write a letter formally expressing your appreciation, even before signing a contract or discussing details. As this is a letter of thanks, the words and phrases must be polite. You do not just express your thanks; you are also writing to confirm the fact that your dealings in the future will be on a friendly basis for both parties.

2. With this type of thank-you letter, there are standard set phrases that are generally used, such as "I once again express our hope for your unending support and kindness now and in the future."

第13課

社内に通知文書を出す

Issuing in-house memos

通知文は、企業において、正確に意思を伝達する役割を担(にな)っています。なかでも、この課で扱う社内文書は、関係者が多数だったり関係部署が複数だったりする場合、重要案件の内容を正確にしかも確実に連絡したい場合、内容を記録し保存(ほぞん)する必要がある場合など、日常の業務でよく使われる重要な文書です。

パソコンなど情報手段のOA化が進むなかにあっても、このような通知文の書き方の重要性はまったく変わりません。

Memos are used in a company to convey information accurately. They are extremely important in the day-to-day operations of that business. As illustrated in the memos in this chapter, there are times when memos are sent to a large number of people or a number of different departments. There are also times when accurate information concerning important issues must be conveyed, and there are times when it is necessary to put something down for the record.

Even in this world of office automation, with personal computers and other information-related equipment, the importance of style in memos has not changed.

13-1 打ち合わせ会議を招集する
Calling a planning meeting

S&A社の山本営業部長は、吉田物産との販売提携開始にあたって打ち合わせを行うため、関係部署の責任者に会議の招集通知を出します。

Mr. Yamamoto, Sales Department Manager of S&A Corporation, issues a memo to the heads of the related sections announcing a meeting to discuss the upcoming opening of business dealings with Yoshida Trading.

営第○○○号
199○年○月○日

工場長殿
資財部長殿
経理部長殿

営業部長　山本良雄（印）

吉田物産納めカーペットの件

このたび、吉田物産(株)とカーペットを中心とする当社製品の販売提携がまとまりました。

従来アトランタ工場渡しであったものが、吉田物産の日本の指定倉庫渡しに切り替わります。数量も、従来と比較して飛躍的な増加が見込まれますので、納入には万全を期したいと思います。

つきましては、下記のとおり打合せを行ないます。各部署の担当者を含めてお集まりください。

記

1．日　時　　○月○日（月）　午前９時から11時30分まで
2．場　所　　支社　#102会議室
3．議　題　　吉田物産へのデュクロン納入について
4．議　事　　⑴吉田物産との契約内容について
　　　　　　　⑵商品の納入期日と数量について
　　　　　　　⑶商品採算と輸送コストの試算について
　　　　　　　⑷アトランタ工場からの輸入品について
　　　　　　　⑸運送業者の指定について
　　　　　　　⑹その他関連事項
5．その他　　⑴各部署において、吉田物産への納入に関する問題点を集約のうえ、ご出席ください
　　　　　　　⑵添付資料
　　　　　　　　商品の納入期日と数量一覧表、商品採算試算表

(写) 支社長

以　上

～納(おさ)め：supplying to ～　販売提携(ていけい)がまとまる：bring about sales tie-up　従来：originally　～渡(わた)し：delivery (from)　指定倉庫：designated warehouse　切り替わる：change　比較する：compare　飛躍(ひやく)的な増加が見込まれる：expect rapid growth　納入(のうにゅう)：delivery　万全(ばんぜん)を期(き)す：take all possible measures (to ensure no mistakes)　各部署の担当者：persons in charge in each section　議事：subject　契約(けいやく)内容：details of contract　期日：set/fixed date　採算(さいさん)：profit　輸送コストの試算：projected calculation of transportation costs　運送業者の指定：designation of transporter　関連事項：related issues　問題点を集約のうえ出席する：attend meeting having put together any queries　添付(てんぷ)資料：attached materials　一覧(いちらん)表：listing

---

Sales Document # ______
Date (year, month, day)

The Honorable Factory Manager
The Honorable Materials Department Manager
The Honorable Accounting Department Manager

Sales Department Manager Yamamoto Yoshio (seal)

RE: Supplying carpet to Yoshida Trading

Recently, we have brought about a sales tie-up with Yoshida Trading (Inc.) whereby they will handle our company's products, especially carpets.

There will be a change in past procedures for deliveries that originated from the Atlanta factory, so that deliveries will now originate from a warehouse in Japan designated by Yoshida Trading. We expect a rapid growth in quantity compared to the past, and we must take all possible measures to ensure smooth deliveries.

In this regard, we will hold a meeting, as detailed below. I ask that all of you and those in charge gather for this meeting.

Details

1. Date, time: (month, day) (Monday) 9:00 A.M.–11:30 A.M.
2. Location: Japan Office, Room #102
3. Subject: Delivery of Dukelon to Yoshida Trading
4. Items of business
   (1) Details of the contract with Yoshida Trading
   (2) Date and quantity of delivery
   (3) Projected calculation of profit and transportation costs
   (4) Importation from Atlanta factory
   (5) Designation of a transporter
   (6) Other related issues
5. Other
   (1) Have your own section or department put together a list of problems related to the delivery to Yoshida Trading and come to the meeting prepared to share these.
   (2) Attached documents:
   a listing of the dates and quantity for delivery, a chart showing a calculation of profits

(copy) Office Manager　(the end)

留意事項

1) 関係部署間の業務連絡のための通知文です。まず会合の目的や趣旨を明らかにし、次に日時、場所、議題(議案)、必要資料などをはっきりと伝えます。

2) 社内文書では、頭語や初めと終わりのあいさつ及び敬語などの儀礼的な表現を一切省きます。また、必要で十分な情報を簡潔に伝えるため、できるだけ箇条書きにします。社内の福利厚生関係の文書には、よりくだけたわかりやすい表現を用います。

3) 宛先は、原則として役職名・部課名を用います。宛先が複数のときは並べて書きます。発信者名は会社によって異なりますが、普通、役員・部長・支店長は役職名及び氏名、その他は役職名とします。

4) 記書きのしめくくりは、社内文書・社外文書とも「以上」とします。

1. This memo is a means of contacting related sections and departments. It first clarifies the objective or purpose of the meeting, then clearly states the date and time, location, subject, and necessary information.

2. Courteous expressions, such as salutations, opening and closing greetings, and polite language are not used at all. If possible, use an itemized format to cover all the necessary information concisely. You may, however, use familiar, easy-to-understand expressions for communications dealing with issues relating to company benefits for company employees.

3. As a rule, memos are addressed to the position or department. When there is more than one addressee, these may be written one after the other. The name of the sender is noted differently in different companies, but usually directors, department managers, and office managers will use their title as well as their name, while others use only their title.

4. In either an in-house document or one directed outside the company, 以上 (the end) is used to indicate the conclusion of the "記書(きが)き" section.

13-2 ＯＡ機器のデモへの出席を求める

Requesting attendance at a demonstration of OA equipment

S&A社のＯＡ化を担当する営業一課は、かねてから導入を進めているコンピュータ・ターミナルのデモンストレーションの日程が遅れたため、日時・場所などを変更し、改めて社内関係者に出席を依頼します。

The sales department, in charge of automating the offices of S&A Corporation, has been promoting the installation of computer terminals for some time, and because the scheduled demonstration was delayed, the time and place had to be changed. The following memo requests that all related employees attend the newly scheduled demonstration.

平成○年○月○日

営業二課長殿

経理課長殿

工場／倉庫総務担当殿

（写）総務課長

営業一課長（印）

YMN社製コンピュータ・ターミナルのデモについて

かねてご案内しました題記の件については、10月１日からの運用開始を予定し９月下旬にはデモを行なう計画のところ、ソフト作成の遅延により、下記のように10月30日（土）のデモとなってしまいました。

なるべく早くシステムの稼働を図りたいので、休日のところ申し訳ありませんが、担当者を出勤させるよう特別のお計らいをお願いいたします。

記

１．日　時　　10月30日（土）　10：00から13：00ごろまで

２．場　所　　営業部営業一課

３．デモ内容　　データのインプット／データの索引作成／月末集計など

以　上

総務担当：in charge of general affairs　コンピュータ・ターミナル：computer terminal　デモ：demonstration　題記の件：the above subject　運用開始：start-up (of use)　下旬(げじゅん)：last third of a month　ソフト作成の遅延(ちえん)：delay in completion of software　システムの稼働(かどう)を図(はか)る：get the system operational　特別のお計(はか)らい：dealing with especially/expressly　データのインプット：input of data　索引(さくいん)：indexing　月末集計：monthly totals

Date (year, month, day)

The Honorable Sales Section Two Chief
The Honorable Accounting Section Chief
The Honorable Person in Charge of General Affairs of the Factory/Warehouse
(copy) General Affairs Chief

Sales Section One Chief (seal)

RE: Demonstration of YMN computer terminal

With respect to this subject about which you were notified earlier, we had originally planned the demonstration for late September in conjunction with a start-up date of October 1. Because of a delay in the completion of the software, however, the demonstration has been moved back to October 30 (Saturday) as noted below.

Though I know this is a day when you normally do not come to the office, I am asking you to expressly direct the persons in charge in your sections to come to work, because we want to get the system operational as quickly as possible. I ask for your cooperation.

Details

1. Date, time: October 30 (Sat.) 10:00 A.M. to about 1:00 P.M.
2. Location: Sales Department, Sales Section One
3. Contents of demonstration: input of data, indexing of data, monthly totals, etc.

(the end)

留意事項

1) 休日出勤など特別な仕事を頼む場合、その旨(むね)を明記することが必要です。
2) 必要で十分な情報だけを箇条(かじょう)書きにして書きます。
3) 文書の写(うつ)しの送付先を受信者に知らせる場合には、宛名(あてな)の下または末尾などに示します。

1. When making special requests of employees, such as reporting to work on their day off, you must make clear notification of these requests.
2. Write concisely in an itemized format only the information they need to know.
3. When informing the recipients of the memo where copies have been sent, note this either at the bottom of the list of recipients or at the bottom of the memo.

13-1と13-2のフローと文例

13-1「打ち合わせ会議を招集する」のフロー

吉田物産納めカーペットの件

このたび、吉田物産(株)とカーペットを中心とする当社製品の販売提携がまとまりました。

従来アトランタ工場渡しであったものが、吉田物産の日本の指定倉庫渡しに切り替わります。数量も、従来と比較して飛躍的な増加が見込まれますので、納入には万全を期したいと思います。 ——①招集するいきさつを説明する

つきましては、下記のとおり打合せを行ないます。各部署の担当者を含めてお集まりください。 ——②招集を通知する

記

1．日　時	○月○日（月）　午前9時から11時30分まで
2．場　所	支社　#102会議室
3．議　題	吉田物産へのデュクロン納入について
4．議　事	(1)吉田物産との契約内容について (2)商品の納入期日と数量について (3)商品採算と輸送コストの試算について (4)アトランタ工場からの輸入品について (5)運送業者の指定について (6)その他関連事項
5．その他	(1)各部署において、吉田物産への納入に関する問題点を集約のうえ、ご出席ください (2)添付資料 商品の納入期日と数量一覧表、商品採算試算表

——③記—通知内容

（写）支社長

以　上

13-2「OA機器のデモへの出席を求める」のフロー

YMN社製コンピュータ・ターミナルのデモについて

かねてご案内しました題記の件については、10月1日からの運用開始を予定し9月下旬にはデモを行なう計画のところ、ソフト作成の遅延により、下記のように10月30日(土)のデモとなってしまいました。 ——①招集するいきさつを説明する

なるべく早くシステムの稼働を図りたいので、休日のところ申し訳ありませんが、担当者を出勤させるよう特別のお計らいをお願いいたします。 ——②招集を通知する

記

1．日　時	10月30日(土)　10：00から13：00ごろまで
2．場　所	営業部営業一課
3．デモ内容	データのインプット／データの索引作成／月末集計など

——③記—通知内容

以　上

（下線の部分は自分の状況に合わせて書いてください。）

①招集（しょうしゅう）するいきさつを説明する

Explaining the circumstances of a gathering

②招集を通知する

Notifying of the gathering

＊下記のとおり打合せを行ないます。各部署の担当者を含めてお集まりください。(13-1)

We will hold a meeting as detailed below. I ask that all of you and those in charge gather for this meeting.

＊休日のところ申し訳ありませんが、担当者を出勤させるよう特別のお計（はか）らいをお願いいたします。(13-2)

Though I know this is a day when you normally do not come to the office, I am asking you to expressly direct the persons in charge in your sections to come to work.

＊創立１周年記念事業に関する第３回打合せ会議を下記のとおり開催（かいさい）いたしますので、関係者全員出席願います。

We will hold the third meeting regarding the first anniversary of the foundation of our business. Would all related persons please attend.

③記――通知内容（日時、場所、議題など）

Description—contents of notification (date, place, topic, etc.)

13-3 取引開始にあたって注意事項を社内に周知させる

Informing employees of matters that require attention as business dealings begin

吉田物産との取引開始にあたって、スミス支社長は、重点取引商品に関する社内会議の決定に基づき、取引先に対する商品納入業務についての注意事項を指示して、関係部署の協力を求めます。

Certain decisions were made at a meeting about the sale of the chief product. As the company begins business dealings with Yoshida Trading, Office Manager Smith issues directions to the heads of related departments concerning matters particularly related to deliveries that require attention. He asks for their cooperation.

重　要

営第　○○○　号
平成○年○月○日

管理部長殿
（輸入・倉庫・運輸・保険　各課）

支社長　（英字サイン）

吉田物産との取引の件
（デュクロンの納入）

かねて検討中であった日本総代理店として、「吉田物産（株）」が起用されることが決定しました。

これに伴い、関連事項、特に重点拡販目標の「デュクロン」について、昨日の社内会議で下記のことが決まりましたので、改めて各課の理解と協力を得たく通知します。

記

1．吉田物産　日本での販売総代理店として、○月から活動を開始する。

2．取扱商品　当社が生産・販売する全商品とするが、洋風化の進む日本向けに重点を置く「デュクロン製品」、特にカーペットを中心とする。日本支社としては、これを全面的にバックアップする。ただし、吉田物産扱いの販売対象地域は、日本国内に限るものとする。

3．商品の出荷・納入手続

通例は、戸田工場から吉田物産の指定倉庫に搬入する。ただし、「デュクロン製カーペット」のデラックス仕様のものはアトランタ工場から通関後、直接納入のこととする。当社の商品納入は、すべて吉田物産の指定倉庫渡しとなる。

4．数　　量　現在、契約により取り決めたものは「デュクロン」標準型カーペットが最低納入数量40,000㎡／月となっている。
デラックス型は都度の発注となる。

5．指定倉庫　吉田物産の指定倉庫は、「富士倉庫」である。

6．運送業者　吉田物産への納入商品の国内輸送は、すべて「大山運輸」を起用する。つまり戸田工場からの輸送、または通関後の富士倉庫までの輸送を「大山運輸」が担当する。

以上、吉田物産との取引は、当社にとって最も重要な取引の一つであり、日本国内の拡販上からも、ぜひともスムーズな展開を期したい。特に、最近デラックス型「デュクロン」製カーペットの生産が遅れ気味なので、輸入担当部門は、生産工程のチェックと督促を忘れないように、また、倉庫・運輸担当部門は、保管・輸送に注意し、納入に万全を期されたい。

以　上

運輸：transportation　保険：insurance　納入：delivery　総代理店：exclusive agency　起用する：appoint　～に伴い：related to ～　関連事項：related matters　重点拡販目標：important objective to expand sales　通知する：inform; give notice　洋風化が進む：westernization is progressing　～向け：aimed at ～　～に重点を置く：put emphasis on ～　全面的にバックアップする：fully support　～扱いの：served by ～　販売対象地域：(object) area for sales　～に限る：limit to ～　～ものとする：I/we decide to ～　出荷：shipping　手続：procedures　通例：as a rule; usually　指定倉庫：designated warehouse　搬入する：transport; carry in　通関後：after customs clearance　～こととする：I/we decide to ～　～渡し：delivery to ～　都度の発注：each order　担当：in charge　拡販上から：from the viewpoint of expanding sales　スムーズな展開を期す：hope for smooth operation　～気味：a tendency to ～　生産工程のチェック：check on the process of production　督促：reminders　保管：storage　万全を期す：take all possible measures (to ensure no mistakes)

Very Important

Sales Document # ______
Date (year, month, day)

The Honorable Executive Department Managers
(Import, Storage, Transportation, Insurance Sections)

Office Manage (English signature)r

RE: Business dealings with Yoshida Trading (Delivery of Dukelon)

It has been decided, after much study, that Yoshida Trading (Inc.) will be appointed as our exclusive agency in Japan.

Related to this, we held an in-house meeting yesterday to deal with the related matters, especially our important objective to expand Dukelon sales, and I want to inform you of the decisions reached at that meeting and to request your understanding and cooperation.

Details

1. Yoshida Trading: will begin serving as our exclusive agency in Japan as of (month).
2. Merchandise to be handled: all of the products that our company manufactures and sells, with a special concentration on Dukelon products, more specifically a carpet that is aimed at the increasingly westernized market in Japan. The Japan Office is in full support of this action. Please note, however, that the sales area Yoshida Trading serves will be limited to the area within Japan.
3. Shipping and delivery procedures: as a rule, merchandise will be transported from the Toda Factory to the Yoshida Trading's designated warehouse. However, deluxe Dukelon carpets will be shipped from the Atlanta factory and taken directly to their warehouse after customs clearance. All of this company's merchandise will be delivered to Yoshida Trading's designated warehouse.
4. Quantity: at the present time, the contract stipulates that they take a minimum of 40,000 square meters of the standard Dukelon carpet per month. The quantity of deluxe carpet will depend on each order.
5. Designated warehouse: Yoshida Trading has designated Fuji Warehouse as its warehouse.
6. Transporter: we have appointed Oyama Transportation to take charge of all of the deliveries to Yoshida Trading within Japan. In other words, Oyama Transportation will be in charge of all deliveries from the Toda Factory, or from customs to the Fuji Warehouse.

In summary, our business dealings with Yoshida Trading are one of the most important we have, and we also hope for smooth operations from the viewpoint of increasing sales within Japan. We note especially that the production of the deluxe Dukelon carpets has a tendency to run behind schedule, and we request that the person in charge of imports check on the progress of production and not forget to issue reminders. We also ask that those in charge of storage and transportation exercise care and take all possible measures to operate without incident.

(the end)

留意事項

1) この通知文では、特に社内関係部署に対して商品取扱上の注意を促(うなが)す意味から、「限るものとする」「期(き)されたい」などの強い表現を使っています。

2) 上の例のように、発信者、受信者の下にかっこ書きをして文書の起案(きあん)者や担当者を示す例があります。

1. As this memo is written to heads of related departments in the company to promote the careful handling of merchandise, strong phrases like 限るものとする (will be limited to) and 期(き)されたい (we expect) are used.

2. This memo illustrates how the titles of

3)特に重要な文書については、「重要」と押印(おういん)します。このほか、特殊(とくしゅ)な文書には、「至急(しきゅう)」(急ぎの文書)、「親展(しんてん)」(特定の相手にあてたもの)、「人事親展」(人事関係の文書で特定の相手にあてたもの)、「秘」(秘密文書)、「極秘(ごくひ)」(秘密度の高いもの)、「社外秘」(社外に対し秘密にしなければならないもの) などがあります。それぞれ、文書の左上部または右上部に朱(しゅ)で押印して表示します。

the persons who drafted the memo or those who are in charge are enclosed within parentheses and noted below the writer and recipients of the memo.

3. In the case of an extremely important document, the words 重要 (very important) are stamped on the face of the memo. Other stamps that are sometimes used include: 至急(しきゅう) (urgent), for memos that must be taken care of immediately; 親展(しんてん) (personal), for memos going to a specific person; 人事親展 (personnel-confidential), for memos related to personnel or directed to a specific person; 秘 (secret), for secret or confidential memos; 極秘(ごくひ) (top-secret), for extremely secret and sensitive memos; 社外秘 (for in-house knowledge only), for memos that absolutely must not be leaked outside the company. Each of these directives is to be stamped in the top left or right corner in red.

13-4 慰労会の案内をする

Issuing an invitation to a thank-you party

S&A社の営業部門では、吉田物産との販売契約が成立したことを祝って部内の慰労会を設けることとなり、案内を出します。

The sales department of S&A Corporation decides to hold an employee thank-you party to celebrate the establishment of business ties with Yoshida Trading and sends out an invitation.

199○年○月○日

部内　各位

営業部営業一課（印）

<u>吉田物産契約成立祝いのお知らせ</u>

かねてから交渉中であった吉田物産との「デュクロン」の販売契約が、めでたく成立しました。

つきましては、交渉開始から今日までの関係者のご苦労をねぎらうため、慰労会の席を設けたいと思います。皆さん、どうか奮ってご参加ください。

記

1.日　時：○月○日（金）午後6時～8時30分

2.場　所：居酒屋「かっぱ」（ＪＲ神田駅北口）

3.会　費：ナシ！

4.その他：当日は、残業しなくても行けるよう頑張って、定時に一同揃って会場に行きましょう。万一、ほかを回って直接会場に来る人は、入口でS&A社の者である旨、店側にお伝えください。
この会には、スミス支社長も出席します。久しぶりに美声が聞けそうです。乞うご期待。

なお、出欠は、○月○日までに営業一課の木村までお願いします。

以　上

------------------------------ 切り取り線 ------------------------------

（ 出席　　欠席 ）します。　　　　氏　名＿＿＿＿＿＿＿＿＿＿

部内各位：all in the department　契約成立祝い：celebration of successful conclusion of contract　めでたく～する：happily do ～　交渉開始：start of negotiations　関係者：people involved　苦労をねぎらう：show appreciation　慰労会：a party held upon the conclusion of a project to show appreciation for everyone's hard work　席を設ける：hold a party　どうか奮って～ください：please feel free to ～　ナシ：free　定時：appointed time　一同揃って：all members together　万一：if ～ should　ほかを回る：go to another place　～旨：to the effect that ～　美声が聞ける：be able to hear a beautiful voice　乞うご期待：please look forward to it　切り取り線：cut line (dotted line to cut along)

Date (year, month, day)

Everyone in the Department

Sales Department Sales Section One (seal)

Notice of a celebration to honor the success of concluding a contract with Yoshida Trading

The negotiations that have been going on for some time for a sales contract with Yoshida Trading to sell Dukelon have happily come to a conclusion.

Therefore, we would like to hold a thank-you party to show our appreciation to everyone involved for the work that you did from the beginning until now. Please feel free to attend.

Details

1. Date, time: (month, day) (Friday) 6:00 P.M.–8:30 P.M.
2. Location: Tavern Kappa (JR Kanda Station, north exit)
3. Cost: Free!
4. Other: On this day, make an effort to complete your work on time so we can all go to the tavern together at the appointed time. If for some reason you are out of the office that afternoon and aim to go directly to the tavern, please tell the tavern employee at the entrance that you are with S&A Corporation. Office Manager Smith will also be present. You'll be able to hear his beautiful voice for the first time in a long time. Please look forward to it.

Please let Mr. Kimura in sales section one know by (month, day) whether or not you will be able to attend.

(the end)

- - - - - - - - - - cut - - - - - - - - - -

(will/will not) attend.　　　Name ＿＿＿＿＿＿＿＿

留意事項

1) 業務に関係した社内行事の案内文なので、宛先は「部内各位」とします。
2) 気軽な会合として全員が参加できるように、親しみのあるくだけた表現を使います。会費をはっきり書き、カラオケなど特別のアトラクションがあるときはそのことも知らせます。

1. Invitations for company work-related activities are addressed to 部内各位 (everyone in the department).
2. To make it a gathering where everyone can casually attend, use friendly and familiar language in the invitation. Clearly note how much it will cost, and let everyone know when you plan to have a special attraction like karaoke.

13-5 社内販売のお知らせ
Notice of in-house sales

S&A社では、社員のために歳暮(せいぼ)用品を市価よりも格安(かくやす)な値段で斡旋(あっせん)して、社内販売を行うことにしました。

At S&A Corporation, articles to be used for year-end gifts will be sold in the company at a reduced rate for employees.

'9○総第○○号

199○年○月○日

社員　各位

総務部（印）

歳暮(せいぼ)用品社内販売のお知らせ

歳末が近づいて参りました。例年どおり、歳暮用品の社内販売を行ないます。価格は、全般(ぜんぱん)に市価の2～3割安(やす)となっております。贈答(ぞうとう)用に、また自家用にご利用ください。

配送は、12月28日までに配達先に到着予定です。

お申し込みは、下記の要領(ようりょう)でお願いいたします。

記

1.申込期限：○月○日（火）

2.申込方法：所定の用紙にご記入のうえ、総務課花山（内線3311）までお出しください。（申込書は総務課にあります。）

3.申込書の記入方法：

(1)申込書は、配達先ごとに分けて別々に記入

(2)注文の品目の数量欄(らん)に注文数量を記入

(3)注文品目ごとの金額を記入

(4)記名押印(おういん)

以　上

添付(てんぷ)資料：カタログ（品目、価格、送料ほか）

(記入例)

歳　暮　用　品　申　込　書

○年○月○日

下記品目を購入します

部課名：営業２課

氏　名：小池桃子（小池）

配達先：染谷寧子　　様

(住所) 葛飾区東立石 2-12-2　　(☎03-3692-1677)

品番	品目	単価（送料とも）	数量	金額	摘要
ア-11	紅鮭新巻	¥6,500	2	¥13,000	
オ-7	コーヒー詰合せ	¥7,000	1	¥7,000	

社員各位：to all employees　歳暮用品：products used as year-end gifts　歳末：year-end　例年どおり：as in past years　全般に：generally　市価：market price　割：(1割＝10 percent)　～安：～ cheaper/below　贈答用：for use as gifts　自家用：for use in one's home　利用する：use (an opportunity)　配送：delivery　到着予定：plan to arrive　下記の要領：procedures below　所定の用紙に記入のうえ：after completing the prescribed form　～ごとに分ける：separate for each ～　数量欄（らん）：column for quantity　記名押印（おういん）：writing name and stamping seal　購入（こうにゅう）する：purchase　部課名：section name　品番：item number　単価：price per unit　送料：postal costs　～とも：including ～　摘要（てきよう）：details

'9X Sales Document # ______
Date (year, month, day)

To All Employees

General Affairs Department (seal)

Notice about the in-house sale of articles to be used for year-end gifts

It's getting close to the end of the year. As in years past, we will sell articles to be used for year-end gifts here in the company, at a cost generally 20–30 percent below market price. Please purchase item as gifts or for use in your own home.

They will be sent out so as to arrive at our planned date of no later than December 28.

To order, follow the procedures below.

Details

1. Deadline for ordering: (month, day) (Tuesday)
2. Method of ordering: Write your order on the prescribed form and turn it in to Ms. Hanayama in the general affairs section (Extension 3311). (Order blanks are available in the general affairs section.)
3. Filling in the order blank:
   (1) Fill out a separate order blank for each destination.
   (2) Indicate the quantity you are ordering in the appropriate column.
   (3) Indicate the cost for each item.
   (4) Write your name and stamp your seal.

(the end)

Attachments: catalog (product names, price, cost of delivery, etc.)

(Example)

Year-End Gift Order Form

Date (year, month, day)

I would like to purchase the following items.

Section: Sales Section Two
Name: Koike Momoko (seal)

Destination: Someya Yasuko (Ms.)
(Address) Katsushika-ku, Higashi-tateishi 2-12-2 (Tel: 03-3692-1677)
Item Number/Name of Item/Price Each (including postal costs)/Quantity/Total Each/Details

留意事項

1) 社員に対する福利厚生（ふくりこうせい）のための案内文です。

2) お知らせの内容はわかりやすく書き、申込書は記入しやすい様式にします。

1. This memo announces a company benefit for employees.

2. The contents should be readily understandable, and the order form easy to fill out.

13-6 休暇届

Notification of requested leave

社員が自分の都合で休暇をとる場合は、事前に所定の様式による休暇届を会社に提出します。

When employees want to take time off for personal reasons, they must present a request form to the company in advance.

休　暇　届

認印				

下記のとおり休暇をとりたいので、お届けします。

10 年12 月3 日

部課名：営業部営業一課

氏　名：高木 秀雄

期　間：10 年12 月 8 日(火) から10 年12 月14 日(月) まで

5 日間

種　類：☑年次有給休暇

□特別休暇（事由：　　　　　　　　　　）

認印：approval seal　　部課名：section name　　年次有給休暇：annual paid vacation

事由：explanation; reason

(approval seal)

Request for time off

I request time off as follows:

(Date: year, month, day)

Section: Sales Section One

Name: Takagi Hideo (seal)

Period of time: From 10/12/8 (Tuesday) to 10/12/14 (Monday), 5 days
Type:
[✓] Annual paid vacation
[ ] Special leave time (Explanation:)

留意事項

1)休暇(きゅうか)については、「就業規則(しゅうぎょうきそく)」などにその取り扱いが決められています。

2)特別休暇には、結婚休暇・服喪(ふくも)休暇・出産休暇・育児休暇・生理休暇などがあります。

1. Rules governing the administration of leave time are found in the company regulations.
2. Special leave time might be granted for such things as weddings, periods of mourning, child birth, child care, and menstrual leave.

第14課

契約違反や取引上のトラブルに対して抗議する

Protesting contract infractions or trouble with business dealings

日常の取り引きのうえでは、商品納入のミス・代金未払い・特許侵害などのトラブルが起こりやすいものです。こうして企業が損害や迷惑を受けた場合は、事実関係をよく確認して、タイミングを失わずに、損害の実態、金額などを明示して先方に抗議を行い、今後の交渉に臨みます。こうした場合、状況を調査確認のうえ、まずトラブル発生の事実を知らせ、そのあとに正式の抗議文を送ります。

抗議を受けた側としては、取りあえずのおわびとあわせて対応処置について回答し、担当部署では社内で上司に事故報告をします。

Due to failure in delivering merchandise, unpaid bills, patent infractions, etc., problems can easily arise in day-to-day business dealings. When a business suffers a loss or is inconvenienced, they should first confirm related facts and then moving quickly to issue a protest to the other party, clearly stating the actual losses and their cost, and then move toward negotiations. In this type of case, after first making an inquiry into what happened, inform the other party that an incident has occurred and then later send a formal letter of protest.

The recipient of the protest first issues an apology along with a response as to what measures you will take, and then the person responsible reports on the accident to company superiors.

14-1 納入商品の汚損に対して抗議する
Protesting the delivery of stained merchandise

吉田物産は、S&A社に対して、納入商品のカーペットのしみ事故について抗議文を出します。
Yoshida Trading issues a letter of protest to S&A Corporation when the carpet they receive is stained.

営本第〇〇〇号
199〇年〇月〇日

S&Aコーポレーション日本支社
営業部長　山本良雄　殿

吉田物産株式会社
営業部長　山田栄三（印）

カーペットしみ事故の件

急啓　本日午前11時電話でご連絡しましたとおり、貴社より弊社指定倉庫の富士倉庫へ搬入されたカーペット「デュクロン」の2,000㎡のうち40㎡に黒いしみが付着しているのを今朝10時過ぎに発見しました。

しみは、機械油状のもので、直径4～6cmから20cmぐらいまで各種、1枚につき数箇所に付着しています。無論、事故品のカーペットは、商品として通用しません。

弊社は、これらカーペットを近日中に丸福デパートその他に納入のため、搬入を依頼しましたので、取引先に迷惑が掛からないよう、至急事故品に替えて正常な品をお送り願います。

併せて、今後このような事故が二度と起きないよう、原因究明と善後処置を徹底的に行なっていただきたいと存じます。

まずは取り急ぎ要用のみ。

不　一

しみ：stain　指定倉庫：designated warehouse　搬入する：deliver; carry in　付着する：stick to　機械油状：(seem) like engine oil　直径：diameter　各種：various　～につき：each ～; per ～　数箇所：several places　無論：needless to say　商品として通用する：be fit as sellable goods　近日中：in the very near future　至急：urgently　正常な品：undamaged goods　併せて：in addition　原因究明：investigation into cause　善後処置：appropriate action; remedial measures　徹底的に行なう：conduct/undertake thoroughly

Sales Document # ______
Date (year, month, day)

S&A Corporation, Japan Office
Sales Department Manager Yamamoto Yoshio (Mr.)

Yoshida Trading, Incorporated
Sales Department Manager Yamada Eizo

RE: Stained carpet

I hasten to say what I reported in a phone call at 11:00 this morning, that at a little after 10:00 A.M. we discovered that 40 square meters of the 2,000 square meters of Dukelon carpet that you had delivered to Fuji Warehouse, our company's designated warehouse, contained black stains.

The stains look like engine oil and are of varied sizes from about 4-6 centimeters to 20 centimeters in diameter, with each piece containing a number of such stains. Needless to say, these damaged pieces of carpet are not fit for sale.

Our company ordered this carpet for the purpose of delivering it to Marufuku Department Store and other stores in the very near future, and we now request that you urgently send us replacements for the damaged carpet so as not to inconvenience these customers.

In addition, we request that you thoroughly conduct an investigation into the cause and take appropriate action so that this type of accident will not happen again in the future.

I hasten here to write only the important details.

Yours truly

留意事項

1) 事実を確認したら、できるだけ早く抗議を行います。まず電話で事故発生の状況を告げ、続いて正式に文書で抗議します。事実確認のためには、先方に現場立ち合いを求めます。

2) 抗議文は、感情的にならずにこちらの被害の実態を告げて、責任の所在がわかるようにします。そのためには、事故の日時、場所、具体的な被害内容、被害金額、前後の状況などの正確な事実関係を伝えます。

3) 次に、先方に対してこちらが求める処置・賠償内容などを明らかにし、今後の交渉に備えます。

4) 今後も同様の事故の再発が懸念されるなどの場合、取引相手に対して改めて注意を促します。

5) 急ぎの文書なので、初めや終わりのあいさつなどは省略し、頭語には「前略」「急啓」、結語には「不一」「草々」などのことばを用います。

6) 緊急の文書ですが、あくまでも最低限のていねいな表現は忘れないようにします。

1. As soon as you can confirm the facts, issue a protest. First, explain the occurrence of the accident by phone, and follow this by writing a formal letter of protest. To confirm the facts, request that the other party come to see what has happened.

2. The protest letter should not express feelings, but rather explain the nature of the accident and make clear where the responsibility lies. For this purpose, you must accurately convey the date and time of the accident, its location, the specifics of the loss, the cost, and what happened prior to and following it.

3. Next, make clear to the other party what measures you want them to take, and what they can do to compensate you for the loss. Then prepare for talks in the future.

4. When there is a fear that this type of accident might occur again, admonish the other party to exercise caution.

5. This letter is written in haste, so leave out opening and closing greetings and use such salutations as 前略(ぜんりゃく) (I hasten to write) or 急啓(きゅうけい) (I begin in haste) and complimentary closes like 不一(ふいつ) or 草々(そうそう) (yours truly).

6. This is an urgent message, but do not forget to use at least a minimum amount of polite language.

14-2 OA機器の納入遅延に対して抗議する
Protesting a delay in the delivery of OA equipment

S&A社は、東京システム販売に対して、OA機器ソフトの開発業務が遅延していることについて厳しく抗議を行います。

S&A Corporation issues a harsh protest to Tokyo System Sales for the delay in the development of their OA software.

営第○○○号
平成○年10月7日

東京システム販売株式会社
代表取締役　赤坂　透　殿

S&Aコーポレーション日本支社
営業部長　山本良雄（印）

YMNソフト開発遅延について

前略　貴社と平成○年2月10日付で契約しました「生産・納品債権管理システム」の開発が、契約による納入完了予定日の「平成○年10月1日」を過ぎ本日に至っても完了しておりません。

ソフト開発に係る貴社との契約をベースに、当社は、従来使用中であった「Pシステム95」の返却を予定する一方、新規にYMN関連機器とその基本ソフトの導入・設置を行ない、業務移行待機体制をとりました。ところが、貴社開発の再三にわたる思いがけない遅延により、やむを得ず旧機器MOPの再リースを行なわざるを得ないこととなりました。

当社としては、YMN機器のシステム開発の着手金・設計料のほか、契約残金の支払いを完了したにもかかわらず、再リース料の支払いに加えて、下期から予定していた電算化計画自体が実施できない状況となっております。

ついては、この間の及び今後の、契約によるシステムの開発・検収・納入完了までの当社損失に係る補償について、先日口頭をもって申し入れましたが、この度確認かたがた本書面をもって当方の考えをお伝えしますので、改めて何分の貴意を得たく存じます。

草　々

ソフト開発：software development　生産・納品債権管理システム：production and delivery credit management system　完了予定日：due date; deadline　返却：return　～一方：while ～　導入：installation　設置：set up　業務移行待機体制をとる：stand by for the transfer to new operations　再三にわたる思いがけない遅延により：based on unexpected and repeated delays　やむを得ず：have no choice but to　再リース：renewal of lease　～ざるを得ない：can only ～　着手金：down payment　設計料：designing fee　契約残金：remaining contracted payment　～にもかかわらず：even though　～に加えて：～ plus; in addition to ～　下期：the last half of the year　電算化計画自体：computerizing plan itself　検収：examination　損失に係る補償：compensation for loss　申し入れる：give notice; request　貴意を得たい：want to get your opinion

---

Sales Document # ______
October 7, (year)

Tokyo System Sales, Incorporated
Representative Director Akasaka Toru (Mr.)

S&A Corporation, Japan Office
Sales Department Manager Yamamoto Yoshio (seal)

RE: The delay in YMN software development

I hasten to inform you that the software for the "production and delivery credit management system" that you promised to develop for us on February 10, (year), was not completed by the deadline of October 1, (year), as you had promised, and is still not finished.

Based on your company's pledge to develop our software, while planning to return the "P System 95" we have been using, we have installed and set up YMN equipment and its basic software, waiting to change over to the new system. Now, however, because of unexpected and repeated delays in your company's development, we have had no choice but to renew our lease on the old MOP equipment.

This means that even though we as a company have put out money for a down payment on the development and designing fee of the YMN machine system, plus paying the remainder of what we agreed to pay, we have also had to pay to renew our lease and are still unable to carry out the computerizing plan that we have been preparing to do in the latter half of this year.

I gave notice when I spoke with you the other day regarding your compensation for the loss we have suffered and will suffer until you have completed the development, examination, and delivery of the system by following the contract. I am using this letter to confirm the situation and to convey to you our thinking. I ask you again to give us your opinion.

Sincerely yours

留意事項

1)出すタイミングが遅れないよう注意します。

2)急ぎの抗議文なので、初めや終わりのあいさつは省略します。

3)相手方の業務遅延によってこちらが受けた損害や日常業務の不利益など、被害の実態をはっきりと伝えて、今後の賠償請求やソフト導入後の交渉に備えます。

1. Timing is essential in sending this letter, so be careful to send it before it is too late.

2. As this is an urgent protest, omit both the opening and closing greetings.

3. Clearly state the actual losses and inconvenience in everyday work schedules that you have incurred because of the other party's work delay in preparation for following up with an invoice for compensation and negotiating with them after the installation is completed.

14-1と14-2のフローと文例

14-1「納入商品の汚損に対して抗議する」のフロー

カーペットしみ事故の件

急啓　本日午前11時電話でご連絡しましたとおり、貴社より弊社指定倉庫の富士倉庫へ搬入されたカーペット「デュクロン」の2,000㎡のうち40㎡に黒いしみが付着しているのを今朝10時過ぎに発見しました。

しみは、機械油状のもので、直径4～6cmから20cmぐらいまで各種、1枚につき数箇所に付着しています。無論、事故品のカーペットは、商品として通用しません。

（①トラブルの発生を知らせ、抗議する）

弊社は、これらカーペットを近日中に丸福デパートその他に納入のため、搬入を依頼しましたので、取引先に迷惑が掛からないよう、至急事故品に替えて正常な品をお送り願います。

（②対処するよう、要求する）

併せて、今後このような事故が二度と起きないよう、原因究明と善後処置を徹底的に行なっていただきたいと存じます。

（③今後の注意を喚起する）

まずは取り急ぎ要用のみ。

不　一

14-2「OA機器の納入遅延に対して抗議する」のフロー

YMNソフト開発遅延について

前略　貴社と平成○年2月10日付で契約しました「生産・納品債権管理システム」の開発が、契約による納入完了予定日の「平成○年10月1日」を過ぎ本日に至っても完了しておりません。

ソフト開発に係る貴社との契約をベースに、当社は、従来使用中であった「Pシステム95」の返却を予定する一方、新規にYMN関連機器とその基本ソフトの導入・設置を行ない、業務移行待機体制をとりました。ところが、貴社開発の再三にわたる思いがけない遅延により、やむを得ず旧機器MOPの再リースを行なわざるを得ないこととなりました。

当社としては、YMN機器のシステム開発の着手金・設計料のほか、契約残金の支払いを完了したにもかかわらず、再リース料の支払いに加えて、下期から予定していた電算化計画自体が実施できない状況となっております。

（①トラブルの発生を知らせ、抗議する）

ついては、この間の及び今後の、契約によるシステムの開発・検収・納入完了までの当社損失に係る補償について、先日口頭をもって申し入れましたが、この度確認かたがた本書面をもって当方の考えをお伝えしますので、改めて何分の貴意を得たく存じます。

（②対処するよう、要求する）

草　々

（下線の部分は自分の状況に合わせて書いてください。）

①トラブルの発生を知らせ、抗議（こうぎ）する

Informing of the occurrence of a problem and objecting

＊本日午前11時電話でご連絡しましたとおり、貴社より弊社（へいしゃ）指定倉庫の富士倉庫へ搬入（はんにゅう）されたカーペット「デュクロン」の2,000m²のうち40m²に黒いしみが付着（ふちゃく）しているのを今朝10時過ぎに発見しました。無論、事故品のカーペットは、商品として通用しません。(14-1)

As I reported in a phone call at 11:00 this morning, that at a little after 10:00 A.M. we discovered that 40 square meters of the 2,000 square meters of Dukelon carpet that you had delivered to Fuji Warehouse, our company's designated warehouse, contained black stains. Needless to say, these damaged pieces of carpet are not fit for sale.

＊○月○日付発注（はっちゅう）書により追加納入（ついかのうにゅう）をお願いしました貴社製品が、納期（のうき）を１週間過ぎても当社に到着しておりません。得意先（とくいさき）からの催促（さいそく）を受け困っております。

The delivery deadline for the additional goods we requested from your company by the order form dated (month, day) was one week ago, and the goods still have not arrived. We have been put in a spot as one of our customers is pressing us (for their order).

＊貴社開発の新システム導入が遅延（ちえん）し、業務移行に少なからず支障（ししょう）をきたしております。

The installation of the new system developed by your company is late, so we are deeply concerned to get things moving.

②対処（たいしょ）するよう、要求する

A demand to deal with a matter

＊取引先に迷惑（めいわく）が掛（か）からないよう、至急（しきゅう）事故品に替えて正常な品をお送り願います。(14-1)

We request that you urgently send us replacements for the damaged carpet so as not to inconvenience our customers.

＊早急にシステム開発を促進（そくしん）し、一日も早く当社への納入（のうにゅう）を実行されるよう申し入れます。

We request that you speed up the development of the system immediately and that its delivery to our company is carried out as soon as possible.

＊実情ご検討のうえ、至急納入（しきゅうのうにゅう）の手配をとられるようお願いします。

Having examined the conditions, please make arrangements for a delivery immediately.

③今後の注意を喚起（かんき）する

Requesting future care

＊今後このような事故が二度と起きないよう、原因究明（きゅうめい）と善後処置（ぜんごしょち）を徹底（てってい）的に行なっていただきたいと存じます。(14-1)

We request that you thoroughly conduct an investigation into the cause and take appropriate action so that this type of accident will not happen again in the future.

＊貴社との取引の信頼関係のためにも、今回のようなことのないよう、万全（ばんぜん）の注意を払（はら）われることを望みます。

For the sake of maintaining trust in our business relations, I hope that the utmost attention will be paid to ensure this kind of thing will not happen again.

＊今後はこのようなことのないよう、十分ご注意されるようお願いします。

Please take great care to ensure this kind of thing does not happen again in the future.

社外 わびる apology

14-3 商品汚損のクレームに対して取りあえず回答する

Making a provisional response to a complaint about stained goods

S&A社は、吉田物産に対してカーペットのしみ事故についておわびするとともに、あわせて対応処置及び事故対策を述べた文書を送ります。

In response to the accident wherein carpet delivered to Yoshida Trading had been stained, S&A Corporation sends a letter apologizing for what happened, and also explains how they are dealing with the accident and how they plan to keep such accidents from happening again.

営本第○○○号

199○年○月○日

吉田物産株式会社

営業部長　山田栄三殿

S&Aコーポレーション日本支社

営業部長　山本良雄（印）

カーペットしみ事故の件

拝復　○月○日の貴社よりのお電話による急報及び同日付貴信をもってお申し越しありました題記事故の件を承り、弊社では、事の重大さに驚いております。

とりわけ本品は、近日中にお取引先に納入予定の由を伺い、この度多大のご迷惑をお掛けいたしましたことを深くおわび申し上げます。

電話連絡をお受けしまして、直ちに代替品カーペット「デュクロン」50m²分を富士倉庫あて急送申し上げました。

この度の事故につきましては、即日、事故調査委員会を設置し、富士倉庫・大山運輸の責任者を交えて原因の究明を開始しました。早急に事故原因を発見し物流業者の管理強化や入出庫時の点検システムの再検討などを実施のこととしました。委細は、改めて遅滞なくご報告申し上げます。

今後は、このような事故の絶無を期して業務に努めて参りますので、なにとぞご海容賜りますようお願い申し上げます。

まずは取り急ぎ書中をもちましておわびかたがたご報告申し上げます。

敬　具

しみ：stain　題記事故の件：matter of the above-mentioned accident　事の重大さ：seriousness of the matter　とりわけ：above all　近日中に：in the very near future　納入(のうにゅう)予定：plan to deliver　直(ただ)ちに：immediately　代替(だいたい)品：replacement goods　～分：amount of ～　即日(そくじつ)：the same day　設置する：set up　運輸(うんゆ)：transportation　責任者を交(まじ)えて：including the responsible people　原因の究明(きゅうめい)：investigation into cause　物流業者の管理強化：reinforcement of management of physical distribution companies　入出庫時の点検システムの再検討：reexamination of the inspection system for loading and unloading at the warehouses　～のこととする：I/we decide to ～　委細(いさい)：details　遅滞(ちたい)なく：without delay　絶無(ぜつむ)を期(き)す：ensure complete stoppage　業務に努(つと)める：work hard at one's job　海容(かいよう)賜(たまわ)る：obtain your forgiveness

---

Sales Document # ______
Date (year, month, day)

Yoshida Trading, Incorporated
Sales Department Manager Yamada Eizo (Mr.)

S&A Corporation, Japan Office
Sales Department Manager Yamamoto Yoshio (seal)

RE: Stained carpet

Salutations: Our company is greatly surprised at the seriousness of the above-mentioned accident, which you conveyed to me in your urgent phone call of (month, day) and then by letter postmarked the same day.

Above all, when I heard that you were planning to deliver the product to a customer in the very near future, I wanted to express my deepest regrets for causing you so much difficulty at this time.

As soon as I received your phone call, I made arrangements for 50 square meters of Dukelon carpet to be sent to the Fuji Warehouse to replace the damaged product.

In regard to this, we set up an investigation committee, including the responsible people at both Fuji Warehouse and Oyama Transportation, that same day and began an investigation into the cause of the accident. We are determined to discover the cause soon and to reinforce our management of physical distribution companies and reexamine the inspection system for loading and unloading at the warehouse. I will send along a detailed report to you without delay.

We will do all we can to see that this kind of accident never happens again and ask for your forgiveness.

I hastened to write, first to apologize and then to report on what we have done.

Sincerely yours

留意事項

1) この文書は、まだ事故原因がはっきりしない段階で、取りあえず相手に出す回答書です。したがって、事故の責任を認める文書ではありませんが、相手のクレームに対する回答として早急に行う対処(たいしょ)の一つです。も

1. This letter is a preliminary response written before the cause of the accident is clearly known. As a result, it does not accept responsibility for the accident, but rather is one way of quickly responding to the other party's complaint. Exchanges that take place

ちろん、電話や現場での誠意のあるやり取りも大切ですが、時期を失わずに部門責任者の文書によるおわびをすることが必要です。

2) 事故の実情をはっきりと確認したうえで、陳謝の気持ちを述べます。さらに、緊急の対応処置の内容を伝えて、再び事故を起こさないよう、対策に万全を期する旨の決意を表明します。

over the telephone or at the site are important, but a written apology in a timely manner from the head of the responsible department is absolutely necessary.

2. After clearly confirming what actually happened, express feelings of apology. Then, explain the immediate measures you have taken and express your determination to do all you can to ensure that such an accident never occurs again.

社内 報告する report

14-4 商品汚損事故について上司に報告する
Reporting an incident involving stained goods to a superior

事故品の納入業務を担当したS&A社営業二課長は、営業部長に対して事故に関する業務報告書を出します。

The manager of sales section two of S&A Corporation, who was in charge of the delivery of the stained merchandise, issues a business report of the incident to his superior, the sales department manager.

営二第○○○号
199○年○月○日

業　務　連　絡　票

営業部長殿

営業二課
課長　橋本　進（印）

「デュクロン」しみ事故発生につき、下記のとおり緊急ご報告する。

記

1．事故状況

⑴取引先　吉田物産株式会社
営業部長　山田栄三殿

⑵事故発見経緯

○月○日（金）午前11時に吉田物産（株）伊藤営業課長よりの電話急報があった。当社が富士倉庫に当日朝搬入した「デュクロン」スタンダード・タイプに、しみが発見された旨の連絡である。

早速、当課から3名が現場へ急行し、現品をチェックしたところ、約40㎡に黒ずんだしみを発見したので、部長あて現地より事故内容について電話報告した。

2．対応処置

伊藤課長より、得意先納入の都合上、代替品の手当ての要請があったので、部長指示に従って同タイプのカーペット50㎡分を即日、富士倉庫あて急送の手続きをとり、納入を完了した。

3．今後の対策

事故調査委員会による原因究明を早急に実施する（物流業者も参加のこと）とともに、物流管理システムの再構築を図る。

また、吉田物産（株）への結果報告に万全を期するとともに、今後厳しく社内に注意を喚起する。

以　上

業務連絡票：business report　しみ：stain　緊急（きんきゅう）：hasten to; urgently　経緯（けいい）：detailed description; circumstances　搬入（はんにゅう）する：deliver; carry in　黒ずんだ：blackened　対応処置（しょち）：measures taken　得意（とくい）先：valued customer　納入（のうにゅう）の都合（つごう）上：because of a scheduled delivery　代替（だいたい）品の手当て：preparation of replacement goods　要請（ようせい）がある：request　指示に従って：complying with directions　～分：amount/quantity of ～　即日（そくじつ）：the same day　急送の手続きをとる：arrange dispatch　完了する：complete　今後の対策：future measures　原因究明（きゅうめい）：investigation into cause　実施（じっし）する：put into action　物流業者：physical distribution company　参加のこと：need to participate　管理システムの再構築（こうちく）を図（はか）る：work on a restructuring of the management system　万全（ばんぜん）を期（き）す：take all possible measures (to ensure no mistakes)　注意を喚起（かんき）する：call for care (to be taken)

Sales Section Two Document # ______
Date (year, month, day)

Business Report

The Honorable Sales Department Manager

Sales Section Two
Chief Hashimoto Susumu (seal)

I hasten to inform you of the details related to the occurrence of stained Dukelon.

Details

1. What happened
(1) Distributor—Yoshida Trading, Incorporated
Sales Department Manager Yamada Eizo (Mr.)
(2) A detailed description of the discovery of the accident
I received an urgent phone call from Mr. Ito, sales section chief of Yoshida Trading (Inc.) at 11:00 A.M. on Friday (month, day), informing me that they had discovered stained areas in the standard type of Dukelon that had been delivered to their Fuji Warehouse that morning. I immediately sent three persons from this department to the location, where they checked the affected product and discovered the blackened stains in about 40 square meters of the merchandise. They reported their findings to you from there by telephone.
2. Measures taken
Chief Ito requested that because of a scheduled delivery to a valued customer, they needed to receive a replacement, and I complied with your directions to send out 50 square meters of the same type of carpet that same day and arranged to have it sent to Fuji Warehouse immediately. That delivery has been completed.
3. Future measures
A committee to investigate the cause of the accident was quickly put into action (including the physical distribution company) and a restructuring of the distribution management system will be worked on.
Also, we will send a report of the results to Yoshida Trading (Inc.), making sure that no mistakes are made, and will call for extreme care within the company in the future.

(the end)

留意事項

1) 事故発生の事実関係・前後の経緯(けいい)などを正確に書くとともに、担当課としての対応及び処理(しょり)の具体的な内容を述(の)べます。

2) 今後の対策は、会社としても重要な事項なので、実効のある提案を具体的に行うこととします。

1. While conveying everything related to the occurrence of the accident and accurately explaining the details of what happened prior to and after the accident, you, as the responsible person, explain specifically what has been done to cope with the situation and what measures will be taken in the future.

2. Measures to be taken in the future are also a very important issue for the company, and therefore you need to clearly spell out an effective proposal.

第15課

トラブルの発生に関して社内関係先に問い合わせる

Making an in-house inquiry to parties related to the occurrence of an incident

同じ会社の中でも、他部門から情報を得る目的で照会をしたり、これに対して回答をしたりすることがあります。

社内の照会文の場合は、社外に対するものと異なり、儀礼を省き実質的な内容を重視します。この場合、同位部門の間では依頼の形をとり、上位者からの場合は指示に近い形をとることとなります。

社内の照会・回答文書のやり取りにあたっては、時間をおかずに対応するように心がけます。

There are times when you conduct an in-house inquiry for the purpose of gaining information from different departments or responding to such inquiries from other sections.

In contrast to a letter of inquiry directed outside the company, an in-house letter of inquiry needs no polite language and focuses on essential information. In this case, it takes the form of a request among departments of the same rank, and, when it comes from a superior, it is very close to being a directive.

In the exchange of in-house letters of inquiry and responses, take care to deal with them promptly.

15-1 汚損事故の原因について担当者に調査を依頼する

Requesting the person responsible to conduct an investigation into the cause of a product being stained

S&A社では、吉田物産に納入した商品に汚損事故が起こったので、山本営業部長が戸田工場長に対して事故原因について照会します。

Because of the incident in which stained merchandise was delivered to Yoshida Trading, Mr. Yamamoto, sales department manager of S&A Corporation, writes a letter of inquiry into the cause of the incident to the manager of the Toda factory.

営第○○○号
199○年○月○日

戸田工場長殿

営業部長　山本良雄（印）

クレーム発生原因調査に係る件（照会）

この度、下記のとおり、吉田物産(株)へ納入の「デュクロン」スタンダード・タイプの汚損事故に対するクレームが発生した。ついては、お手数ながら貴工場において状況を至急調査のうえ、○月○日までに当方あて調査結果をご通知願いたく、ご照会する。

記

1．事故発生状況

○月○日午前11時、吉田物産(株)伊藤営業課長から、富士倉庫の「デュクロン」にしみが発見された旨の電話通知が当部にあった。(本品は、当日午前10時に大山運輸が搬入したもの)

通報を受けて、直ちに当部の担当者が現場検証したところ、約40㎡に汚れ・しみが認められた。これは、油類の付着によるもののように思われる。

2．調査事項

(1)○月○日から○日までの間の貴工場での加工部門及び荷捌部門の本品取扱い時の状況並びに検品関係の記録・伝票類のチェック

(2)上記日時の間、貴工場から運輸会社が本品を搬出した際のハンドリング状況並びに関係の記録・伝票類のチェック

(3)その他参考事項

以　上

追って、今後の対策を含めて、

(1)当部としては、社内調査と並行して、富士倉庫の庫内受渡しや運輸会社の取り扱い状況などについて詳細にチェックを行い、事故原因の発見に努めたい。

(2)また、本件の処理完了後は、この機会に、改めて物流業者の管理強化、入出庫時の点検、支社・工場間の連絡などの関係システム見直しを実施することといたしたく、その節は、貴工場よりもよろしくご協力のほどをお願いする。

了

照会：inquiry　納入：delivery　しみ：stain　通知：notice; report　運輸：transportation　搬入する：deliver; carry in　通報を受ける：receive report; be informed　直ちに：immediately　現場検証する：inspect the location　油類の付着による：according to the kind of oil stuck on　調査事項：items to be investigated　加工部門：manufacturing department　荷捌部門：handling and storage department　検品関係の記録：inspection-related records　伝票類：order slips　搬出した際のハンドリング状況：the handling conditions at the time of transporting　今後の対策：future measures　〜と並行して：along with 〜　庫内受渡し：delivery within the warehouse　詳細に：in detail　処理完了後：after completing the handling　物流業者の管理強化：reinforcement of the management of physical distribution companies　入出庫時の点検：inspection for loading and unloading at the warehouse　関係システム見直しを実施する：put into effect the reexamination of related systems　〜こととする：I/we decide to 〜

Sales Document # __________
Date (year, month, day)

The Honorable Toda Factory Manager

Yoshio Yamamoto, Sales Department Manager (seal)

RE: Investigation into the cause of the incident generating the complaint (inquiry)

Recently, as noted below, a complaint was made because of the delivery of stained standard-type Dukelon to Yoshida Trading (Inc.). With relation to this, I am sorry to trouble you, but I request that you conduct an immediate investigation into the situation at your factory and report your findings to me by (month, day).

Details

1. Details of incident
At 11:00 A.M. on (month, day), our department received a phone call from Yoshida Trading's (Inc.) Sales Section Chief Ito informing us that they had discovered stains in the Dukelon carpet at Fuji Warehouse. (This merchandise was delivered to them by Oyama Transportation at 10:00 that morning.)
As soon as we received the report, the person responsible for this department went to inspect that location and confirmed that there were stains on about 40 square meters, probably caused by some sort of oil.
2. Items to be investigated
(1) Check the conditions of all of the manufacturing departments and the handling and storage department of your factory, as they handled this merchandise, and also check the inspection records and order slips from (month, day) to (day).
(2) Check what happened in the handling of the merchandise when it was loaded for delivery by the transportation company, and also check the inspection records and order slips for the above period of time.
(3) Other items to be considered

(the end)

In addition, future measures to be taken include:
(1) As a department (in our search for the cause of this incident), along with conducting an in-house investigation, we are carrying out a detailed check into both the delivery procedures at Fuji Warehouse and the handling conditions at the transportation company.
(2) After this incident has been resolved, we will take this opportunity to reinforce our management of the physical distribution companies and reinvestigate related systems, including inspection procedures for loading and unloading at the warehouse and communication measures between the branch office and the factories. As we undertake this, we also ask for the cooperation of all at the factory.

(completed)

留意事項

1) 照会(しょうかい)文は、取引先の照会・商品在庫の照会・人物照会などの日常業務について、社外または社内に対して問い合わせを行う文書です。
2) まず照会の趣旨(しゅし)や目的をはっきり説明し、何を調査するのか照会内容を具体的に箇条(かじょう)書きでわかりやすく示します。また、照会する側の見解も、できる限り相手に知らせるようにします。
3) この例の追って書きのように、必要があれば、クレームの事後処理(しょり)についての協力に触れることがあります。
4) 取引先からのクレームに対して回答を急ぐという事情があるので、文書のはじめに回答期限を決めています。
5) 社内文書なので、頭語(とうご)と結語(けつご)、初めと終わりのあいさつは省(はぶ)きます。
6) 追って書きの文の終わりには、「了」(または「完」)と書きます。

1. Letters of inquirys, called 照会(しょうかい)文, deal with matters relating to trading partners, warehousing, and personnel, both inside and outside the company.
2. First explain the aim or purpose of the inquiry, and then outline simply and specifically in an itemized statement what you want investigated. You, as the inquirer, also express your own opinion as clearly as you can.
3. As in the postscript of this example, if necessary, touch on the need for cooperation in what should be done after the settlement of the complaint.
4. Because of the need to respond to the complaint of a dealer as soon as possible, set a deadline for a response to the in-house letter of inquiry.
5. As this is an in-house communication, omit the salutation, complimentary close, and opening and closing greetings.
6. At the end of a postscript, write either 了 or 完 (completed).

15-2 商品の納入遅延について担当者に照会する

Referring a problem regarding a delay in the supply of goods to the person responsible

S&A社の山本営業部長は、戸田工場長に対し、営業倉庫への納期遅滞について緊急に問い合わせる文書をファックスで送ります。

S&A Corporation's Sales Department Manager Yamamoto faxes an urgent letter of inquiry to the manager of the Toda factory concerning missing a deadline for a delivery to the sales warehouse.

営第○○○号

199○年○月○日

戸田工場長殿

営業部長　山本良雄（印）

倉庫納期の遅延の件

この度、吉田物産(株)より下記商品の営業倉庫（富士倉庫）への搬入遅滞に関して、照会及び督促の申し入れがあったので、至急調査のうえ、折り返しファックスにより当部へご回示願いたい。

記

1．商　品　名	「デュクロン」スタンダード・タイプ		
	商品番号　DC-dx-0995		
2．荷主(寄託者)	吉田物産(株)営業部		
3．内　　容	(1) No.富士00551	8,000m²	約定納期○月○日
	(2) No.富士00671	6,000m²	約定納期○月○日
	(3) No.富士00690	16,000m²	約定納期○月○日
4．納期遅滞状況	吉田物産(株)営業部より「入庫通知書」未着のため、本日午前9時当部へ連絡があり、担当者が現地倉庫において入庫遅滞の事実を確認した。		
5．調査事項	上記商品について、貴工場から運輸会社－富士倉庫への搬出、搬入、ハンドリングなどの状況及び一連の受け渡し書類をチェックし、確認のうえファックス願いたい。		

以　上

納期：delivery deadline　搬入：delivery; carry-in　照会：inquiry　督促の申し入れ：pressing notification　至急：urgently　折り返し：by return　回示：response　荷主：to be delivered　寄託者：depositor　約定納期：contractual deadline　遅滞状況：situation of delay　入庫通知書：receiving report; tender storage　運輸会社：transportation company　搬出：transporting　ハンドリングなどの状況：conditions of handling, etc.　一連の受け渡し書類：all of the documented receipts

Sales Document # ________
Date (year, month, day)

The Honorable Toda Factory Manager

Sales Department Manager Yamamoto Yoshio (seal)

RE: Missing the delivery deadline

We have received a letter of inquiry and reminder from Yoshida Trading (Inc.) regarding a late delivery of the products listed below to their sales warehouse (Fuji Warehouse). We request that you look into this urgently and fax back your response.

Details

1. Product name: Dukelon, standard-type
   Product No. DC-dx-0995
2. To be delivered to (Depositor) Yoshida Trading (Inc.) Sales Department
3. Contents
   (1) No. Fuji 00551—8,000 square meters—contractual deadline (month, day)
   (2) No. Fuji 00671—6,000 square meters—contractual deadline (month, day)
   (3) No. Fuji 00690—16,000 square meters—contractual deadline (month, day)
4. Situation of delivery delay: Yoshida Trading's Sales Department informed us at 9:00 this morning that a receiving report had not arrived, and the responsible person confirmed with the warehouse that the delivery was late.
5. Items of investigation: check the transporting, delivery, and handling of the above merchandise from your factory to the transportation company to Fuji Warehouse, including all of the documented receipts, and fax us a copy of what you find out.

(the end)

留意事項

1) 特に回答を急ぐ場合には、ファックスで照会し、回答もファックスで求めます。回答期限については、上の例では特に指定していませんが、急ぐ場合ははっきり示します。

2) 一般的にファックス文書では、要点をなるべく簡潔に書くようにします。

3) 調査事項は、具体的に箇条書きではっきりと示します。また、社内文書なので、頭語や結語、その他のあいさつは必要ありません。

1. Particularly with letters that need a speedy reply, send the inquiry by fax and request that it be answered by fax. Do not stipulate a deadline for the reply, but indicate the need for expediency.

2. Generally speaking, in letters to be faxed, you concisely write only the most important points.

3. Items to be investigated are spelled out in outline form. As these are in-house communications, there is no need to include salutations, complimentary closes, or words of greeting.

15-1と15-2のフローと文例

15-1「汚損事故の原因について担当者に調査を依頼する」のフロー

クレーム発生原因調査に係る件（照会）

この度、下記のとおり、吉田物産(株)へ納入の「デュクロン」スタンダード・タイプの汚損事故に対するクレームが発生した。ついては、お手数ながら貴工場において状況を至急調査のうえ、○月○日までに当方あて調査結果をご通知願いたく、ご照会する。

①調査を依頼するいきさつを説明する

②調査を依頼する＋回答日時、方法を知らせる

記

1．事故発生状況

○月○日午前11時、吉田物産(株)伊藤営業課長から、富士倉庫の「デュクロン」にしみが発見された旨の電話通知が当部にあった。(本品は、当日午前10時に大山運輸が搬入したもの)

通報を受けて、直ちに当部の担当者が現場検証したところ、約40㎡に汚れ・しみが認められた。これは、油類の付着によるもののように思われる。

2．調査事項

(1)○月○日から○日までの間の貴工場での加工部門及び荷捌部門の本品取扱い時の状況並びに検品関係の記録・伝票類のチェック

(2)上記日時の間、貴工場から運輸会社が本品を搬出した際のハンドリング状況並びに関係の記録・伝票類のチェック

(3)その他参考事項

以　上

③記——調査依頼内容

追って、今後の対策を含めて、

（後略）

了

15-2「商品の納入遅延について担当者に照会する」のフロー

倉庫納期の遅延の件

この度、吉田物産(株)より下記商品の営業倉庫（富士倉庫）への搬入遅滞に関して、照会及び督促の申し入れがあったので、至急調査のうえ、折り返しファックスにより当部へご回示願いたい。

②調査を依頼する＋回答日時、方法を知らせる

記

1．商　品　名	「デュクロン」スタンダード・タイプ 商品番号　DC-dx-0995		
2．荷主(寄託者)	吉田物産(株)営業部		
3．内　　　容	(1) No.富士00551	8,000㎡	約定納期○月○日
	(2) No.富士00671	6,000㎡	約定納期○月○日
	(3) No.富士00690	16,000㎡	約定納期○月○日
4．納期遅滞状況	吉田物産(株)営業部より「入庫通知書」未着のため、本日午前9時当部へ連絡があり、担当者が現地倉庫において入庫遅滞の事実を確認した。		
5．調査事項	上記商品について、貴工場から運輸会社ー富士倉庫への搬出、搬入、ハンドリングなどの状況及び一連の受け渡し書類をチェックし、確認のうえファックス願いたい。		

③記——調査依頼内容

以　上

（下線の部分は自分の状況に合わせて書いてください。）

①調査を依頼するいきさつを説明する

Explaining the circumstances of a request for an investigation

②調査を依頼する + 回答日時、方法を知らせる

Requesting an investigation and specifying a date and measures for a reply

＊お手数ながら貴工場において状況を至急（しきゅう）調査のうえ、〇月〇日までに当方あて調査結果をご通知願いたく、ご照会（しょうかい）する。(15-1)

I am sorry to trouble you, but I request that you conduct an immediate investigation into the situation at your factory and report your findings to me by (month, day).

＊この度（たび）、吉田物産(株)より下記商品の営業倉庫（富士倉庫）への搬入遅滞（はんにゅうちたい）に関して、照会（しょうかい）及び督促（とくそく）の申し入れがあったので、至急（しきゅう）調査のうえ、折り返しファックスにより当部へご回示願いたい。(15-2)

We have received a letter of inquiry and reminder from Yoshida Trading (Inc.) regarding a late delivery of the products listed below to their sales warehouse (Fuji Warehouse). We request that you look into this urgently and fax back your response.

＊下記につき、至急（しきゅう）調査のうえご回答頂（いただ）きたく、取り急ぎご照会（しょうかい）いたします。なお、〇月〇日までにご返信願います。

We hasten to make this inquiry regarding the following matter and ask that you reply after conducting an immediate investigation. Please note that your reply is requested by (month, day).

③記——調査依頼内容（調査対象、調査事項など）

Description—contents of request for investigation (object of investigation, issues of investigation, etc.)

15-3 汚損事故の原因について調査結果を回答する（責任がある場合）

Announcing the results of an investigation into the cause of an accident (when you are responsible)

納入商品のカーペットの汚損事故について調査の結果、工場側に責任があることが判明したので、戸田工場長は、その旨、回答します。

The results of an investigation into the cause of the stained merchandise prove that the responsibility lies with the factory, and the Toda factory manager explains this to the sales department manager.

戸工第〇〇〇号
199〇年〇月〇日

営業部長殿

戸田工場長　田山　明（印）

クレーム発生原因に係る件

〇月〇日付営第〇〇〇号題記貴信をもってお申し越しの「デュクロン」スタンダード・タイプ汚損事故クレームの件につき、当工場の調査結果を下記のとおり報告する。

本件については、事故原因が当方の荷捌部門の取扱い不注意によることが判明し、誠に申し訳なく存ずる次第である。改めて、支社長に報告するとともに、貴部及び社外関係とも早急に打ち合せ、事故品の処理に当り、併せて今後の改善策を講じたく、ご協力のほど重ねてお願いいたしたい。

記

1．事故発生の原因

〇月〇日午後3時ごろ当工場の荷捌倉庫Ａ号内で本品の庫移し作業を行なった。その際、パレット上の「デュクロン」に、作業中のフォークリフトの機械油が飛散したものと思われる。

大山運輸及び富士倉庫のハンドリング関係の使用機械について詳細に調査したが、今回のしみ・汚れの油は、両社が日常使用しているものではなく、当工場の油と同一であった。また、フォークリフトのタイヤが不具合で、運転の際に振動があった旨の担当者の報告があった。

2．検品状況

当日の検品担当者の報告書類には事故の指摘がなく、荷捌関係者も事故に気付いていない。油の飛散時点では、ほとんど目につかない状態であったかと考えられる。

3．当面の処置

当工場の加工部門及び荷捌部門において、庫内の整理整頓の徹底、運搬荷捌器具の整備点検など工場内管理の全般にわたりチェックを実施中であり、同時に関係書類や伝票・記録類の見直しを行なっている。

品質管理の面についても、今後は貴部と充分な打ち合せをいたしたい。

以　上

荷捌部門：handling and storage department　不注意：carelessness　判明する：be proved; come to light　～次第である：we must say that ～　処理に当る：handle; deal with　改善策を講じる：devise measures for improvement　庫移し：moving (merchandise) within a warehouse　パレット：palette　フォークリフト：forklift　飛散する：spatter; splash　～ものと思われる：it is believed/thought that ～　ハンドリング関係：handling-related　詳細に：in detail　しみ：stain　不具合：not functioning properly　振動がある：shake; vibrate　検品：inspection of goods　指摘がない：no report/notice　当面の：for the time being　加工：manufacturing　整理整頓の徹底：thorough reorganization　器具の整備点検：maintenance check of equipment　全般にわたり：general; thorough　実施中：in the middle of conducting　伝票：order slips　見直しを行う：undertake a reexamination　品質管理の面：with regard to quality control

---

Toda Factory Document # __________
Date (year, month, day)

The Honorable Sales Department Manager

Toda Factory Manager Tayama Akira (seal)

RE: Cause of the complaint

Following is a report of our factory's investigation into the complaint concerning stained standard-type Dukelon, as requested in your document # __________ of (month, day).

With regard to this, it has been proved that the stain accident occurred because of carelessness by our handling and storage department, and we must say that we are extremely sorry that it happened. We will report this to the office manager and consult with your department and others outside the company as soon as possible, taking care of the damaged merchandise and at the same time devising a plan for future improvements. We ask for your continued cooperation.

Details

1. Cause of the accident

At about 3:00 on the afternoon of (month, day), we moved the merchandise within Building A of our storage warehouse. We believe that engine oil splattered on the Dukelon carpet on a forklift palette that was being used at the time.

We conducted a detailed investigation of the equipment used for handling by both Oyama Transportation and Fuji Warehouse and found that the oil that caused these stains was different from what they are presently using and that it matched the oil we use at the factory. The person responsible also reported that the forklift tires were not functioning properly, so it shook when in use.

2. Inspection status

There was no record of an incident in the reports of the inspector on that day, and no one in the handling department noticed anything. We can only assume that when the oil splattered, it went almost completely unnoticed.

3. Dealing with the matter now

The manufacturing department and the handling and storage department of the factory are now conducting a general check of the factory management, including a thorough reorganization of the warehouse and a maintenance check of equipment used in the handling of merchandise. At the same time, we are also undertaking a reexamination of the related documents, order slips, and records.

With regard to quality control, we would like to conduct a thorough discussion with your department.

(the end)

留意事項

1)調査は早急に実行し、回答も遅れないようにします。

2)上の例は、事故発生の責任部署として関係部長にわびるとともに、調査結果について報告する文書となっています。

3)調査結果の回答書においては、記書(きが)きとして、事故発生の原因・日時・状況・対応処置(しょち)などをできるだけ具体的に正確に書くとともに、責任部署として善後策(ぜんごさく)についての意見を提示するようにします。

4)急ぐときはファックスを使い、あとで文書を郵送する場合もあります。

1. The investigation is carried out immediately, and a prompt response is sent.

2. The above example was sent by the person responsible to the manager involved to apologize and to report the results of the investigation.

3. In responding with the results of the investigation, include in the "記書(きが)き" section as much specific detail as possible about the cause of the accident, the date and time, the conditions, and measures taken. The person responsible should also suggest possible preventive measures for the future.

4. When time is of the essence, fax your response and then send the letter later by mail.

15-4 汚損事故の原因について調査結果を報告する(責任がない場合)

Announcing the results of an investigation into the cause of an accident (when you are not responsible)

納入商品の事故原因調査の結果、工場側に責任がないことが判明したので、戸田工場長は、その旨、営業部長に回答します。

As a result of the investigation into the cause of the accident, the factory proved not to be responsible, so the Toda factory manager conveys this fact to the sales department manager.

戸工第○○○号
199○年○月○日

営業部長殿

戸田工場長　井上　明（印）

クレーム発生原因の件（回答）

○月○日付営第○○○号貴信をもってお申し越しのあった「デュクロン」スタンダード・タイプ汚損事故クレームの件については、当方は無関係であることが判明したのでご通知する。

調査内容等は、下記のとおりである。

記

1．調査内容

(1)○月○日から○日までの間における当工場の加工・荷捌両部門の取扱い時の状況並びに検品関係の記録・伝票類をそれぞれ担当者とともにチェックしたが、問題はなかった。

(2)同上期間において、運輸会社の本品搬出、受け渡しの際の担当者の作業状況に問題となる点はなかった。

2．その後、貴部から富士倉庫側の庫内作業に起因する旨の連絡を受けた。本件を他山の石として、今後、工場内の作業管理の再チェックを行なうこととしたい。

以　上

無関係である：have no relation　判明する：be proved; come to light　通知する：inform; report　加工・荷捌両部門：both manufacturing and handling divisions　検品関係の伝票・記録類：order slips and records related to inspection　運輸会社：transportation company　搬出：transporting　～に起因する：caused by ～　本件を他山の石とする：take this as a lesson　作業管理の再チェックを行う：undertake a reevaluation of the operations management　～こととする：I/we decide to ～

Toda Factory Document # __________
Date (year, month, day)

The Honorable Sales Department Manager

Toda Factory Manager Inoue Akira (seal)

RE: (Response) Cause of the incident generating the complaint

This is to inform you that it has been proved that this party has no relation to the complaint about stained Dukelon (standard type) mentioned in your document # __________, dated (month, day).
The results of our investigation are as follows:

Details

1. Contents of the investigation
 (1) The person responsible for both the manufacturing and handling divisions of the factory and I examined the handling conditions and records and order slips of the inspection for (month, day) through (day) and found no problems.
 (2) During the same period, no problems were found with regard to the working conditions of the transportation company's employee who were responsible for handling and delivering the merchandise.
2. Later, we received word from your department that a problem had occurred in operations at Fuji Warehouse. We want this to serve as a lesson and will soon undertake the reevaluation of the management of operations within the factory.

(the end)

留意事項

1) この文書は、15-3 の文書とは反対に、戸田工場側には事故責任がない場合のものです。
2) まず調査方法を述(の)べ、次いで調査結果、社内外の関係者の関与の有無(うむ)などについて報告します。必要があれば、資料を添付(てんぷ)します。
3) 調査結果の報告は、できる限り早く出します。まずファックスを送って、あとから文書を送るという方法もあります。

1. This letter, in contrast to the one shown in 15-3, is one in which Toda factory is not responsible for the accident.
2. First, explain how the investigation was conducted, then indicate the results of the investigation and report on how related persons both within and outside the company were or were not involved. Attach documentation if necessary.
3. The report of the investigation should be sent as soon as possible. You can first fax the report and then send it later by regular mail.

第16課

契約違反や取引上のトラブルについて事後処理をする

Dealing with broken contracts or troublesome business dealings

取引の相手先からのクレームに対しては、おわびの文書をできる限り早く出すようにします。このような文書を「陳謝文」といいます。陳謝文では、状況の詳細な報告や相手がこうむった損害への対処をはっきり示すことが大切です。場合によっては、今後の信頼を失わないために、文書を出すだけでなく相手先を訪ねて事情説明とおわびをします。回答に時間がかかる場合は、取りあえずその間の中間報告を行います。

なお、クレーム発生について事故に無関係であった場合には、相手方に対して反駁（他から受けた非難に対して、逆に論じ返すこと）の文書を出します。

In response to a complaint filed by someone with whom you do business, a letter of apology (陳謝(ちんしゃ)文) should be sent as soon as possible. It is important in this letter to make a detailed report of the circumstances and clearly indicate what measures will be taken for losses suffered by the other party. In some cases, you may also need to visit the other party in person to explain what happened and to apologize, so as not to lose their trust in the future. If it will take some time to formulate a complete response, send an interim report in the meantime.

If you were not involved in the accident that caused the complaint, issue a rebuttal letter, refuting the complaints issued by the other party.

16-1 事故原因の調査結果を報告し、おわびをする

Announcing the results of an investigation into the cause of an accident and apologizing

S＆A社は、納入商品に汚損事故が起こったことについて吉田物産におわびをするとともに、今後の善後策について約束します。

S&A Corporation, with regard to the stained merchandise delivered to Yoshida Trading, apologizes and promises to take corrective measures in the future.

営本第◯◯◯号
平成◯年◯月◯日

吉田物産株式会社
　営業部長　山田栄三殿

S＆Aコーポレーション日本支社
営業部長　山本良雄（印）

拝復　初秋の候　貴社ますますご隆昌のこととお喜び申し上げます。

平素より格別のご愛顧のほど深謝申し上げます。

さて、◯月◯日付貴信によるカーペットしみ事故の件につきましては、貴社に対し一方ならぬご迷惑をお掛けいたしまして、誠に申し訳なく、深くおわび申し上げます。

つきましては、早速昨◯日に現地富士倉庫において、貴社の営業二課の方々並びに弊社より小職、工場長、営業部員のほか物流業者の責任者が立ち会い、事故の調査確認を実施いたしました。その結果、弊社戸田工場の庫内入れ替え作業中にフォークリフトの機械油が落ちたために、今回のしみができたものと判明しました。

弊社といたしましては、今後再びこのような事故のないよう、社内はもとより倉庫・運輸業者に対しても厳しく周知徹底させますので、この度の事故につきましては、なにとぞご海容のほどお願い申し上げます。

まずは、取り急ぎ書中をもちまして、おわびかたがたご報告申し上げます。

敬　具

格別のご愛顧：your special patronage　深謝：deep thanks　現地：the spot (place)　小職：I　物流業者の責任者：responsible person(s) from the physical distribution company　立ち会う：attend; be present at　実施する：put into effect　庫内入れ替え作業中：during reorganizing operations within the warehouse　フォークリフト：forklift　判明する：be proved; come to light　～はもとより：not to mention ～　運輸業者：transportation company　周知徹底させる：make widely known to all　海容のほどお願い申し上げる：I ask for your kind forgiveness

Sales Document # ______
Date (year, month, day)

Yoshida Trading, Incorporated
Sales Department Manager Yamada Eizo (Mr.)

S&A Corporation, Japan Office
Sales Department Manager Yamamoto Yoshio (seal)

Salutations: At this the beginning of autumn, may I congratulate your company on its increasing prosperity.

Allow me to express our deepest thanks for your special, continuing patronage in our day-to-day operations.

Now with regard to the problem of the stained carpet mentioned in your letter of (month, day), I am truly sorry to have caused your company this completely inexcusable inconvenience and offer my sincere apologies.

In this regard, personnel from your company's sales section two, along with myself, the factory manager, employees of our sales department, and the person responsible from the physical distribution company gathered at the Fuji Warehouse yesterday, (day), where we confirmed the nature of the accident. Our investigation proved that the stain was caused by engine oil, which dropped from the forklift during an operation at the Toda factory warehouse, where the merchandise was being reorganized.

Our company will, as a matter of course, make it well known to our staff, as well as to the warehouse and transportation companies, that this type of accident is not to happen again. So with respect to this accident, we ask for your kind forgiveness.

I hasten now to use this letter first to apologize and then to report on what we have done.

Sincerely yours

留意事項

1) 陳謝(ちんしゃ)文では、①まず、おわびと当面の処置(しょち)を述(の)べた文書を取りあえず送り、そのあとで事故の調査結果などを報告する場合と、②調査結果が早く判明して、おわびとともに調査報告や善後策(ぜんごさく)を書いた文書を出す場合とがあります。この文書は、②の例です。

2) こちら側のミスや不注意によって相手に損害(そんがい)を与えた場合の陳謝文は、事実関係を具体的に正確に示し、おわびのことばを述べて誠意(せいい)をもって善後策を提案するようにします。

3) こちら側のミスでなく、天候や第三者による原因で相手が損害を受けたときは実情をよく説明して、はっきりと釈明(しゃくめい)します。

4) この例では、初めと終わりのあいさつを書いていますが、急ぐ場合には、これらを省略(しょうりゃく)して用件に入ります。

1. There are two types of letters of apology. In the first, you begin with an apology and an explanation of the immediate measures taken, followed by a report on the results of the investigation. In the second, when the investigation quickly proves what happened, along with the apology you can include a full report of the investigation and explain what corrective measures are needed. This is an example of the latter type.

2. A letter of apology, written when the other party has incurred a loss due to your mistake or carelessness, clearly explains the relevant facts; it also contains words of apology and a sincere proposal to take corrective measures.

3. When you are not at fault, but the other party has incurred a loss because of either the weather or a third party, explain the situation thoroughly and clearly vindicate yourself.

4. An opening and closing greetings have been included in this example but may be omitted when you are in a hurry.

社外 わびる apology

16-2 ＯＡ機器の納入の遅延をおわびする
Apologizing for the delay in the delivery of OA equipment

ＯＡ機器会社の東京システム販売は、ソフト開発業務の遅延によって、契約の納期日が守れなかったことに対しておわびをします。

Tokyo System Sales, an office equipment company, apologizes for not being able to meet the delivery deadline because of a delay in software development.

営第○○○号
199○年○月○日

Ｓ＆Ａコーポレーション日本支社
営業部長　山本良雄殿

東京システム販売株式会社
代表取締役　赤坂　透（印）

YMNソフト開発遅延に関する件

拝復　掲題に関する○月○日付貴状拝承いたしました。

契約の納入期日に遅れを生じましたこと誠に申し訳なく、おわび申し上げます。

目下のところ、10月30日のデモで、貴社のご要望を満たすオペレーションが可能と考えておりますので、当日システム納入を行ない、ご検収いただく方向で取り進めたいと存じております。

当初予定の10月１日運用開始が、ソフト仕様追加のため１カ月遅れとなってしまい、お手数をお掛けしましたこと誠に申し訳なく、改めてお伺いのうえ、当方の事情などご説明させていただきたく存じますが、本件なにとぞご寛大なご処置のほどお願い申し上げます。

敬　具

ソフト開発遅延：delay in software development　掲題に関する：regarding the above issue　契約：contract　納入期日に遅れを生じる：cause a delay in meeting the delivery deadline　目下のところ：at this time　デモ：demonstration　貴社の要望を満たす：fulfill your company's wishes　オペレーションが可能：operation is possible　システム納入を行なう：system delivery　検収する：examine　～方向で取り進めたい：want to (continue in the direction of) ～　当初予定：original plan　運用開始：beginning to use　ソフト仕様追加：addition of software specifications　当方の事情：our situation　寛大な処置のほど：granting ～ some leeway

Sales Document # ______
Date (year, month, day)

S&A Corporation, Japan Office
Sales Department Manager Yamamoto Yoshio (Mr.)

Tokyo System Sales, Incorporated
Representative Director Akasaka Toru (seal)

RE: The delay in YMN software development

Salutations: I received your letter of (month, day) regarding the above issue.

I am very sorry to have caused the delay in meeting the delivery deadline specified in our contract and apologize for this.

I believe that the October 30 demonstration to be given by our employees will show you an operation that fulfills your wishes. Therefore, we want to deliver the system on that day and have you examine it at that time.

Our original plan to begin operations on October 1 had to be delayed for one month because of the addition of software specifications, and we are truly sorry for the trouble this has caused you. I would like to meet with you later to explain our situation and ask that you grant us some leeway.

Sincerely yours

留意事項

1) まず相手に与えた損害（そんがい）（この場合は納入（のうにゅう）が遅れたこと）を率直（そっちょく）におわびし、次いで今後の対処（たいしょ）（今後のスケジュールや業務の見通し）について、きちんと明示します。

2) 事務的な文書の例なので、初めと終わりのあいさつを省きますが、おわびのことば及び今後の対処についてはっきり示し、相手の信頼を失わない誠意（せいい）のある内容を示します。また、一度文書を出すだけでなく、相手に対して常に報告・連絡をしておくことが大切です。

1. First, apologize frankly for the loss you caused the other party (in this case it was a delay in delivery) and then explain clearly what you plan to do about it (herein is an overview of the schedule and the work to be done).

2. Because this is an example of a business communication, omit the opening and closing greetings. Clearly state your sincere apology and plans for dealing with the problem, so as not to lose the trust of the other party. It is important not to stop with writing just this letter, but follow up with frequent reports and contacts with the other party.

16-1と16-2のフローと文例

16-1「事故原因の調査結果を報告し、おわびをする」のフロー

拝復　初秋の候　貴社ますますご隆昌のこととお喜び申し上げます。

　平素より格別のご愛顧のほど深謝申し上げます。

　さて、○月○日付貴信によるカーペットしみ事故の件につきましては、貴社に対し一方ならぬご迷惑をお掛けいたしまして、誠に申し訳なく、深くおわび申し上げます。

①迷惑をかけたことをわびる

　つきましては、早速昨○日に現地富士倉庫において、貴社の営業二課の方々並びに弊社より小職、工場長、営業部員のほか物流業者の責任者が立ち会い、事故の調査確認を実施いたしました。その結果、弊社戸田工場の庫内入れ替え作業中にフォークリフトの機械油が落ちたために、今回のしみができたものと判明しました。

②調査結果を報告する

　弊社といたしましては、今後再びこのような事故のないよう、社内はもとより倉庫・運輸業者に対しても厳しく周知徹底させますので、この度の事故につきましては、なにとぞご海容のほどお願い申し上げます。

③対処方法を知らせる
＋
許しを求める

　まずは、取り急ぎ書中をもちまして、おわびかたがたご報告申し上げます。

敬　具

16-2「OA機器の納入の遅延をおわびする」のフロー

拝復　掲題に関する○月○日付貴状拝承いたしました。

　契約の納入期日に遅れを生じましたこと誠に申し訳なく、おわび申し上げます。

①迷惑をかけたことをわびる

　目下のところ、10月30日のデモで、貴社のご要望を満たすオペレーションが可能と考えておりますので、当日システム納入を行ない、ご検収いただく方向で取り進めたいと存じております。

　当初予定の10月１日運用開始が、ソフト仕様追加のため１カ月遅れとなってしまい、お手数をお掛けしましたこと誠に申し訳なく、改めてお伺いのうえ、当方の事情などご説明させていただきたく存じますが、本件なにとぞご寛大なご処置のほどお願い申し上げます。

③対処方法を知らせる
＋
許しを求める

敬　具

（下線の部分は自分の状況に合わせて書いてください。）

①迷惑をかけたことをわびる

Apologizing for causing trouble

＊○月○日付貴信によるカーペットしみ事故の件につきましては、貴社に対し一方ならぬご迷惑をお掛けいたしまして、誠に申し訳なく、深くおわび申し上げます。(16-1)

With regard to the problem of the stained carpet mentioned in your letter of (month, day), I am truly sorry to have caused your company this completely inexcusable inconvenience and offer my sincere apologies.

＊掲題に関する○月○日付貴状拝承いたしました。契約の納入期日に遅れを生じましたこと誠に申し訳なく、おわび申し上げます。(16-2)

I received your letter of (month, day) regarding the above issue. I am very sorry to have caused the delay in meeting the delivery deadline specified in our contract and apologize for this.

＊今回の貴社への商品納入の遅滞につきましては、一方ならぬご迷惑をお掛けいたしまして、誠に恐縮に存じます。

With regard to the delay in the delivery of the goods to your company, I am very sorry for the inexcusable inconvenience it has caused you.

②調査結果を報告する（調査日時、立会人、発生原因など）

Reporting the results of an investigation (date of investigation, witnesses, cause of incident, etc.)

③対処方法を知らせる＋許しを求める

Informing about ways to deal with an incident and asking for forgiveness

＊弊社といたしましては、今後再びこのような事故のないよう、厳しく周知徹底させますので、この度の事故につきましては、なにとぞご海容のほどお願い申し上げます。(16-1)

Our company will make it well known that this type of accident is not to happen again. So with respect to this accident, we ask for your kind forgiveness.

＊今回の汚損事故につきましては、本日より５日以内に、担当の営業部長からご連絡申し上げますので、よろしくご了解のうえ、今しばらくお待ちくださいますようお願い申し上げます。

With regard to the stained goods accident, the sales manager responsible will be in touch with you within the next five days. I request for your understanding and ask that you wait for a short while.

＊取りあえず、不足分の商品を別便をもってご送付申し上げましたので、お納め願います。今後二度とこのようなことのないよう十分に注意いたしますので、なにとぞご寛容くださいますようお願いいたします。

Please accept the remainder of the goods I initially sent you by separate mail. We will take great care to ensure that this kind of thing never happens again in the future, so we ask for your kind forgiveness.

16-3 事故原因調査の中間報告をする

Issuing an interim report on the investigation into the cause of an accident

S＆A社は、納入商品の事故について、その原因調査にしばらく時間がかかるので、取りあえず事情を説明し了解を求める文書を出します。

With respect to the merchandise delivery incident, S&A Corporation, seeing that the investigation into the cause would take time, issues an interim report explaining the situation and requesting understanding.

営本第○○○号
平成○年○月○日

吉田物産株式会社
営業部長　山田栄三殿

S＆Aコーポレーション日本支社
営業部長　山本良雄（印）

「デュクロン」事故の件

拝啓　平素よりの格別のご厚誼に深謝申し上げます。

さて、この度の「デュクロン」スタンダード・タイプのしみ事故発生につきましては、一方ならぬご迷惑をお掛けいたしまして、誠に恐縮に存じます。取りあえず事故品のカーペット40m²については、即時弊社で引き取り代替品50m²を本日納入させていただきました。

弊社におきましては、かねてより社内はもちろん、運輸・倉庫業者など物流業者に対しても、月例会議などの機会を捉えて、その都度取扱商品について、正確でていねいなハンドリングの周知徹底を図り、指導に努めてまいりました。

今回のような事態が起こるとは信じがたい思いでありますが、直ちに社内に事故委員会を設け、業者を含めて原因究明に入りました。同時に、今後の商品取扱の万全を期して、営業・工場部門のチェックシステムの再検討に着手しました。

本件事故の調査結果につきましては、判明次第改めてご報告し、ご了承を得たく存じます。

ここに取りあえず書中をもって中間ご報告申し上げますとともに、改めておわび申し上げる次第でございます。

敬　具

格別の厚誼：special kindness　深謝：deep appreciation　即時：immediately　代替品：replacement goods　納入する：deliver　運輸：transportation　倉庫業者：warehouseman　物流：physical distribution　月例会議：monthly meetings　機会を捉えて：taking an opportunity　その都度：every time　周知徹底を図る：plan to let all know　指導に努める：try to instill　事態が起こる：incident occurs

信じがたい思いである：difficult to believe　直ちに：immediately　事故委員会を設ける：form an accident committee　原因究明に入る：enter an investigation into the cause　万全を期す：take all possible measures (to go without incident)　～部門：departments　チェックシステムの再検討に着手する：begin reevaluation of check system　判明次第：as soon as it becomes clear　了承を得る：obtain your understanding　～する次第である：upon (doing) ～

Sales Document # ______
Date (year, month, day)

Yoshida Trading, Incorporated
Sales Department Manager Yamada Eizo (Mr.)

S&A Corporation, Japan Office
Sales Department Manager Yamamoto Yoshio (seal)

RE: Dukelon incident

Salutations: Allow me to express our deep appreciation for the special kindness you continually extend to us.

Now, with regard to the stains on the Dukelon standard carpet, we have caused great inconvenience to you and are indeed sorry for this. First of all, with regard to the 40 square meters of damaged carpet, we immediately picked it up and delivered 50 square meters of replacement as of today.

As a company, we have held regular monthly meetings and worked both in-house and with the physical distribution company—both transportation and the warehouse—taking every opportunity to instill in them the need for accurately and carefully handling our merchandise.

It is difficult to believe that an accident such as this recent one could occur, but we immediately formed an in-house accident committee, and an investigation into the cause has begun with other workers involved. At the same time, we began a reevaluation of the check system in both our sales and factory departments to ensure that all merchandise is handled without mistakes.

As to the results of the investigation into the recent incident, we will report our findings to you as soon as they are clear. We ask for your understanding in this matter.

At this point, I am writing to give you an interim report and also once again to express our apologies for what has happened.

Sincerely yours

留意事項

1) この例では、クレームに対する取りあえずの中間報告として、事実関係を説明して相手方の了解を求めています。

2) 事故原因調査の報告としては、まず相手への迷惑に対してのおわびをし、次に代替品手当てなど、どのような応急処置をしたか・するかについて報告します。

3) そして、平素から商品取扱いについては十分注意して対処してきた旨を述べ、最後に事故調査に対する態勢と今後の対応を示して中間報告とします。

1. In this example, you are writing an interim report in response to the complaint, explaining related facts and asking for the other party's understanding.

2. As a report of the investigation into the cause of the accident, first apologize for inconveniencing the other party and then report on what emergency measures you have taken to make up for the inconvenience, i.e. providing replacement.

3. Then explain that you have always exercised adequate care in the handling of merchandise, and lastly, report on the way the accident is being investigated, and show what measures will be taken in the future.

16-4 クレームに対して反駁(はんばく)する

Refuting a complaint

S&A社は、納入(のうにゅう)商品の事故について関係者に対する調査を行った結果、同社は事故発生に無関係であったという反駁(はんばく)文（他から受けた非難(ひなん)に対して逆に論じ返す文書）を出します。

The results of the investigation of persons related to the delivery of the stained merchandise proved that S&A Corporation was in no way involved in the accident. The company now writes a letter to those who issued the complaint, refuting their claim.

営本第○○○号
平成○年○月○日

吉田物産株式会社
営業部長　山田栄三殿

Ｓ＆Ａコーポレーション日本支社
営業部長　山本良雄（印）

カーペットの汚損(おそん)クレームに関する件(回答)

拝復(はいふく)　頭記に関する○日付貴信拝承(はいしょう)しました。

早速弊社(さっそくへいしゃ)の製造・倉庫・運輸(うんゆ)各担当部門の関係者及び業者について調査いたしました結果は、次のとおりでございます。

製造・倉庫関係：

製造に当っては、完了時の品質検査と工場保管時の外装(がいそう)検査を行なっておりますが、品質検査はもちろん合格し、その際、汚損箇所(かしょ)の発見は報告されておりません。

検査後は、包装紙(ほうそうし)を巻き、その上にビニール製カバーをつけて工場保管といたしますが、工場保管の入出庫時の外装検査は、いずれも異常なしとなっております。

なお、工場内の保管場所には、油類は一切(いっさい)保管しておりません。

ご参考までに、工場の品質検査報告書と保管時の入出庫伝票の写(うつし)を同封いたします。

運輸関係：

工場の保管場所から貴社ご指定の「富士倉庫」までの輸送には、「大山運輸」を使用しておりますので、大山運輸についても調査を行ないました。

その結果は、大山運輸は、油類を積載(せきさい)したことのないトラックを使用しており、富士倉庫納入(のうにゅう)の際の受け渡(わた)しには、異常なしのクリーンレシートを受け取っております。念のため、富士倉庫の入庫通知書の本紙を同封しました。

まずは、貴照会(しょうかい)信に対し弊社の見解を申し上げます。

敬　具

同封書類：富士倉庫の入庫通知書　１式

汚損：damage by staining　頭記：the above topic　拝承する：receive　運輸：transportation　各担当部門の関係者：person(s) concerned from each of the departments responsible　業者：company　製造に当っては：in manufacturing　品質検査：quality inspection　工場保管時：when stored at the warehouse　外装検査を行う：undergo an external inspection　包装紙を巻く：wrap in packing paper　入出庫時：when entering and leaving the storage area　一切～ない：absolutely no ～　参考までに：for your reference　伝票の写：copy of order slips　同封する：include　貴社指定の：your company's designated ～　輸送：transport　積載する：carry　納入の際の受け渡し：passing on at the time of delivery　クリーンレシート：clean receipt　照会信：letter of inquiry　見解：opinion

---

Sales Document # ______
Date (year, month, day)

Yoshida Trading, Incorporated
Sales Department Manager Yamada Eizo (Mr.)

S&A Corporation, Japan Office
Sales Department, Yamamoto Yoshio (seal)

Response RE: Stained carpet complaint

Salutations: We received your letter of (day) concerning the above topic.

Following are the results of the immediate investigation involving all concerned staff from the departments responsible for manufacturing, storage, and transportation, respectively, and the related physical distribution companies.

Manufacturing and storage:

In manufacturing, a quality inspection was conducted at the time the merchandise was completed, an external inspection was made when it was put into storage in the warehouse, but the merchandise, of course, passed the quality inspection, and there was no report of stains being discovered at that time.

After the inspection, the merchandise was wrapped in packing paper and then covered with vinyl and stored in the factory warehouse, but nothing strange was discovered at the time of the external inspection, when it entered and left the storage area.

In addition, there is absolutely no oil kept in the storage area of the factory.

For your reference, I am including copies of the quality inspection report from the factory and the slips showing the placing of merchandise in the storage area.

Related to transportation:

We employ Oyama Transportation to transport goods from our factory storage area to your designated Fuji Warehouse, and we conducted an investigation of Oyama Transportation. The results show that they used a truck that has never hauled carry oil products, and they received a clean receipt at the time they delivered the merchandise to Fuji Warehouse. For your reference, I have included the original copy of Fuji Warehouse's receiving report.

With my regards, I would like to share with you our company's interpretation of the inquiry your company sent us.

First of all, with regard to your inquiry, I am sending our opinion.

Sincerely yours

Enclosures: A set of Fuji Warehouse receiving reports.

留意事項

1)反駁文は、取引先からのクレームに対して、こちら側のミスによるものではないという見解を述べるものです。

2)相手方を非難するような表現は避けて、こちら側の調査方法と結果を客観的に報告します。

3)できるだけ証拠資料(必要ならば現場写真など)を提示するなどして事実関係を示し、相手を納得させるようにします。また、事故原因について参考になることがあれば、相手に知らせます。

1. A letter of rebuttal is written in response to a complaint made by a business associate in which you state your interpretation that the accident was not caused by you, as the accused.

2. Avoid using phrases that criticize the other party, but rather report on the method and results of your investigation from an objective point of view.

3. Do your best to convince the other party by presenting as many pieces of evidence as you can (send on-the-spot photos, if necessary) to show relevant facts. If you have any information related to the cause of the accident, share it with the other party.

第17課

トラブルについて社内に報告する

Making an in-house report regarding an incident

企業としては、日常の業務のなかで起こる取り扱い商品の事故・代金未払い・契約違反・特許侵害などのトラブルに対して、特に的確で迅速な対応が必要です。

トラブルが起こった関係部署では、事故発生状況・対応処置などの事実関係を正確に述べた社内報告書を上司に対して提出することが求められます。この報告書をもとに、相手先への対応処置や事故再発防止策の実施、担当部門への処置などが進められます。

In everyday business dealings, a variety of problems occur that require prompt and accurate responses, such as the mishandling of merchandise, unpaid bills, contract violations, and patent infringements.

In the department where the trouble occurs, an in-house report must be presented to one's superior, accurately explaining the situation leading to the incident and what measures were taken to deal with it. Based on this report, the company will take the next step, as follows: appropriate measures will be taken for the other party; preventive measures against recurrence will be put into effect; and decisions will be made on how to deal with the responsible department.

17-1 汚損事故の経過と事後処理について上司に報告する
Reporting to one's superior on the progress of an incident and the action being taken

S&A社の山本営業部長は、スミス支社長に対して、納入商品の汚損事故に対するクレーム処理について報告書を出します。

Mr. Yamamoto, sales department manager of S&A Corporation, sends a report on the handling of a complaint about stained merchandise to Mr. Smith, the office manager.

営一第○○○号
平成○年○月○日

支社長殿

営業部長　山本良雄（印）

クレーム処理報告書

吉田物産(株)で発生したカーペット「デュクロン」のクレーム処理に関し次のとおり報告します。

1．クレーム発生状況

平成○年○月○日午前11時ごろ、吉田物産の伊藤課長から、当社が同日搬入したスタンダード・タイプにしみがある旨の電話連絡を受けた。早速富士倉庫に赴き、現物をチェックしたところ、約40m²にわたり汚れとしみが付いていた。取りあえず不良品を引き取るとともに原因調査を約束。

2．事故原因

社内の担当部門、倉庫業者、運送業者を呼んで、原因を調べたところ、当社戸田工場で貨物の入れ替え作業中にフォークリフトの油がカーペットに落ちたものと判明。

3．吉田物産に対する補償

40m²分を新品の物と取り替えるとともに、迷惑料として10m²分を無償提供。

4．大山運輸に対する処置

(1)50m²相当額を弁償させる。

(2)当社あてに「事故報告書」を出させる。

5．再発防止策

(1)すべての取扱業者に「取扱注意」の指示文書を出す。

(2)社内にプロジェクト・チームを作り、出荷管理システムの再検討を行なう。

なお、今回の事故につき、営業部長としての監督不行届きを深く反省し再びこのようなことのないよう最善を尽くす所存であります。

以　上

クレーム処理(しょり)：handling a complaint　発生する：occur　搬入(はんにゅう)する：deliver; carry in　赴(おもむ)く：go　～にわたり：covering ～; over ～　担当部門：responsible departments　倉庫業者：warehouseman　貨物：freight; merchandise　入れ替え作業中：during reorganizing operations　フォークリフト：forklift　判明：become clear　補償(ほしょう)：compensation　～分：amount/quantity of ～　無償(むしょう)提供：offer free of charge　処置(しょち)：measures taken　～相当額：amount (of money) equal to ～　弁償(べんしょう)する：compensate　再発防止策：preventive measures against recurrence　出荷管理システムの再検討を行なう：undertake a reevaluation of the shipping management system　監督不行届き(かんとくふゆきとどき)：negligence in supervision　最善を尽(つ)くす所存である：plan to do one's best

---

Sales One Document # ________
Date (year, month, day)

The Honorable Office Manager

Sales Department Manager Yamamoto Yoshio (seal)

Report on handling a complaint

I would like to report, as follows, on how Yoshida Trading's complaint concerning Dukelon carpet was handled.

1. The situation causing the complaint

At about 11:00 A.M. on (year, month, day) we received a phone call from Yoshida Trading's Sales Section Chief Ito stating that the standard-type we delivered that morning was stained. We immediately went to Fuji Warehouse, and upon checking the actual merchandise found dirt and stains on about 40 square meters of carpet. We initially took back the defective merchandise and promised to investigate the cause.

2. Cause of the accident

We called together the responsible departments within the company and the warehouse and transportation companies to study the cause and discovered that oil had fallen on the carpet from a forklift at the time it was being moved during a reorganization at the Toda factory.

3. Compensation to Yoshida Trading

In addition to sending 40 square meters of new carpet in exchange for the damaged merchandise, we included 10 square meters extra as payment for their inconvenience.

4. Measures related to Oyama Transportation

(1) Have them pay an amount equal to the value of 50 square meters of carpet.
(2) Have them send a report of the accident to our company.

5. Preventive measures against recurrence

(1) Issued a notice to all handlers concerning handling precautions.
(2) Put together an in-house project team to reevaluate our management system of shipping.

In addition to this accident, I deeply regret that I have been so negligent in my supervisory role as sales department manager and plan to do my best so that this type of thing never happens again.

(the end)

留意事項

1) 事故の報告書では、項目を立てて、まず事故の発生状況を説明し、その原因を述(の)べます。次いで、相手先への補償(ほしょう)やミスをおかした部門への処置(しょち)・再発防止策を述べ、反省(はんせい)のことばで結びます。事実関係を正確に報告し、故意(こい)に一部を省(はぶ)いたり誇張(こちょう)した表現を使わないように留意します。

2) 報告の文書では、一般に「である」体が使われますが、最近は会社によっては、「です」「ます」体を使うところもあります。

3) 社内文書なので、頭語(とうご)・結語(けつご)や初めと終わりのあいさつは省きます。

1. Divide your accident report into sections, first explaining how the accident happened and then relating the cause. Next, explain what compensation will be made to the other party, the measures taken toward the department causing the accident, and what preventive measures are being taken. Tie the letter together with words of reflection. Report relevant facts accurately, being careful neither to omit parts of them intentionally nor to use exaggerated expressions.

2. It is generally accepted procedure to use the *de aru* (plain) form for reports, but recently companies sometimes use the *desu-masu* (polite) form.

3. As this is an in-house communication, omit salutations, complimentary closes, and opening and closing greetings.

17-2 OA機器の導入の遅れと事後処理(しょり)について関係部門に連絡する

Contacting the related department with regard to the delay in OA installation and subsequent actions

山本営業部長は、OA機器会社からシステム導入遅延(ちえん)の通知を受けて、これまでの経緯(けいい)を社内各部門に報告し、いつから利用できるかを知らせます。

Sales Department Manager Yamamoto receives the notice regarding the delay in installation of system software and reports what has happened in this regard so far, letting the people concerned know when it will be operational.

営企第○○○号
平成○年○月○日

総務部長殿
経理部長殿
工場長殿

営業部長　山本良雄（印）

OA機器導入遅延(ちえん)に関する件（連絡）

東京システム販売(株)のコンピュータ・ターミナル設置(せっち)遅延につき、次のとおり連絡いたしますのでご了承(りょうしょう)ください。(担当は、営業企画課)

1)状況：かねて取り進め中のコンピュータ・ターミナルは、当初10月１日運用開始の予定であったところ、グラフィック機能不具合(ふぐあい)で約定の期限の運用開始は不可能となった。

2)原因：調査の結果、ハード部分とソフト部分の双方(そうほう)に欠陥(けっかん)があることが判明。目下(もっか)、業者の東京システム販売が持ち帰り修復中。

3)今後の見通し：業者の連絡によれば、ハード改修とソフトのデバッグともに10月20日ごろまでに完了、10月末当社でテストランのうえ、引渡(ひきわた)し可能とのこと。従って、10月１日の運用開始は１カ月遅れのこととなる見込み。

4)納入(のうにゅう)業者に対する処置(しょち)：納入の期日遅延につきクレームを申し入れたところ、別紙のような返書があった。１カ月の遅延のため、11月１日運用開始を厳守(げんしゅ)のこと及び今後のメンテなどに手落ちのないようアテンドすることを条件に今回は不問(ふもん)にすることといたしたく、ご了承(りょうしょう)願う。

5)その他：前記のとおり、11月１日の運用開始のため10月30日(土)にテスト・ランの予定につき、あらかじめお含みおき願いたく。

以　上

(添付(てんぷ)の参考書類）東京システム販売(株)の返書　　１通

遅延：delay　コンピュータ・ターミナル設置：installation of computer terminal　了承する：understand　担当：responsible for ～　当初：originally; at first　グラフィック機能不具合：glitch in the graphics program　約定の期限：agreed deadline　双方に欠陥がある：have defects in both　判明：be discovered; come to light　目下：now　修復中：in the middle of repairs　今後の見通し：future prospects　改修：repairs　デバッグ：debugging　テストランのうえ引渡し：pass on after a test run　納入業者：installer; supplier　クレームを申し入れる：file a complaint　厳守：strict observance; without fail　メンテ：maintenance　手落ちがない：no mistake　アテンドする：attend　～を条件に：on condition that ～　不問にする：overlook　前記のとおり：as written above　含みおく：keep in mind　添付の：enclosed

Sales Planning Document # ________
Date (year, month, day)

The Honorable General Affairs Department Manager
The Honorable Accounting Department Manager
The Honorable Factory Manager

Sales Department Manager Yamamoto Yoshio (seal)

RE: Delay in the installation of OA equipment (Communication)

Regarding the delay in the installation of computer terminals by Tokyo System Sales, I will make the following announcement and ask for your understanding (Sales Planning Section responsible).

1. Conditions: It will not be possible to begin operations on the originally planned date of October 1, due to a glitch in the graphics program.
2. Cause: Upon investigation, defects were discovered in both the hardware and software, resulting in it being returned to Tokyo System Sales, where it is now being repaired.
3. Prospect for the near future: According to Tokyo System Sales employees, the hardware repairs and software debugging should be completed by about October 20, so that they can pass the system on to us around the end of October after a test run. We anticipate this to mean that the plan to begin operating the system October 1 has been delayed by one month.
4. Measures taken with regard to the installer: When we filed a complaint against the installer for the installation delay, we received the response shown on the attached sheet. We will overlook the delay this time on the condition that they have the system operational by November 1, without fail, and then attend to future maintenance, etc. with the utmost care. We ask for your understanding.
5. Other: As written above, in order to become operational on November 1, we are planning to conduct a test run on Saturday, October 30, and I would like to invite you to attend.

(the end)

(Enclosed materials for reference) Tokyo System Sales (Inc.) reply—1 letter

留意事項

1) OA機器導入遅延にいたる間のやむを得ない事情を各部門に了解してもらい、システム稼働の際に、全社の協力を得ることがこの手紙の目的です。

2) 社内文書なので、頭語や結語、あいさつのことばなどは書きません。本文は項目ごとに簡潔でわかりやすいように箇条書きにし、本文の最後は「以上」で終わります。

3) 本文書にあるように、必要に応じて、参考書類を添付します。

1. The purpose of this letter is to gain the understanding of each department for the unavoidable delay in OA equipment installation and to receive the cooperation of the entire company when the system does become operational.

2. As this is an in-house communication, you do not write a salutation, complimentary close, or greeting. This example is separated into topics and written concisely and simply in the outline form, closing with 以上 (the end).

3. As in this example, attach materials whenever necessary.

17-1と17-2のフローと文例

17-1「汚損事故の経過と事後処理について上司に報告する」のフロー

クレーム処理報告書

吉田物産(株)で発生したカーペット「デュクロン」のクレーム処理に関し次のとおり報告します。 ―①報告する

1．クレーム発生状況

平成○年○月○日午前11時ごろ、吉田物産の伊藤課長から、当社が同日搬入したスタンダード・タイプにしみがある旨の電話連絡を受けた。早速富士倉庫に赴き、現物をチェックしたところ、約40㎡にわたり汚れとしみが付いていた。取りあえず不良品を引き取るとともに原因調査を約束。

2．事故原因

社内の担当部門、倉庫業者、運送業者を呼んで、原因を調べたところ、当社戸田工場で貨物の入れ替え作業中にフォークリフトの油がカーペットに落ちたものと判明。

3．吉田物産に対する補償

40㎡分を新品の物と取り替えるとともに、迷惑料として10㎡分を無償提供。

(中略)

―②報告内容

なお、今回の事故につき、営業部長としての監督不行届きを深く反省し再びこのようなことのないよう最善を尽くす所存であります。

以　上

17-2「OA機器の導入の遅れと事後処理について関係部門に連絡する」のフロー

OA機器導入遅延に関する件（連絡）

東京システム販売(株)のコンピュータ・ターミナル設置遅延につき、次のとおり連絡いたしますのでご了承ください。（担当は、営業企画課） ―①報告する

1)状況：かねて取り進め中のコンピュータ・ターミナルは、当初10月1日運用開始の予定であったところ、グラフィック機能不具合で約定の期限の運用開始は不可能となった。

2)原因：調査の結果、ハード部分とソフト部分の双方に欠陥があることが判明。目下、業者の東京システム販売が持ち帰り修復中。

3)今後の見通し：業者の連絡によれば、ハード改修とソフトのデバッグともに10月20日ごろまでに完了、10月末当社でテストランのうえ、引渡し可能とのこと。従って、10月1日の運用開始は1カ月遅れのこととなる見込み。

4)納入業者に対する処置：納入の期日遅延につきクレームを申し入れたところ、別紙のような返書があった。

(後略)

―②報告内容

以　上

(添付の参考書類) 東京システム販売(株)の返書　　1通

（下線の部分は自分の状況に合わせて書いてください。）

①報告する

Reporting

＊吉田物産(株)で発生したカーペット「デュクロン」のクレーム処理に関し次のとおり報告します。(17-1)

I would like to report, as follows, on how Yoshida Trading's complaint concerning Dukelon carpet was handled.

＊東京システム販売(株)のコンピュータ・ターミナル設置遅延につき、次のとおり連絡いたしますのでご了承ください。(17-2)

Regarding the delay in the installation of computer terminals by Tokyo System Sales, I will make the following announcement and ask for your understanding.

＊その経緯、処置並びに今後の対応について下記のとおりご報告するので、ご了承願いたい。(17-3)

With regard to this, following is a report of what happened and how we dealt with it, and what future measures we will take. I ask for your acknowledgment.

②報告内容（状況説明、調査結果、対処方法、今後の姿勢、見通しなど）

Contents of report (explanation of circumstances, results of investigation, ways of handling issue, future position, estimate, etc.)

〈状況の書き方〉

How to write about the circumstances

＊現物をチェックし**たところ**、約40m²にわたり汚れとしみが付い**ていた**。(17-1)

Upon checking the actual merchandise, we found dirt and stains on about 40 square meters of carpet.

＊当初10月1日運用開始の予定であっ**たところ**、グラフィック機能不具合で約定の期限の運用開始は不可能**となった**。(17-2)

It will not be possible to begin operations on the originally planned date of October 1, due to a glitch in the graphics program.

〈調査結果の書き方〉

How to write about the results of an investigation

＊原因を調べ**たところ**、フォークリフトの油がカーペットに落ちたもの**と判明**。(17-1)

We studied the cause and discovered that oil had fallen on the carpet from a forklift.

＊調査**の結果**、～に欠陥がある**ことが判明**。**目下**、業者が持ち帰り修復**中**。(17-2)

Upon investigation, defects were discovered in . . . , resulting in it being returned to the manufacturer, where it is now being repaired.

17-3 汚損事故の経過と事後処理について本社に報告する

Reporting to headquarters on the progress of an incident and actions taken

S&A社のスミス支社長は、米国の本社あてにカーペット汚損事故の状況と事後処理について報告します。

Mr. Smith, manager of the Japan Office of S&A Corporation, sends a report to the company's headquarters located in the United States, explaining the stained merchandise incident and what action has been taken.

営一第○○○号
199○年○月○日

S&Aコーポレーション本社
「デュクロン」部長殿

S&Aコーポレーション日本支社
支社長　ハワード　G. スミス
(サイン)

「デュクロン」汚損事故発生のご報告

平素より当支社業務につきご支援をいただき、厚く御礼申し上げる。

さて、この度、当支社において題記の事故が発生した。ついては、その経緯、処置並びに今後の対応について下記のとおりご報告するので、ご了承願いたい。

以上取りあえずご報告まで。

記

1．事故の経緯・処置

(1)199○年○月○日午前11時業務提携先の吉田物産(株)から、当社が同日午前中に取引倉庫内に搬入した「デュクロン」スタンダード・タイプに汚れとしみが発見された旨の電話があった。直ちに当社営業担当者が現場に直行し、検証したところ、約40㎡に汚れとしみの付着を認めた。

(2)現地において事故品を引き取り、取りあえず代替品補充の処置をとった。

(3)事故委員会の調査により、当社戸田工場で庫内作業中にフォークリフトの機械油が飛散したものと判明した。損害額は、商品代金その他で70万円となるが、全額を大山運輸（庫内作業担当）に求償している。

2．今後の対応

当分の間、入出庫時の点検、倉庫管理状況などについて、随時当社の担当者を派遣して、チェックを行なう。また、物流業者への監督強化や社内各部門・工場間の連絡システムの再構築を図るなど万全を期したい。

以　上

支援（しえん）：support　題記：the above issue　経緯（けいい）：circumstances; events　処置（しょち）：treatment; measures taken　今後の対応：future measures　了承（りょうしょう）：understanding; acknowledgment　提携先（ていけい）：company to tie up with; tie-up partner　搬入（はんにゅう）する：deliver; carry in　直（ただ）ちに：immediately　検証する：inspect　付着（ふちゃく）：sticking to　認める：confirm　代替品補充（だいたい・ほじゅう）：supplement with replacement　庫内作業中：during operations within the warehouse　フォークリフト：forklift　飛散（ひさん）する：spatter; splash　判明する：come to light; be discovered　損害額（そんがいがく）：value of damage　求償（きゅうしょう）する：seek compensation　当分の間：for the time being　入出庫時の点検：inspection when moving into and out of the warehouse　倉庫管理：organizing of warehouse　随時（ずいじ）：whenever necessary　派遣（はけん）する：dispatch　チェックを行う：undertake an inspection　物流業者：physical distribution company　監督（かんとく）強化：strengthening of supervision　各部門：each department　〜間の連絡システムの再構築（こうちく）を図（はか）る：try to restructure the communication system between 〜　万全（ばんぜん）を期（き）す：take all possible measures (to go without incident)

Sales One Document # ＿＿＿＿＿
Date (year, month, day)

S&A Corporation Headquarters
The Honorable Manager of Dukelon

S&A Corporation, Japan Office
Office Manager Howard G. Smith
(signature)

Report of the stained Dukelon incident

Allow me to express my deep gratitude for the support you continually give to our office.

Now, the above incident occurred recently in our office. With regard to this, following is a report of what happened and how we dealt with it, and what future measures we will take. I ask for your acknowledgment.

I am reporting this for your information.

Details

1. Details of the accident and how we dealt with it

(1) At 11:00 A.M. on (year, month, day), we had a phone call from our distributor, Yoshida Trading (Inc.), reporting that they had discovered stains in the standard-type Dukelon we had delivered to their warehouse that morning. The person in charge of our sales department immediately went to their location, and upon inspection, confirmed that 40 square meters were stained.

(2) We returned the damaged merchandise to our location, and for the time being replaced it with new carpet.

(3) An investigation by the accident committee proved that it had been spattered with engine oil from a forklift used during operations within our company's Toda factory.
The value of the damaged merchandise, etc., amounted to 700,000 yen. We are seeking compensation for the entire amount from Oyama Transportation (which was in charge of operations within the warehouse).

2. Future measures

For the time being, whenever necessary, we will dispatch an assigned person from our company to go and check on the inspections conducted when moving merchandise into and out of the warehouse and the way in which the warehouse is organized. We are also strengthening the supervision of the physical distribution company, and trying to restructure the communication system between the various departments of the company and the factory in an effort to have everything run smoothly.

(the end)

留意事項

1) 上の例は、本社の担当部長が組織のうえでは支社長と同格の地位にある場合です。このような場合は、「である」体の文章でもかまいません。
2) 事故発生の状況を具体的に説明して、クレームに対する処置(しょち)を述べ、今後の取引関係に不安がないこと及び今後の改善策(かいぜんさく)を報告します。
3) クレームに対する対応が的確(てきかく)で取引先の信頼を失わず、事後処理(しょり)もきちんと行われた旨(むね)、明示します。
4) 社内・社外文書とも、記書(きが)きの終わりは「以上」でしめくくります。

1. In the above example, the manager in charge at the company headquarters is on the same level as the office manager, so it is permissible to use the *de aru* (plain) form of sentence structure.
2. Give specifics in explaining the incident, state the measures taken with regard to the complaint, then report that there is no dissatisfaction with the business dealings and share plans for improvement.
3. After stating the above, explain that the measures taken are the right way to handle the complaint, that you have not lost the business associate's trust, and that you have taken all necessary steps to bring closure to the incident.
4. In both in-house and out-going documents, the "記書(きが)き" section should be pulled together with 以上 (the end).

社内 報告する・わびる〈始末書〉 report/apology

17-4 汚損事故に関して始末書を書く

Sending a written apology with regard to an incident involving stained goods

S&A社の橋本営業二課長は、支社長に対してカーペット汚損事故の担当課長として事故の発生とその後の状況を述べ、始末書を書きます。

S&A Corporation's Sales Section Two Chief Hashimoto, as the person in charge of the stained carpet incident, sends a letter of apology to the office manager, explaining how the incident occurred and the situation that followed.

<u>始　末　書</u>

(「デュクロン」汚損事故の件)

199○年○月○日

支　社　長　殿

営業部営業二課

課長　橋本　進（印）

私は、この度、頭記事故につき会社に対し損害をお掛けし、取引先の信頼を失う結果を招き、誠に申し訳なく存じます。

ここに事故の始末を申し述べてご報告します。

記

1．事故の経緯

199○年○月○日午前11時ごろ、吉田物産(株)伊藤営業課長から富士倉庫の庫内に当社が当日午前中に搬入した「デュクロン」スタンダード・タイプにしみが発見された旨の電話がありました。私と担当者2名が倉庫へ直行し、現物の検証に当ったところ、約40㎡に汚れとしみの付着を認めました。

現地から営業部長にこの旨を報告し、指示を仰ぎました。

2．処置

部長の指示により現地において事故品を引き取り、取りあえず代替品補充の処置をとりました。

その後、事故委員会の調査結果として、当社の庫内作業中にフォークリフトの機械油が飛散したものと原因が判明しました。

損害額は、商品代金その他で約70万円となりますが、全額大山運輸側に求償のこととなっております。

3．反省と今後の対策

新取引先なので、入出庫時の点検、倉庫管理状況の掌握など随時当社担当者を派遣しチェックすべきであったと思います。また、工場の貨物取扱い状況の把握が不十分な点がありました。

今後は、物流業者の監督強化や社内・工場間の連絡システムの再構築を図りたく、改めて対案をご報告します。

以　上

頭記：the above issue　損害を掛ける：cause loss　～結果を招く：bring about results of ～　経緯：circumstances; events　庫内：inside the warehouse　搬入する：deliver; carry in　現物の検証に当る：inspect the product　付着：sticking to　認める：confirm　指示を仰ぐ：seek direction　処置：measures taken　代替品補充：supplement with replacement　フォークリフト：forklift　飛散する：spatter; splash　判明する：come to light; be discovered　損害額：value of damage　運輸：transportation　求償：seek compensation　今後の対策：future measures　入出庫時の点検：inspection when moving in and out of the warehouse　倉庫管理状況の掌握：control of organizing inside warehouse　随時：whenever necessary　派遣する：dispatch　貨物取扱い状況の把握：control of freight handling　物流業者：physical distribution company　監督強化：strengthening supervision　～間の連絡システムの再構築を図る：try to restructure the communications system between ～　対案：counterproposals

<u>Written Statement</u>

(RE: Soiled Dukelon incident)

Date (year, month, day)

The Honorable Office Manager

Sales Department Sales Section Two
Chief Hashimoto Susumu (seal)

I am truly sorry for causing a loss to the company due to the above incident, and bringing about the loss of trust on the part of our business associate.

Following is a report of how the incident was settled.

Details

1. Circumstances of the incident

At about 11:00 A.M. on (year, month, day), we had a phone call from Sales Section Chief Ito of Yoshida Trading reporting that they had discovered stains in the standard-type Dukelon we delivered to Fuji Warehouse that morning. Two persons in charge and I went straight to the warehouse and, upon inspection, confirmed that about 40 square meters were stained.

I notified the sales department manager from the warehouse and sought his direction.

2. Measures taken

At the direction of the manager, we removed the damaged merchandise and chose to replace it for the time being.

Later, as a result of the investigation conducted by the accident committee, it was discovered that the stain was caused by engine oil that had been spattered from a forklift used during operations within our company's Toda factory.

The value of the damaged merchandise was approximately 700,000 yen, and we are seeking compensation for the entire amount from Oyama Transportation.

3. Reassessment and future measures

As this was a new business associate, we should have dispatched the responsible person, whenever necessary, to see that the inspection of merchandise moving in and out of the warehouse and the way in which the warehouse was organized was under control. There were also inadequacies in the control of the situation in the factory's handling of freight.

In the future, we will strengthen the supervision of the physical distribution personnel and try to restructure the communications system between the company and the factory, and later I will report to you on counterproposals.

(the end)

留意事項

1) 始末書は、普通、社員が業務上または業務外で会社に損害を与えたり、信用を落とすような行為をした場合に、上司・会社のトップに対して出す文書です。人事に関係するので、その重要性・機密性は一般の社内文書とは異なります。

2) まず、事故状況と担当者としてとった対応処置を述べます。特に反省すべき点は率直に認めるとともに今後の心構えを報告します。以上を述べて、最善の努力をした旨を訴えることが必要です。

1．始末(しまつ)書 is usually written by a company employee who has caused the company to suffer a loss or done something to cause a diminishing of trust, whether work-related or non-work-related, to a superior or head of the company. This is personnel-related, and is therefore different from regular in-house communications in its importance and confidentiality.

2．First, state the situation of the incident and what measures you took as the person responsible. Next, while candidly reflecting on what you should do, report on your preparations for the future. After explaining all of this, make an appeal explaining that you have done the best you could.

17-5 汚損事故に関して進退伺を出す

Indicating a desire to resign because of an incident

大山運輸の川村管理部長は、会社のトップに対し、作業中の事故について大きな責任があるとして、自分の進退の処置を仰ぎます。

Supervision Manager Kawamura of Oyama Transportation offers his resignation to the head of the company to take major responsibility for the incident that occurred during operations.

平成○年○月○日

代表取締役　太田虎造殿

管理部長　川村直道（印）

進　退　伺

10月○日 S&A コーポレーション戸田工場の庫移し作業中にフォークリフトの機械油が漏れ、同社のカーペット「デュクロン」40m²にしみを付ける事故を起こしました。その結果、S&A 社とその得意先に多大の迷惑を掛け、また会社に対して重大な損害を与え、会社の信用を傷つけました。

これは、ひとえに私の監督不行き届きによるもので、責任を痛感しております。将来、再びこのような失態のないよう、深く注意いたす所存でございます。

上記により、ここに小職の進退につきお伺い申し上げます。

以　上

庫移し作業中：during moving operations within the storage area　フォークリフト：forklift　得意先：valued customer　重大な損害を与える：suffer great loss　信用を傷つける：wound one's trust　監督不行き届きによるもの：due to negligence in supervision　責任を痛感する：feel keenly one's responsibility　失態：blunder　小職の進退：my resignation

Date (year, month, day)

Managing Director Ota Torazo (Mr.)

Supervision Manager Kawamura Naomichi (seal)

Letter of Resignation

On October (day), engine oil from the forklift leaked out during moving operations at S&A Corporation's Toda factory, causing the staining of 40 square meters of that company's Dukelon carpet. As a result, a great inconvenience was caused to both S&A Corporation and to their distributor, our company suffered a heavy loss, and its trust has been wounded.

As this is all because of my negligence in supervision, I am keenly aware of my responsibility. It is my thought that we must be extremely careful that this type of blunder not happen again in the future.

Because of the above, I hereby tender my resignation.

(the end)

留意事項

1) 社員が業務上または業務外で会社に対して損害を与え、会社の信用を失うような行為を行ったときは、会社の内規により退職事由にあたるものとして取り扱われます。このような場合、普通、「進退伺」を出して処置を会社に委ね、後は指示を待ちます。状況に応じて社員が自発的に書きますが、上司が書くことを指示することもあります。

1. When an employee causes the company to suffer a loss or does something to cause a diminishing of trust, whether work-related or nonwork-related, according to company regulations, it is treated as a cause for resignation. In a case like this, the employee will turn in a 進退伺 (a letter of resignation) and wait for direction, leaving it up to the company to decide how to handle it. Depending on the situation, the employee usually submits the resignation voluntarily, but sometimes a superior will order it to be submitted.

第18課

社内に指示や通達を出す

Issuing in-house directives and notices

企業活動は、経営者や管理者の指示・命令に従って実行されます。その指示を伝える文書のうち重要なものとしては、⑴経営方針の指示、⑵会社組織・諸規則などの制定・改正の告知、⑶人事に関する辞令などがあります。このような文書は、普通、経営トップの名で発信されますが、日常業務では、担当役員や部門の長から部下に対して出されることもあります。

指示文では、社内でも秘扱いとするもの、社外秘とするものがあり、機密事項が漏れないよう取り扱いに注意が必要です。

Business is carried out at the direction or command of the manager or supervisor. The most important of the documents that convey those directives include (1) directives on management policy, (2) notices establishing, or revising, company organization and regulations, and (3) personnel appointments. These are normally sent out under the name of the company president, but there are times when matters related to daily concerns are sent out from the person responsible or department manager to his or her subordinates.

Among the directives, there are those that are confidential, even within the company, and those that must not go outside the company. It is necessary to take care not to leak any confidential information.

18-1 事故再発防止のための対策を指示する

Presenting a plan to prevent the recurrence of an accident

スミス支社長は、納入品カーペットの事故が発生したことに関して、関係の各部門に対して事故原因を指摘し、具体的な改善策の実施を指示します。

Office Manager Smith, in connection with the occurrence of the carpet incident, points out the cause of that accident to all related departments and directs the implementation of a specific plan for improvement.

営第○○○号

199○年○月○日

営業・製造・資財・運輸

各部門関係　各位

支社長（印）

<u>吉田物産納めカーペット事故の件</u>

吉田物産が当社と提携し、日本におけるS&A製品の販売に大きな力となっていることは、皆さんのご承知のとおりです。

最近、その吉田物産に納入しているデューク社開発のカーペット「デュクロン」に汚損事故が発生しました。調査の結果、汚損は製造後、当社戸田工場内での積み替え時に、フォークリフトから油漏れしたものと判明しました。

クレームは、担当の営業部門の敏速な処理によって、汚損の現品を全量当社で回収し、代替品を再出荷するということで事なきを得ました。

しかし、今回の事故は、一つ誤ればせっかく滑り出した提携関係にヒビを入れかねないものであり、当社もこのため余分な作業と予定外の出費を余儀なくされました。

このような事故を二度と繰り返さないために、各位が次のことを励行するよう望みます。

①日本の当社倉庫はもとより、アトランタ工場などの外地倉庫出荷時の品質検査書をファイルしておくこと。

②包装は充分に行なうこと。

③高価品には、「取扱注意」、「水漏れ、油漏れ厳禁」、「フック厳禁」などのラベルを用意し、貼付を励行すること。

④クレームが発生したときは、自分だけの一存で処理しないで、営業その他関係者と連携して、会社全体として総合的な対策を講ずること。

⑤クレーム処理は、誠意をもって迅速に行なうこと。特に時間が大切。処理を適切迅速に行なえば、かえって当社に対する客先の信頼が増すものであることを認識すること。

以　上

（写）上記以外の各部

資材：materials　運輸：transportation　～納め：delivered to ～　提携する：tie up　納入する：deliver　汚損：damage by staining　フォークリフト：forklift　判明する：come to light; be discovered　クレーム：complaint　敏速な処理：prompt action　回収する：take back; withdraw　代替品：replacement goods　再出荷：redeliver　事なきを得る：settle problem smoothly　一つ誤れば：if a mistake takes place　滑り出す：begin　ヒビを入れかねない：can cause a rift　余儀なくされる：be forced to　励行する：strive　～はもとより：not to mention ～　品質検査書：quality check records　包装：packaging　～厳禁：protect from ～; No ～　フック：hook　貼付：pasting　～の一存で処理する：take/handle on one's own　連携する：work in cooperation　対策を講ずる：devise measures　クレーム処理：handling a complaint　誠意をもって：with sincerity　適切迅速に行う：handle properly and promptly　かえって：all the more　認識する：recognize

Sales Document # __________
Date (year, month, day)

Everyone related to the following departments:
Sales, Manufacturing, Materials, Transportation

Office Manager (seal)

RE: Incident involving carpet delivered to Yoshida Trading

You all are aware of how the sale of S&A merchandise in Japan has been strengthened by our tie-up with Yoshida Trading.

Recently, stains were discovered in Dukelon, the carpet developed by Duke Corporation, that had been delivered to Yoshida Trading. The results of an investigation proved that the staining occurred after manufacturing—at our Toda factory when it was being moved to another place—by oil that leaked from a forklift.

Because of the prompt action of the sales department people responsible, taking back all of the stained merchandise and delivering new merchandise in its place, the complaint was settled smoothly.

This incident, however, could well have caused a rift in an only recently begun relationship, if a big mistake had taken place. Our company unavoidably had to spend extra time and unexpected expense on account of the incident.

In order to prevent the repetition of this type of incident, I hope each of you will strictly enforce the following.

(1) File all quality check records from the shipment related to our company's warehouse in Japan as well as overseas factories like the Atlanta factory.
(2) Package every item adequately.
(3) Prepare labels that say "Handle with care," "Protect from liquid spills," and "No hooks," and paste them on all high-priced items.
(4) When a complaint occurs, do not try to take care of it by yourself, but rather work together with other related persons and devise comprehensive steps to deal with it at the company level.
(5) Complaints should be handled promptly and with sincerity. Timing is especially important. Be aware that prompt, appropriate handling of complaints may lead to an increase, rather than a decrease, in the customer's level of trust.

(the end)

(Copies) to all departments not included above

留意事項

1)指示・通達の文書は、特に重要な文書なので、後日問題となることのないよう事前に関係部門と周到(しゅうとう)な意見調整をしたうえで発信するようにします。

2)実務に即(そく)した注意事項（上の例では業務システムの改善）を列挙(れっきょ)します。

3)重要事項の場合は、関連する他部門へも同文の写(うつし)を配布します。

4)一般に社内文書では、頭語(とうご)・結語(けつご)や初めと終わりのあいさつを省(はぶ)き、文書末は「以上」とします。

1. Directives and notices are particularly important documents, so it is sometimes important to carefully obtain the views of related departments before sending them out, in order to avoid problems later.

2. List the matters requiring attention (in the above example, they deal with systems of doing business) to meet the needs of the directive.

3. When important matters are concerned, distribute a copy to all relevant departments.

4. Generally speaking, salutations, complimentary closes, and opening and closing greetings are omitted for in-house documents. Use 以上 (the end) to indicate the close of a document.

18-2 経費節減の方策を指示する
Directing a plan for cost reduction

スミス支社長は、各部門長に対して、経営方針としてコスト節減について全社をあげて取り組むよう指示します。

Office Manager Smith directs all department managers to engage in a management policy of cost reduction across the entire company.

総第○○○号
199○年○月○日

各部長・工場長殿

支社長　ハワード　G. スミス
(サイン)

コスト節減に係る件

戦後最長の不況といわれる現在、当社は、企業の永続的な発展のため、下記のとおりコスト節減の諸方策を実施のこととした。

ついては、この趣旨を全社に周知徹底させ、収支改善に努められたい。

記

1．事務所賃料

ビル賃借料が低落している現在、契約更新時も近いので、交渉に当っては、厳しい線で臨みたい。併せて、経費節減のため事務所移転も含めて検討のこととしたい。

2．3Kの見直し

いわゆる3K（広告費、交際費、交通費）については、平常からも、費用対効果の点から注意してきたことであるが、この際、全面的に見直しのこととする。総務部及び経理部において月間実績を作成、報告のこと。

3．事務経費

コピー、ファックス、電話、通信費、書類等急送便、文具用紙類など事務経費については、総務部においてチェック・リストを作成、毎月の数字を報告のこと。

4．健康管理

社員全員が各自の健康管理に努めることは、結局、会社としても家族としても最大の経費節減である。

以上、全社的に、公私ともムダ、ムリ、ムラなく、永続的な発展を期したい。

以　上

コスト節減：cost reduction　永続的な発展：continued development　諸方策を実施：put various measures into effect　趣旨：aim　周知徹底させる：thoroughly let all know　収支改善：improving of income and expenditure　賃料：rent　低落する：experience decline　契約更新時が近い：the time for renewing contracts is near　厳しい線で臨む：take a tough stance　経費：costs　移転：movement　検討：examining　見直し：reexamining　交際費：social expenses　費用対効果の点から：from the viewpoint of cost performance　月間実績：monthly results　公私とも：in both private and public matters　ムラ：inconsistency; unevenness　～を期す：look forward to ～

General Affairs Document # ______
Date (year, month, day)

The Honorable Managers of all departments and the factory

Office Manager Howard G. Smith
(signature)

RE: Cost reduction

Because we are presently experiencing the longest recession since the war, for the continuing development of business, this company has put into effect the following policies related to cost reduction.

Therefore, I would like to make all of the company thoroughly aware of the aims to improve our income and expenditures.

Details

1. Office rental
   As we are presently experiencing a decline in the rent from tenants and the time for the renewal of contracts is drawing near, I want us to take a tough stance as we approach these negotiations. Along with this, I would like to examine moving our offices as a way of reducing costs.
2. Reexamining the three soft expenses
   With regard to the three soft expenses (advertising, social expenses, and travel), we have normally been careful from the viewpoint of cost performance, but at this time I want to conduct an overall reexamination. The general affairs department and the accounting department will put together monthly results and report them to us.
3. Office expenses
   The general affairs department will construct a check list for office expenses, which include copying, fax machine, telephone, mailing, express mailing of documents, and stationery items, then report monthly figures.
4. Health
   Having each individual employee work at maintaining his or her own health is a major factor in cost reduction both for the company and for the family.

In closing, I look forward to continued development, without waste, without overwork, and without inconsistency in both public and private matters.

(the end)

留意事項

1)社内に徹底するよう、箇条書きで具体的に実施項目を指示します。

2)経営トップの経営方針を示す文書として、全社員に対して理解しやすく書き、日常業務のなかで実行できる内容を具体的に示します。

3)社内文書ですから、頭語や結語、初めと終わりのあいさつなどは省略します。

4)記書きを用いて簡潔に重要事項を列記し、指示内容を際立たせ、読む者の注意を促します。記書きは「以上」で終わります。

1. Using the outline form, be specific when indicating the areas to be enforced throughout the company.

2. As it is a document showing the management policies of the top management, write so that all employees will easily understand, showing specifically how the policies can be carried out in daily business practices.

3. This is an in-house document, and so salutation, complimentary close, and opening and closing greetings are omitted.

4. Concisely list the important items in the "記書(きが)き" section, so that the directives are emphasized and the reader is encouraged to notice. Use 以上 (the end) to indicate the conclusion of the section.

18-1と18-2のフローと文例

18-1「事故再発防止のための対策を指示する」のフロー

吉田物産納め(おさ)カーペット事故の件

吉田物産が当社と提携(ていけい)し、日本におけるS&A製品の販売に大きな力となっていることは、皆さんのご承知のとおりです。

最近、その吉田物産に納入(のうにゅう)しているデューク社開発のカーペット「デュクロン」に汚損(おそん)事故が発生しました。調査の結果、汚損は製造後、当社戸田工場内での積み替え時に、フォークリフトから油漏(も)れしたものと判明しました。

クレームは、担当の営業部門の敏速(びんそく)な処理(しょり)によって、汚損の現品を全量当社で回収し、代替(だいたい)品を再出荷するということで事なきを得ました。

しかし、今回の事故は、一つ誤(あやま)ればせっかく滑(すべ)り出した提携関係にヒビを入れかねないものであり、当社もこのため余分な作業と予定外の出費を余儀(よぎ)なくされました。

——①指示するいきさつを説明する

このような事故を二度と繰り返さないために、各位が、次のことを励行(れいこう)するよう望みます。——②指示する

①日本の当社倉庫はもとより、アトランタ工場などの外地倉庫出荷時の品質検査書をファイルしておくこと。

②包装(ほうそう)は充分に行なうこと。　(後略)

——③記—指示内容

以　上

(写(うつし)) 上記以外の各部

18-2「経費節減(けいひせつげん)の方策を指示する」のフロー

コスト節減(せつげん)に係(かかわ)る件

戦後最長の不況といわれる現在、当社は、企業の永続的な発展のため、下記のとおりコスト節減の諸(しょ)方策を実施(じっし)のこととした。——①指示するいきさつを説明する

ついては、この趣旨(しゅし)を全社に周知徹底(しゅうちてってい)させ、収支改善に努(つと)められたい。——②指示する

記

1．事務所賃料(ちんりょう)

ビル賃借料が低落している現在、契約更新(けいやくこうしん)時も近いので、交渉(こうしょう)に当っては、厳(きび)しい線で臨(のぞ)みたい。併(あわ)せて、経費(けいひ)節減のため事務所移転も含めて検討のこととしたい。

2．3Kの見直し

いわゆる3K（広告費、交際費、交通費）については、平常からも、費用対効果の点から注意してきたことであるが、この際、全面的に見直しのこととする。総務部及び経理部において月間実績を作成、報告のこと。（後略）

——③記—指示内容

以上、全社的に、公私ともムダ、ムリ、ムラなく、永続的な発展を期(き)したい。

以　上

（下線の部分は自分の状況に合わせて書いてください。）

①指示するいきさつを説明する（現状報告、今後の影響など）

Explaining the circumstances of instructions (reporting the present state of affairs, future influences, etc.)

②指示する

Instructing

＊このような事故を二度と繰(く)り返さないために、各位が次のことを励行(れいこう)するよう望みます。(18-1)

In order to prevent the repetition of this type of incident, I hope each of you will strictly enforce the following.

＊この趣旨(しゅし)を全社に周知徹底(しゅうちてってい)させ、収支改善に努(つと)められたい。(18-2)

I would like to make all of the company thoroughly aware of the aims to improve our income and expenditures.

＊「国内旅費規定」について、次のとおり一部を改正し、本日より実施(じっし)することとなったので通知する。

With regard to our domestic travel cost regulations, note that a part of it has been revised and becomes valid today.

③記――指示内容

Description—contents of instructions

〈指示内容の書き方〉

How to write the contents of instructions

＊クレームが発生した**ときは**、自分だけの一存(いちぞん)で処理(しょり)し**ないで**、会社全体として総合的な対策を講ずる**こと**。(18-1)

When a complaint occurs, do not try to take care of it by yourself, but devise comprehensive steps to deal with it at the company level.

＊クレーム処理(しょり)**は**、誠意(せいい)をもって迅速(じんそく)に行なう**こと**。(18-1)

Complaints should be handled promptly and with sincerity.

＊事務経費(けいひ)**については**、総務部においてチェック・リストを作成、毎月の数字を報告**のこと**。(18-2)

The general affairs department will construct a check list for office expenses and report monthly figures.

18-3 人事異動の辞令を出す
Announcing personnel appointments

S&A社では、臨時の人事異動を発令することとなり、営業二課長に対して異動の辞令を出します。
At S&A Corporation, a temporary personnel change is announced whereby the sales section two chief will be notified of a change in position.

辞　令

営業部営業二課長
橋本　進

戸田工場倉庫課長を命ずる

199○年○月○日
S&A コーポレーション日本支社
(社印)

Official Announcement of Appointment

Sales Section Two Chief
Hashimoto Susumu

is appointed as Toda Factory Warehouse Section Chief

(year, month, day)
S&A Corporation, Japan Office
(company seal)

留意事項

1)辞令は、採用・昇進・昇給・勤務部署の異動・退職などの場合に、会社が役員・社員に対して交付する文書です。

2)辞令は普通、社長または担当役員や部門長から手渡されますが、本人に口頭で申し渡すこともあります。

3)辞令の用紙は、やや厚手のものが一般的です。大きさや様式、縦書きか横書きかなどは、会社によって決まっています。

1. Official announcements of appointment are delivered to officers and employees by the company at the time of employment, promotion, raise in salary, change in work assignment, and retirement.

2. Official announcements of appointment are usually handed out personally by the office manager, office in charge, or section chief, but sometimes the person involved is told by word of mouth.

3. A fairly heavy weight of paper is used for these official announcements. The size and style, and whether it is written vertically or horizontally, is decided by the company.

18-4 人事異動の通達を出す

Issuing an official notice of personnel changes

S&A社の人事担当部門は、社内に人事異動の通達を出します。

The personnel section of S&A Corporation issues a notification of personnel changes within the company.

社内回覧

総人第○○○号
199○年○月○日

総務部長　青山忠夫（印）

社内人事異動につき次のとおり通知する。

社内人事異動通知（○月）

日　　付	氏　名	新	旧
199○年○月○日	橋本　進	戸田工場倉庫課長	営業部営業二課長
199○年○月○日	中山四郎	営業部営業二課長	戸田工場倉庫課長
199○年○月○日	山川孝夫	営業部営業一課	総務部総務課

社内回覧：in-house circular notice

In-house circular notice

General Personnel Document # ________
Date (year, month, day)

General Affairs Department Manager
Aoyama Tadao (seal)

Giving notice on account of personnel changes within the company.

Notification of personnel changes within the company (Month)

Date	Name	New position	Former position
(Year, month, day)	Hashimoto Susumu	Toda Factory Warehouse Section Chief	Sales Department Sales Section Two Chief
(Year, month, day)	Nakayama Shiro	Sales Department Sales Section Two Chief	Toda Factory Warehouse Section Chief
(Year, month, day)	Yamakawa Takao	Sales Department Sales Section One	General Affairs Department General Affairs Section

留意事項

1) 新採用・昇進・昇給・勤務部署の異動・退職など役員・社員の人事に関する異動事項は、人事通達（または人事通知）として社内に周知されます。

2) 発令月日、氏名、新旧役職名、所属場所等を明記します。

3) 人事異動の場合、辞令は本人に渡し、異動の通知は社内に回覧します。

1. Matters related to the personnel moves (either officers or employees), such as through new employment, promotions, a raise in salary, changes in work assignment, and retirements, are made known within the company by means of personnel notices.

2. Make clear the effective date, name, new and former positions, location of assignment, and so on.

3. In the case of personnel moves, the official announcement is given to the person and the notification of that move is circulated within the company.

18-5 履歴書
Résumé

S&A社は、社員の採用にあたって履歴書の提出を求め、日時を決めて採用試験をします。クラークさんは、同社の海外部門の採用試験に応募するため、履歴書を書きます。

When hiring new employees, S&A Corporation asks them to submit a résumé, and then sets a date for an employment examination. Ms. Clarke writes a résumé for the purpose of applying to take the employment examination for the company's overseas department.

写真を貼る必要がある場合
1. 縦 36 ~ 40 mm
横 24 ~ 30 mm
2. 本人単身胸から上

履 歴 書 1998年 12月 1 日現在

ふりがな りさ じぇーん くらーく	※男·女 (女)
氏名 Lisa Jane Clarke	印 LJ Clarke
1969年 10月 20日生 (満 29 才)	本籍 アメリカ合衆国 ※ 都道府県

ふりがな とうきょうと せたがやく せいじょう 現住所 東京都世田谷区成城 7-30-11 〒(157-0066) 山田 方	電話 市外局番(03) 3453-2797 (方呼出)
ふりがな 連絡先（現住所以外に連絡を希望する場合のみ記入） 〒(-)	電話 市外局番( ) (方呼出)

年	月	学歴·職歴（各別にまとめて書く）
		学　歴
1988	9	ハワイ大学社会科学部入学（経済学専攻）
1992	6	同校卒業
1992	9	ハワイ大学経営学大学院修士課程入学
1994	6	同課程修了
		MBA（経営学修士）取得
		職　歴
1994	9	NTA International (California) に入社
		営業部勤務　現在に至る
		（顧客開拓を担当）
		賞　罰
		なし
		以上

本籍：legal domicile　満～歳：～ years of age　～方呼出：care of ～　経営学修士取得：graduated with master of business administration　職歴：work experience　現在に至る：currently still doing　顧客開拓：cultivation of customers　賞罰：(record of) awards and penalties　特技：specialties　扶養家族：family dependents　配偶者：spouse　～を除く：except for ～　保護者：contact person; sponsor　未成年者：persons under 20

年	月	免許・資格
1995	2	日本語能力試験２級合格

特技・好きな学科・志望の動機など	
マーケティング論 水泳、スキー、旅行	勤務開始可能日　月　日 最寄駅　線　駅 通勤時間　約　時間 50 分 配偶者　※ 有・無（無に○） 配偶者の扶養義務　※ 有・無 扶養家族数(配偶者を除く)　なし　人

本人希望記入欄(特に給料・職種・勤務時間・勤務地・その他についての希望があれば記入)
貴社海外部門を希望

備考欄

保護者(本人が未成年者の場合のみ記入) ふりがな		電話 市外局番(　　) － (　　方呼出)
氏　名	住　所(〒　　－　　)	

採用者側の記入欄(応募者は記入しないこと)

Résumé December 1, 1998

Name: Lisa Jane Clarke (seal), Female (circled)
Date of birth: 1969, October 20 (29 years of age) Legal domicile: America (U.S.A.)
Present address: Tokyo-to, Setagaya-ku, Seijo 7-30-11, c/o Yamada, Code 157-0066
Telephone: 03-3453-2797

Schooling, work experience (write each category together):
Schooling
1988/September—Entered College of Social Sciences, University of Hawaii (major in economics)
1992/June—Graduated from same
1992/September—Entered graduate course, College of Business Administration, University of Hawaii
1994/June—Graduated from same
with MBA (Master of Business Administration)
Work experience
1994/September—Entered NTA International (California)
Still working in the sales department
(responsible for cultivation of customers)
Record of rewards and penalties: None

(the end)

Licenses, certifications:
1995/February—Passed Japanese language strength test, second level

Specialties, favorite subjects, etc.:
Marketing theory, swimming, skiing, traveling

Commuting time: 50 minutes Spouse: no (circled) Family dependents: None

Special requests (salary, type of work, commuting time, duties, etc.):
I request the overseas department in your company.

留意事項

1) 履歴書(りれき)の用紙は、市販のものか会社所定のものを使い、封筒に入れて出します。その際、封筒の中央より左下に「履歴書在中」と赤で書いておきます。
2) できるだけていねいな、わかりやすい文字で書きます。万年筆かボールペンを使って自筆で書きます。
3) 学歴・職歴などは、それぞれ別々にまとめて書きます。学歴・職歴の「年月」は、古いものから順番に書くようにします。学歴は普通、大学入学のときから書き、職歴は勤務先や仕事について最初から現在までを書きます。
4) 「賞罰(しょうばつ)」には、普通、「なし」と書きますが、公的または社会的な賞を受けた場合は、その旨(むね)を書きます。
5) 「賞罰」のあとに、「以上」と書きます。

1. When writing a résumé, use either a form you can buy or one furnished by the company. Place it in an envelope and send it by mail. Write 履歴書在中 (résumé included) in red in the lower left corner of the envelope.
2. Write as politely and clearly as you can. Write by hand, using either a fountain pen or ballpoint pen.
3. When describing schooling or work experience, write in chronological order, beginning with your earliest experience and progressing toward the present. Start with your entrance into college or university. For work experience, include everything from your first job to your present job.
4. Usually you will have nothing to write in the Record of Rewards and Penalties section, so write なし (none). If you have received a public award, include it here.
5. Write 以上 (the end) after the Rewards and Penalties section.

第19課

取引先を招待する

Sending invitations to business associates

取引先やお世話になった相手を、役員交代や創業記念、支店開設などのパーティーのほか、新製品発表会などの会合や催しに招待して、お互いの関係を深めることがあります。また、役員や担当者をゴルフや食事などに招待することもあります。

招待にあたっては、準備や当日の催しの進行について十分な心配りが必要です。

There are times when you will invite business associates and others to whom you are indebted to attend gatherings or functions, such as receptions for new officers, anniversaries of the founding of the company, or parties for the opening of a new branch, as well as exhibitions for new products, and so on, to deepen your relationship with them. You might also invite company officials or responsible persons to play golf or have dinner.

It is necessary to make adequate preparations in advance, and then facilitate running the event on the day it takes place.

社外　招待する〈招待状〉 invitation

19-1 取引成立のお礼に、紹介者を宴席に招待する

Inviting the person responsible for introducing a company to a banquet to thank him for a contract to be concluded

S＆A社のスミス支社長は、吉田物産との取り引きがまとまったので、紹介者である東京商事の小川営業部長を食事に招待します。

Office Manager Smith of S&A Corporation invites Sales Manager Ogawa of Tokyo Shoji to dinner to thank him for what he did to make the tie-up between S&A Corporation and Yoshida Trading possible.

拝啓　晩秋の候　ますますご清栄のこととお慶び申し上げます。平素は格別のご愛顧にあずかり深謝申し上げます。

過日は、ご多用のところ、わざわざ吉田物産株式会社の山田営業部長殿をご紹介賜り、誠にありがとうございました。

その後、同社と「デュクロン」の販売取引につき交渉中でしたが、このほど価格など取引条件が整い、契約締結の運びとなりました。

今回の成約は、ひとえに貴台のご厚情、ご支援によるものと改めて御礼申し上げる次第でございます。

つきましては、諸事ご多端の折からとは存じますが、御礼までに粗餐を差し上げたく、左記によりご出席くださいますようお願い申し上げます。

右、取りあえず書中ご案内申し上げます。

敬具

記

一、日　時　十一月二十六日(木曜日)　午後六時三十分より

二、場　所　料亭「田辺」　中央区築地八—五—四

（電話　三八八四—一一三八）

なお、当方出席者は、私及び営業部長山本の二名でございます。

再拝

平成十年十一月四日

S&Aコーポレーション日本支社

日本支社長　ハワード　G・スミス

（サイン）

東京商事株式会社

営業部長　小川　正様

侍史

格別の愛顧にあずかる：receive special support　深謝する：thank deeply　過日：some time ago　取引条件が整う：work out business terms　契約締結の運びとなる：be at the stage of signing a contract　成約：conclusion of a contract　貴台のご厚情：your kindness　支援：support　～によるもの：due to ～　諸事ご多端の折からとは存じますが：I know you are extremely busy now, but . . .　粗餐：dinner　料亭：(Japanese-style) restaurant

Salutations: As autumn draws to a close, allow me to congratulate you on your good health and well-being. Allow me also to express my deep appreciation for your special support at all times.

Thank you for taking the trouble the other day, when you were very busy, to introduce us to Mr. Yamada, the sales department manager of Yoshida Trading, Incorporated.

After that, we negotiated with that company about the sale of Dukelon, and we have finally worked out terms, such as price, and are now at the stage of signing a contract.

Conclusion of the contract at this time is entirely due to your kindness and support, and again I wish to express my appreciation.

In this regard, I know that you are extremely busy now, but I would like to offer you a dinner, as set out below, to thank you for your assistance, and I ask that you kindly agree to attend.

I am sending you this invitation at this time.

Sincerely yours

Details

1. Date, time: November 26 (Thursday), beginning at 6:30 P.M.
2. Location: Tanabe Restaurant Chuo-ku, Tsukiji 8-5-4 (TEL: 3884-1138)

Please note that two of us will be attending from here, myself and Sales Department Manager Yamamoto.

Thank you again.

November 4, 1998

S&A Corporation, Japan Office
Office Manager Howard G. Smith
(signature)

Tokyo Shoji, Incorporated
Sales Department Manager Ogawa Tadashi (Mr.)
Respectfully

留意事項

1) この例は、あらかじめ相手の都合(つごう)を口頭(こうとう)で聞いてから手紙を出すケースで、出欠の返事などには触れていません。このように、日時などだいたいのことは、あらかじめ秘書などを通じて打ち合わせ、招待状(しょうたい)は確認の意味を持つだけのことがあります。その場合にも、接待(せったい)の前日には、招待する側から再度出席を確かめるようにします。

2) 前文で日ごろの好意(こうい)に対してお礼を述(の)べてから、招待の趣旨(しゅし)、内容を書きます。日時、場所などは箇条(かじょう)書きにします。場所の案内図などを同封しておくと便利です。招待する側の出席者を書いておくことも大切です。

3) 招待文では、最近は横書きも見られます。横書きのときは「左記」は「下記」となります。

4) 宛名(あてな)の左下の「侍史(じし)」は、書き手の謙遜(けんそん)の気持ちを表すことばです。

1. This example does not mention how the invited party should reply that he will be able to attend or not. This is because he has already been contacted, and it was found that he could attend. In this way, there are cases when the invitation is sent only to confirm the information, having contacted the other party through his secretary, etc., and arranging in advance such general things as date and time. Even in a case like this, it is still advisable that the person issuing the invitation call the day before to reconfirm whether the other party can still attend.

2. After offering thanks for the goodwill of the other person in the opening sentence, write the purpose and details of the invitation. Put the date, time, and location in outline form. It is handy to include a map showing how to get to the location. It is also important to tell who will be present.

3. Invitations written in the horizontal style are sometimes seen these days. When written in this way, 左記 (left) becomes 下記 (below).

4. The word 侍史(じし) (respectfully), written to the left of the address's name, expresses the writer's humility.

19-2 記念パーティーに招待する
Issuing an invitation to an anniversary party

Ｓ＆Ａ社は、日本支社の昇格一周年を記念してパーティーを開き、取引先などを招待します。
On the first anniversary of S&A Corporation's Tokyo Office becoming the Japan Office, the company holds a party and invites business associates and others to attend.

謹啓　時下ますますご清栄のこととお慶び申し上げます
　平素は格別のご高配にあずかり誠にありがたく御礼申し上げます
　さて　この度　弊社は支社昇格一周年を迎えることとなりました
　つきましては　別記により小宴を催しご挨拶申し上げたく存じますので　ご繁忙のところ恐縮でございますが　なにとぞご来臨賜りたくご案内申し上げます　　敬具

Ｓ＆Ａコーポレーション
日本支社長
ハワード　Ｇ．スミス

記

1．日　時　　199○年○月○日（火曜日）
　　　　　　午前11時30分から
　　　　　　午後1時30分まで
2．場　所　　帝国ホテル
　　　　　　パール・ルーム
　　　　　　（7階）
　　　　　（別添の案内図をご覧ください）

なお　お手数ですが　ご都合のほどを同封のハガキにより○月○日までにご回示賜りたく
また　ご出席の際は本状封筒を受付にお出しくださいますようお願い申し上げます

格別の高配にあずかる：receive special consideration　昇格：upgrading　～周年を迎える：reach our ～th anniversary　小宴を催す：host a small party　繁忙のところ：when being extremely busy　ご来臨賜りたく：hope you can attend　別添の：attached; included　ご都合のほど：whether or not you can attend　回示賜る：receive your reply

(left side)

Salutations: Allow me to congratulate you on your good health and well-being at this time.

I am extremely grateful for the special gift of consideration you continually give us.

Now, our company is reaching its first anniversary since being upgraded to the Japan Office.

Because of this, we will host a small party, as noted elsewhere, and extend our greetings to you. Though I know you are extremely busy, I hope it will be possible for you to attend.

Sincerely yours

S&A Corporation

Japan Office

Howard G. Smith

(right side)

Details

1. Date, time: (year, month, day) (Tuesday),
   11:30 A.M.-1:30 P.M.
2. Location: Imperial Hotel
   Pearl Room (seventh floor)
   (Map included)

In addition, it is a bother, but I would like to ask you to return the enclosed postcard indicating whether you will be able to attend or not by (month, day). When you arrive, please present the envelope at the reception table.

留意事項

1) 招待状(しょうたい)では、句読点(くとうてん)を省略(しょうりゃく)することがあります。

2) 招待状には、日時（曜日、開始時刻・終了時刻）、場所などを明記します。また、会場への案内図を添(そ)えます。

3) 終わりのあいさつは、この例のように省略することがあります。

4) 上の例では、一周年記念である旨(むね)の通知を兼(か)ねた形になっています。

5) 多数の人が参加するパーティーでは、期限を示した出欠回答のはがきを同封するようにします。19-5に回答の書き方例があります。

1. You may omit punctuation marks in an invitation.

2. The date, day of the week, starting and closing time, and location are written clearly. Also include a map of the location.

3. As in this example, the closing greeting may be omitted.

4. This example is not only an invitation but also an announcement of the company's first anniversary.

5. When a number of people are being invited to a party, include a return postcard indicating whether they will attend or not. An example of such a postcard is found in 19-5.

19-1と19-2のフローと文例

19-1「取引成立のお礼に、紹介者を宴席に招待する」のフロー

①招待する理由を述べる

拝啓　晩秋の候　ますますご清栄のこととお慶び申し上げます。平素は格別のご愛顧にあずかり深謝申し上げます。

過日は、ご多用のところ、わざわざ吉田物産株式会社の山田営業部長殿をご紹介賜り、誠にありがとうございました。

その後、同社と「デュクロン」の販売取引につき交渉中でしたが、このほど価格など取引条件が整い、契約締結の運びとなりました。

今回の成約は、ひとえに貴台のご厚情、ご支援によるものと改めて御礼申し上げる次第でございます。

②招待する

つきましては、諸事ご多端の折からとは存じますが、御礼までに粗餐を差し上げたく、左記によりご出席くださいますようお願い申し上げます。

右、取りあえず書中ご案内申し上げます。

敬具

記

③記――招待内容

一、日　時　十一月二十六日(木曜日)　午後六時三十分より

二、場　所　料亭「田辺」　中央区築地八―五―四

（電話　三八八四―一一三八）

なお、当方出席者は、私及び営業部長山本の二名でございます。

再拝

19-2「記念パーティーに招待する」のフロー

①招待する理由を述べる

謹啓　時下ますますご清栄のこととお慶び申し上げます

平素は格別のご高配にあずかり誠にありがたく御礼申し上げます

さて　この度　弊社は支社昇格一周年を迎えることとなりました

②招待する

つきましては　別記により小宴を催し　ご挨拶申し上げたく存じますので　ご繁忙のところ恐縮でございますが　なにとぞご来臨賜りたくご案内申し上げます　　敬具

S＆Aコーポレーション
日本支社長
ハワード　G．スミス

記

③記―招待内容

1．日　時　199○年○月○日（火曜日）
午前11時30分から
午後1時30分まで

2．場　所　帝国ホテル
パール・ルーム
(7階)
(別添の案内図をご覧ください)

なお　お手数ですが　ご都合のほどを同封のハガキにより○月○日までにご回示賜りたく
また　ご出席の際は本状封筒を受付にお出しくださいますようお願い申し上げます

（下線の部分は自分の状況に合わせて書いてください。）

①招待する理由を述べる

Giving a reason for an invitation

＊過日は、ご多用のところ、わざわざ吉田物産株式会社の山田営業部長殿をご紹介賜り、誠にありがとうございました。その後、同社と「デュクロン」の販売取引につき交渉中でしたが、このほど価格など取引条件が整い、契約締結の運びとなりました。今回の成約は、ひとえに貴台のご厚情、ご支援によるものと改めて御礼申し上げる次第でございます。(19-1)

［お礼のための招待の場合］

Thank you for taking the trouble the other day, when you were very busy, to introduce us to Mr. Yamada, the sales department manager of Yoshida Trading, Incorporated. After that, we negotiated with that company about the sale of Dukelon, and we have finally worked out terms, such as price, and now are at the stage of signing a contract. Conclusion of the contract at this time is entirely due to your kindness and support, and again I wish to express my appreciation. [An invitation when offering thanks]

＊この度　弊社は支社昇格一周年を迎えることとなりました　(19-2)［記念行事の場合］

Now, our company is reaching its first anniversary since being upgraded to the Japan Office. [In the case of a commemorative event]

＊この度の商品汚損事故につきましては、関係者一同反省し、二度とこのような失態を起こさないよう努める覚悟でございます。　［わびのための招待の場合］

Regarding the stained products, our staff concerned, having reflected on our business, are prepared to see that this type of accident never happens again. [In the case of inviting to make an apology]

②招待する

Inviting

＊諸事ご多端の折からとは存じますが、御礼までに粗餐を差し上げたく、左記によりご出席くださいますようお願い申し上げます。(19-1)　［お礼のための招待の場合］

I know that you are extremely busy now, but I would like to offer you a dinner, as set out below, to thank you for your assistance, and I ask that you kindly agree to attend. [An invitation when offering thanks]

＊別記により小宴を催し　ご挨拶を申し上げたく存じますので　ご繁忙のところ恐縮でございますが　なにとぞご来臨賜りたくご案内申し上げます　(19-2)

We will host a small party, as noted elsewhere, and extend our greetings to you. Though I know you are extremely busy, I hope it will be possible for you to attend.

＊お詫びかたがた、左記により、ささやかながら一席を設けたく存じますので、何卒ご出席下さいますよう、ご案内申し上げます。　［わびのための招待の場合］

By way of apologizing, we would like to hold what is merely a small party, as follows, so I ask that you kindly agree to attend. [In the case of inviting to make an apology]

③記——招待内容（日時、場所、当方の出席者、［返答日時、方法の明示］など）

Description—contents of invitation (date, place, attendants from the host company, [reply date, method of reply] etc.)

社外 通知する〈欠席通知〉 giving notice

19-3 招待の欠席を知らせる
Notifying that you will not be able to accept an invitation

S&A社の山本営業部長は、急用のため招待ゴルフを欠席することとし、その旨返事を出します。
Mr. Yamamoto, sales department manager of S&A Corporation, is not able to accept an invitation to play golf because of emergency business. He conveys this by letter.

拝復　晩秋の候　ますますご清栄のことと大慶に存じます。
平素より格別のご高配にあずかり厚く御礼申し上げます。
さて、この度は貴社ご恒例の「インテックス」杯ゴルフ会にお招きいただきまして、いつもながらのご芳情重ねて御礼申し上げます。
つきましては、○月○日当日は、急用にて海外に出張のこととなりましたので、誠に残念ながら、欠席とさせていただきたく存じます。
取りあえず御礼かたがたご連絡まで申し上げます。

敬　具

一九九○年○月○日

S&Aコーポレーション日本支社
営業部長　山本良雄　㊞

株式会社インテックス
営業部長　高橋吉男殿

格別の高配にあずかる：receive special consideration　恒例：customary　～杯：～ cup　いつもながらのご芳情：your kindness at all times

Salutations: As autumn ends, I rejoice at your increased good health and well-being.
I am extremely grateful for the special gift of consideration you continually give us.
Now, I thank you for inviting me to participate in Intex's customary golf tournament and also for your kindness at all times.
In this regard, because it has become necessary for me to be out of the country on business that day (month, day), I am sorry to say I will not be able to attend.
Again, I thank you for the invitation, but wanted to inform you of this.

Sincerely yours

Date (year, month, day)

S&A Corporation, Japan Office
Sales Department Manager Yamamoto Yoshio (seal)

Intex, Inc.
Sales Department Manager Takahashi Yoshio (Mr.)

留意事項

1)特に重要な相手先からの招待(しょうたい)などでは、電話だけの断りでは失礼なので、文書によってはっきりと通知します。

2)ゴルフなどのグループ行事を欠席するときはメンバー編成の迷惑(めいわく)になるので、なるべく早く返事を出すように気をつけます。

3)まず招待へのお礼を述(の)べてから、欠席のおわびをします。

1. Especially when you receive an invitation from an important business associate, saying you cannot attend only by phone is considered impolite, so put your refusal in writing and send it by mail.

2. When you do not participate in group activities, such as golf, this may cause trouble in organizing the event, so it is important to let them know as soon as possible that you will not attend.

3. First, thank the other party for the invitation and then apologize for not being able to attend.

19-4 私的な接待へ招待する

Issuing an invitation to a private reception

東京商事の小川部長は、ごく親しい友人のスミスを電話で相撲見物に誘いましたが、改めて招待の手紙を出します。

Manager Ogawa of Tokyo Shoji has called his good friend, Mr. Smith, and invited to go to a sumo tournament with him, and again repeats the invitation in a letter.

199○年○月○日

ハワード　G．スミス様

小　川　　正

（サイン）

拝呈　ご健勝のこととおよろこび申し上げます。

日本へのご着任以来、すっかりこの国のビジネスにとけこんで、ご活躍の趣を伺い誠に心強く、うれしく存じております。

さて、この度、折り好く大相撲の正月場所の枡席の券を手に入れましたので、ぜひご夫妻おそろいでおいで願いたく、ご案内申し上げます。家内もお久しぶりで奥様にお会いできるのを楽しみにいたしております。

どうぞ、当日は、午後4時ごろまでに、両国国技館の案内所へおいでください。

枡席の券2枚を同封しました。

では当日を楽しみに。

草　々

着任以来：since arriving　活躍の趣：doing a lot of business　折り好く：luckily　～場所：(name for each of the annual sumo tournaments)　枡席：box seats　手に入れる：get; obtain　夫妻おそろいで：you and your wife　両国国技館：(the arena in Tokyo where three of the six annual sumo tournaments are held)

Date (year, month, day)

Howard G. Smith (Mr.)

Ogawa Tadashi
(signature)

Greetings: Congratulations on your fine health.

I have been happy and encouraged to hear how you have become so used to business practices in Japan since you arrived in the country and are now doing business so widely.

Now, I was lucky to get tickets for box seats at the New Year's Sumo Tournament and would like you and your wife to attend. My wife is looking forward to seeing your wife again after such a long time.

Please come to the information desk at the Ryogoku Kokugikan by about 4:00 P.M. that day.

I am enclosing two box seat tickets.

I look forward to the day.

Yours truly

留意事項

1) この例は、ごく親しい間柄（あいだがら）の私的な手紙なので、堅苦（かたくる）しい表現を避けます。

2) 相手が場所をよく知らないと思われるときは、いつ、どこで待ち合わせるかなどを事前に確かめておきます。

3) 親しい相手に対しては、手書きにすることもあります。

1. This example is a personal letter between good friends, so avoid the use of stiff expressions.

2. When you do not think the other party will know much about the location, set up a meeting place ahead of time.

3. Letters written to good friends are sometimes written by hand.

19-5 出欠のはがき
Reply postcard (to indicate attendance/absence)

東京商事の小川部長は、パーティーの招待(しょうたい)を受けて、出席の返事を出します。(19-2参照)

Manager Ogawa of Tokyo Shoji receives an invitation to a party, and returns the reply postcard, indicating he will be able to attend. (See 19-2 for the invitation.)

(オモテ)

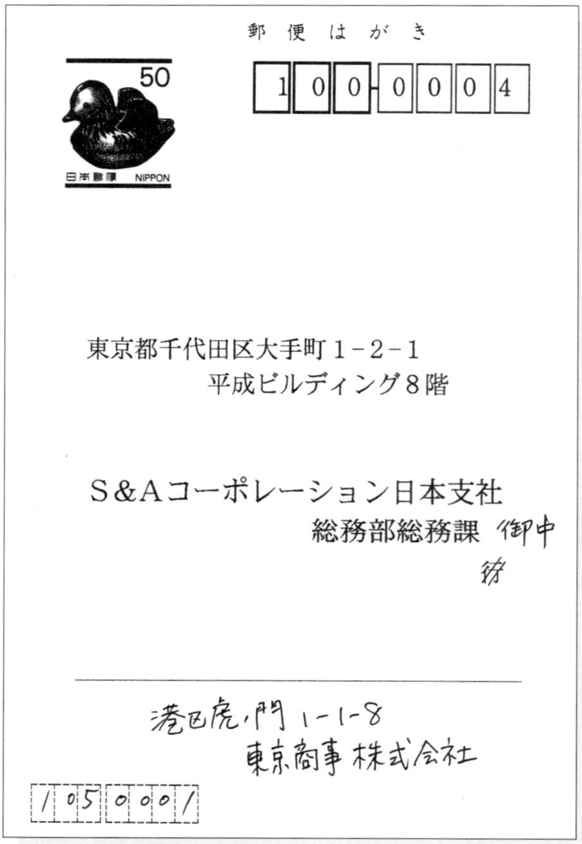

郵便はがき

100-0004

東京都千代田区大手町1-2-1
平成ビルディング8階

S&Aコーポレーション日本支社
総務部総務課 御中
~~様~~

港区虎ノ門1-1-8
東京商事株式会社
105 0001

(ウラ)

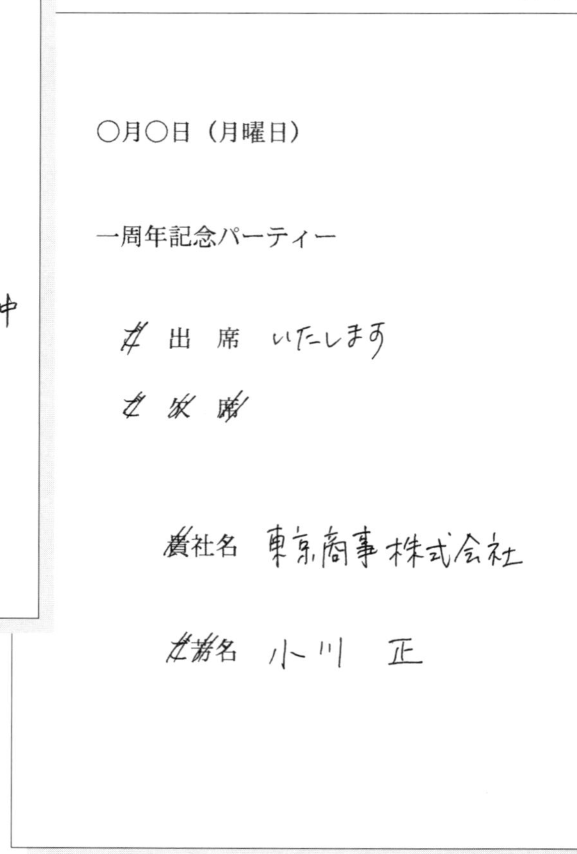

○月○日（月曜日）

一周年記念パーティー

~~御~~出席 いたします

~~御欠席~~

~~貴~~社名 東京商事株式会社

~~御芳~~名 小川 正

Month, day (Monday)
Anniversary Party
Will attend (circled)
Company name: Tokyo Shoji, Incorporated
Name: Ogawa Tadashi

留意事項

1) 出欠の返事は、できるだけ早く出します。
2) 宛名(あてな)の「行」は消して、「御中(おんちゅう)」(会社や団体宛) または「様」(個人) とします。
3) 「ご出席」「ご欠席」は、該当(がいとう)しないほうを消し、該当するほうについては「ご」を取って「いたします」を加え、「出席(欠席)いたします」とします。また、「貴社名」の「貴」や「ご芳名(ほうめい)」の「ご芳」を消しておきます。

1. Return the reply postcard as soon as possible.
2. Strike out the 行 (to) in the address, and write in the honorific 御中(おんちゅう) (for a postcard addressed to a company or organization) or 様 (if it is addressed to an individual).
3. Strike out whichever answer is not appropriate, and also strike out the honorific ご of the answer you select, since it applies to yourself, and add いたします (humble "will do") after that answer. Also eliminate other honorifics applied to your company or yourself, as the "貴" of 貴社名 and the "ご芳(ほう)" of ご芳名.

第20課

さまざまなあいさつ状

A variety of greetings

ビジネス文書には、業務を遂行するための公的な文書ばかりではなく、個人的な文書もあります。こういう社交文は、日常の業務文とは違い、企業やビジネスマン自身のいわば「品格」「人柄」を表すものとなります。

このような文書としては、災害・病気・時候（暑中／寒中）の見舞い、死去に対するお悔やみ、年賀状や喪中の欠礼あいさつ、お礼状などがあります。

Business letters are not only official documents for the carrying out of business. Sometimes you must write personal letters, too. These social letters, unlike regular business letters, are an expression of your own or your business's character.

These more personal letters include those sent in times of a disaster or illness, midsummer or end-of-the-year greetings, condolences, New Year's cards, in-mourning cards, and thank-you letters.

20-1 暑中見舞い
Midsummer greeting (letter of inquiry)

東京印刷は、関係先に出す暑中見舞いのはがきを作成します。
Tokyo Printing puts out a midsummer greeting to send to related businesses and persons.

暑中御見舞い申し上げます

例年にない暑さでございます
皆々様にはくれぐれもご自愛のほどお祈りいたします

一九九九年盛夏

〒一〇三-〇〇〇〇 東京都中央区八重洲三―五―一
有限会社 東京印刷
代表取締役 只野三平

例年にない暑さ：much hotter than in normal years くれぐれも：especially (used for emphasis) 自愛のほどお祈りする：pray you will be careful of your health 盛夏：midsummer 有限会社：limited (liability) company

We wonder how you are doing
in the heat of the summer.

It is much hotter than in normal years.
We pray that you will all be especially careful of your health.
1999 Midsummer

103-0000 Tokyo-to, Chuo-ku, Yaesu 3-5-1
Tokyo Printing, Ltd.
Representative Director Tadano Sanpei

留意事項

1)企業の PR 的なことばを入れる場合もあります。また、個人宛(あて)には、手書きで短いあいさつを入れると親しみが出ます。

2)差出人は、会社名のほかに代表者名などを入れる例が多く見られます。

3)季節のあいさつの手紙では、句読点(くとうてん)を書かない場合もあります。

1. Some businesses include a short phrase for public relations purposes. When sending to individuals, including a short note by hand adds familiarity.

2. In the place for the sender's name, you often see the name of the head of the company in addition to the company name.

3. Letters for seasonal greetings are not punctuated at times.

20-2 年賀状
New Year's card

S&A 日本支社長スミスは、年賀状を作成します。
S&A's Japan Office Manager Smith prints a New Year's card.

謹賀新年

旧年中のご愛顧を感謝いたしますとともに
本年もなお一層のお引き立てを賜りますよう
お願いいたします

一九九九年元旦

〒一〇〇-〇〇〇四 東京都千代田区大手町一の二の一
平成ビルディング八階
S&Aコーポレーション日本支社
支社長 ハワード G・スミス

謹賀新年：Happy New Year 旧年中のご愛顧を感謝する：thank you for the kindness you have shown in the past year なお一層の：even more お引き立てを賜る：receive more support 元旦：New Year's Day

Happy New Year

While thanking you for the favor you have shown us during the past year, I ask for even more support during this coming year.

1999 New Year's Day

100-0004 Tokyo-to, Chiyoda-ku, Otemachi 1-2-1
Heisei Building, Eighth Floor
S&A Corporation, Japan Office
Office Manager Howard G. Smith

留意事項

1)年賀状は、なるべく１月１日に着くように出します。郵便局の所定の受け付け日までに出すと、ほぼ間違いなく１月１日に配達されます。

2)印刷の本文は、定型的表現となるので、手書きで個人的なあいさつを書き添(そ)えると親しみが表わされます。

3)季節のあいさつの手紙では、句読点(くとうてん)を書かない場合もあります。

1. New Year's cards should be sent so that they will arrive on January 1. If you mail them by the deadline set by the post office, you can be almost certain they will be delivered on New Year's day.

2. Greetings printed on New Year's cards are fairly set and standard phrases, so you can add familiarity by writing a short personal note, too.

3. Letters for seasonal greetings are not punctuated at times.

20-3 喪中のはがき

In-mourning postcard

東京商事の小川部長は、私信で喪中のはがきを出し、新年のあいさつを欠礼します。

Manager Ogawa of Tokyo Shoji sends a private message to say that as he is in mourning, he will refrain from sending New Year's greetings this coming year.

亡母の喪中につき年末年始の
ご挨拶をご遠慮申し上げます

十月一日に母　文子が八十七才で永眠いたしました
皆々様一層のご自愛のほどお祈りいたします

一九九八年十二月

〒一一三-〇〇三二　東京都文京区弥生町二丁目五番三〇号
小　川　　正

亡母の喪中につき：because of being in mourning for my mother　年末年始の挨拶を遠慮する：refrain from sending year-end or New Year's greetings　永眠する：pass away　一層のご自愛のほどお祈りする：pray you will take care of yourself more

I will refrain from sending year-end or New Year's greetings this year because I am in mourning for my mother.

My mother, Fumiko, passed away on October 1, at the age of 87.

It is my prayer that you will take care of yourselves.

1998 December

113-0032 Tokyo-to, Bunkyo-ku, Yayoi-cho 2-5-30
Ogawa Tadashi

留意事項

1) 親族が亡くなったときには、翌年の年賀状は出しません。そして、その旨をあらかじめはがきで知らせておきます。普通、十二月の上旬ごろまでに出すようにします。
2) このはがきには、誰がいつ亡くなったかについて簡単に書き添えます。
3) 年月は、「十二月」とだけ書き、「日」は省きます。
4) 句読点は省略されることがあります。

1. When a relative dies, you do not send out New Year's cards the next year. Instead, you send out cards ahead of that time, informing everyone of the death. Try to send them out by the beginning of December.
2. Include a note simply explaining who died and when.
3. Write only the month and year. Do not include the day.
4. You may eliminate punctuation.

20-4 プレゼントのお礼の手紙

Letter of thanks for a gift

S&A日本支社長のスミスは、東京商事の小川部長から日本の「武者人形」を贈られました。それに対してお礼状を出します。

S&A's Japan Office Manager Smith received a samurai doll from Manager Ogawa of Tokyo Shoji. He sends a thank you for the gift.

謹啓　春暖の候　貴台には、ますますご清祥のことと大慶至極に存じ上げます。

　このたび、小生ことS&A日本支社長を命ぜられ、ニューヨーク本社より東京に着任いたしましたところ、早速に貴台よりご懇篤なるご祝詞を賜りご芳情のほど深謝申し上げます。また、重ねてこのほどは、誠に結構な日本伝統の「武者人形」の逸品をご恵贈にあずかり、改めてご友情に感佩いたしております。日本在勤の記念として、永く我が家に飾らせていただきたく存じます。

　妻も、米国でのご家族ともどものご交際を懐かしく回想し、再びご縁を得ましたことを心より喜んでおります。

　どうぞ今後とも相変わりませずご厚誼のほどお願いいたします。

　なお、末筆ながら貴台いよいよご自愛、ご発展のほど祈念いたします。取りあえず書中御礼まで申し述べます。

敬白

一九九〇年〇月〇日

ハワード・G・スミス
（サイン）

小川　正様

小生こと：I　着任する：arrive at one's new position　懇篤なる祝詞を賜る：receive a kind congratulatory message　ご芳情のほど：your kindness　深謝する：thank deeply　結構な：fine　武者人形：samurai doll　逸品：superb item　恵贈にあずかる：receive (a gift)　友情に感佩する：be grateful for your friendly consideration　懐かしく回想する：recall fondly　再び：again　縁を得る：have an opportunity to associate with　相変わりませず：as always　厚誼のほど：kindness　いよいよ：more and more; continued　自愛：taking care of your health　発展のほど祈念する：pray for development

Salutations: As the season begins to get warmer, I congratulate you greatly on your continuing good health and well-being.

On the occasion of my arrival in Tokyo from the New York headquarters to assume the job of S&A Corporation Japan Office manager, I received such a kind congratulatory message from you. Thank you very much. In addition, I recently received a very fine traditional Japanese samurai doll and am extremely grateful for your friendly consideration. We will display it in our home for a long time in commemoration of the time I will work here in Japan.

My wife also remembers fondly the times we spent together as families in the United States and is glad to have such an opportunity again.

As always, please continue to extend us your kindness in the future.

As I come to the end of the letter, I pray for your continued health and development.

I put my thanks into writing.

Yours truly

Date (year, month, day)

Howard G. Smith
(signature)

Ogawa Tadashi (Mr.)

留意事項

1) この例のような特に改(あらた)まった儀礼(ぎれい)的なあいさつ状の場合は、横書きでなく縦(たて)書きで書きます。

2) 個人的な手紙なので、会社名は省(はぶ)き、住所は（差出人も受取人も）個人の住所とします。

1. This type of formal letter of greeting is written in the vertical style, not the horizontal style.

2. This is a personal letter of thanks, so do not use the company name. Use personal addresses for both the sender and the addressee.

20-5 見舞(みま)いの手紙

Get well letter

S&A日本支社長のスミスは、病院に入院している東京商事の小川部長に対し、個人的に見舞状(みまいじょう)を出すとともに別便(べつびん)で見舞いの品を贈(おく)ります。

S&A's Japan Office Manager Smith sends a personal get well letter to Manager Ogawa of Tokyo Shoji, who is in the hospital, and he also sends a gift separately.

平成○年○月○日

小川　正様

ハワード　G. スミス
（サイン）

前略(ぜんりゃく)　このたび、貴台(きだい)には大学OBのサッカー対抗(たいこう)試合に出場の際、アキレス腱(けん)を切り、急遽(きゅうきょ)、慶応大学病院に入院された由(よし)承(うけたまわ)り、びっくりいたしました。平素(へいそ)から頑健(がんけん)そのもの、公私ともにご活躍(かつやく)の日常にて、病院などとは無縁(むえん)の方と、かねがねうらやましく存じていました。ご家族の皆様もさぞ驚かれたことと思います。

この際、まずは骨休めのひとときと受けとめられて、ご養生専一(ようじょうせんいつ)のうえ、一日も早く日頃のお元気なお姿に接(せっ)したく存じます。

別便(べつびん)にて心ばかりのお品をお届けさせていただきましたので、ご笑納(しょうのう)ください。

不日(ふじつ)、改(あらた)めてお見舞いに参上いたしますが、取り急ぎ書中をもってお見舞い申し上げます。

不　一

貴台(きだい)：you　OB：alumni　対抗試合(たいこうしあい)：match　アキレス腱(けん)を切る：tear Achilles' tendon　急遽(きゅうきょ)：suddenly; hastily　頑健(がんけん)そのもの：a picture of health　公私ともに：both publicly and privately　活躍(かつやく)：being active　～とは無縁(むえん)の方：the type who doesn't ～　かねがね：for a long time　うらやましく存じます：I envy (you)　さぞ：no doubt　まずは：first of all　骨休めのひとときと受けとめる：take this opportunity to rest　養生専一(ようじょうせんいつ)のうえ：concentrate on getting well　心ばかりの品：small gift　笑納(しょうのう)：accept　不日(ふじつ)：in the near future

Date (year, month, day)

Ogawa Tadashi (Mr.)

Howard G. Smith
(signature)

I hasten to write to express my surprise at hearing that you were suddenly hospitalized at Keio University Hospital because of a torn Achilles' tendon that you injured at a university alumni soccer match. I have envied you for a long time for always being so healthy and active, both publicly and privately, with never a need to go to the hospital. No doubt, your family must have been very surprised.

First of all, take this opportunity to rest and concentrate on getting well, so that you will soon be your healthy self once again.

I have taken the liberty of sending a small gift separately. Please accept it.

I will visit you in the near future, but am sending this written get well greeting in haste.

Yours truly

留意事項

1) 事態(じたい)を知ったら、すぐ手紙を出します。
2) 見舞(みま)いの文では、文頭のことばは省(はぶ)いて、直(ただ)ちに見舞いの用件に入ります。

1. Send a letter as soon as you hear of the situation.
2. In a get well letter, get directly to the business of wishing the other party well. Do not write an opening seasonal greeting.

20-6 お悔やみの手紙
Letter of condolence

S&A日本支社長のスミスは、東京商事の小川部長の母親が逝去したことを知って、お悔やみ状を出し、花を贈ります。

When S&A's Japan Office Manager Smith hears that the mother of Mr. Ogawa, manager of Tokyo Shoji, has died, he sends a letter of condolence and arranges to have flowers sent.

199◯年◯月◯日

東京商事株式会社
営業部長　小川　正様

S&Aコーポレーション
日本支社長　H. G. スミス
(サイン)

先日ご紹介いただきました吉田物産(株)との契約が成立しましたことのご報告を兼ね、一席設けたく存じましてご連絡しましたところ、ご母堂様のご不幸があったとの由承りました。気が付かぬこととは申しながら、今日まで存じませず、誠に申し訳ございません。深くおわび申し上げます。

皆様のお嘆きも一方でないこととお察し申し上げます。心よりお悔やみ申し上げ、ご冥福をお祈りいたします。

遅ればせながら、生花一対お届け申し上げましたので、ご仏前にお供えいただければと存じます。

いずれお目にかかりましたうえ、改めてごあいさつ申し上げますが、取りあえず書中をもちまして、おわびかたがたお悔やみ申し上げます。

契約が成立する：sign a contract　～を兼ねる：～ and at the same time　一席設ける：invite (to a party)　ご母堂様：your mother　ご不幸がある：die　気が付かぬこととは申しながら：though I just hadn't been aware　嘆きも一方でない：(your) sorrow is extremely deep　察する：guess　お悔やみを申し上げる：express condolences　冥福を祈る：pray for the repose of a person's soul　遅ればせながら：although it is late　生花一対：a set of flowers　仏前に供える：place near memorial tablet

Date (year, month, day)

Tokyo Shoji, Incorporated
Sales Department Manager Ogawa Tadashi (Mr.)

S&A Corporation
Japan Office Manager H. G. Smith
(signature)

When I was about to write to inform you that we had signed a contract with Yoshida Trading, to whom you had introduced us, and to invite you to a party to celebrate the event, I heard of the death of your mother. Even though I did not know about it until today, I feel badly not to have been aware sooner. Please forgive me.

I can only guess at the deep sorrow you all must be feeling. Allow me to express my deep condolences and to pray for the repose of your mother's soul.

Although it is late, I have sent flowers and ask that you place them near the memorial tablet for your deceased mother.

When I see you, I will once again express my condolences, but first I'll send this letter and again ask for your forgiveness.

留意事項

1) お悔(く)やみの文では、文頭のことばは省(はぶ)いて、いきなり弔慰(ちょうい)の用件に入ります。
2) 「重(かさ)ねて」「たびたび」「再び」などの繰(く)り返す意味のことばは、お悔やみの文では使わないようにします。また、追って書きも避けます。
3) 上の例は、会社で送るお悔やみ状なので、個人名でなく会社の立場で出しています。内容的にも定型的な表現を用いています。
4) 手紙を出すのが遅れた場合でも、知った時点ですぐに出します。

1. Go directly to the business of expressing your condolences in this type of letter. Do not write an opening seasonal greeting.
2. Do not use words that imply repetition, such as 重(かさ)ねて, たびたび, or 再び. Also avoid adding a postscript.
3. The above example is sent by a company. It is sent from a company standpoint, not that of an individual. Therefore use standard set expressions in the body of the letter.
4. Even though you are late in sending the letter, send it as soon as you hear of the sad event.

巻　末

資　料

1 ビジネス文書によく出てくることば
Words frequently appearing in business letters

次の語句で、「(ご) ～」「(お) ～」となっているものは、先方の動作にのみ使います。たとえば、「(先方が) ご査収くださる・ご査収になる」などとはいっても、「(こちらが) ご査収した・査収した」とはいいません。

Of the following words, those starting with ご or お are used when addressing the other party. For example: using (先方が) ご査収くださる・ご査収になる, and so on, would be correct when referring to the other party's action, but we could not say (こちらが) ご査収した・査収した when referring to our own actions.

◀ あ ▶

愛顧	patronage
あしからず	I am sorry that ～
(～に)与る	take a hand in ～
改めて～する	do ～ at another time; do ～ again
案件	the matter in question
意向	intention
一報	information
承る	understand; receive
鋭意	in earnest
恐れ入る	be overwhelmed; be astonished
追って	afterward; soon after
(～の)趣	the content/purport/meaning of ～ (a letter, etc.)
及び	and (as well as)
折り返し	by return (mail, etc.)

◀ か ▶

格別の～	particular ～; special ～; noticeable ～
重ねて	add; repeat
かねてより・かねてから	for some time past
(～を)期す	take all possible measures; ensure
恐縮	obligation
(ご)忌憚のない	(your) frank/open (option, etc.)
くれぐれも	extremely (used for emphasis)
件	a matter; a case; an affair
懸案	a pending problem/question
賢察	understand; consider
公私	public and private affairs
厚情	kindness; favor
(～ば、)幸甚に存じます	I would be very glad (if ～)
心ばかりの～	a small ～ (gift, etc.)
この度	on this occasion
この程	on this occasion
今後とも	and from here on; in the future

◀ さ ▶

(～ば、)幸いに存じます	It would make me happy (if ～)
(ご)査収	receipt
早速	immediately
さて	now
(ご)自愛	(your) health
しかるべく	properly
事情	the circumstances/situation
時節柄	(unsettled) season
謝意	thanks
従来(より)	(from) the past; up to now

(ご)主旨・趣旨(しゅし)	(your) point/aim
(ご)笑納(しょうのう)	(your) acceptance
所見	one's opinion
所存である	it is one's intention
書中	a letter; a document
先般(せんぱん)(来(らい))	some time ago (for some time)
早急に	urgently
その節	at that time

◀ た ▶

ただし	but; provided that ~
賜る(たまわる)	grant; give; award
(~の)段	~ stage
頂戴(ちょうだい)する	receive
つきましては(ついては)	in this regard
当初	at first
とりあえず	for the time being; right away
取り急ぎ	hurry
(お)取り計(はか)らい	manage; deal with

◀ な ▶

なお	in addition to ~; besides; furthermore
何かと	one way or another
何卒(なにとぞ)	please
何分の	some; some way or another
何分(とも)よろしくお願いします	I would appreciate it if you would please see to it.
並びに	and
何なりと	whatever; anything

◀ は ▶

拝承(はいしょう)する	receive
拝受(はいじゅ)する	accept
(~する)運びとなる	(~) becomes settled
(お)引(ひ)き立(た)て	favor; patronage
一重(ひとえ)に	earnestly
一方(ひとかた)ならぬ	extraordinary; uncommon; unusual
平素(へいそ)は	ordinarily
平素より	as usual

◀ ま ▶

前向きに検討する	give favorable consideration
誠(まこと)に	really/extremely (grateful, etc.)
~旨(むね)	to the effect that ~
(お)申し越し	a request
申し上げる	say
申し入れる	offer; propose
申し添(そ)える	attach/add (to)
目下(もっか)	presently

◀ や ▶

やむを得ず	unavoidably; out of necessity
用件	business; a matter (of business)
由(よし)	the reason; the significance; the cause

◀ ら ▶

了承(りょうしょう)	understanding; acknowledgment

◀ わ ▶

わざわざ	purposely; specially

2 ことばの前や後についてよく用いられる表現
Phrases often used by adding them to the beginning or end of words

◀ あ ▶

(〜した)上(で)　in addition to 〜ing; besides 〜ing

(〜に)おいて・おきまして
on〜; in〜; at〜; as to〜; in the matter of 〜

(〜に)おける　in; at

◀ か ▶

(〜にも)かかわらず　regardless of 〜; nevertheless

〜かたがた〜まで

お知らせかたがたお礼まで　I tell you this with thanks.

お詫(わ)びかたがたお願いまで　I send my apologies and request (you deal with the above).

〜(し)かねる　cannot 〜

お受けしかねる　cannot accept

お引き受けしかねる　cannot accept

(〜に)関する・関します/(〜に)関して・関しまして
regarding 〜; concerning 〜

貴〜　your 〜

貴社　your company

貴状・貴信　your letter

〜記　a description

下記　described below

上記　described above

題記　the issue above

頭記　the issue above

別記　the issue written elsewhere

既(き)〜　already 〜

来(きた)る〜　coming 〜; next 〜
e.g., 来る5月20日　coming May 20th

(〜日)現在　as of 〜　e.g., 20日現在 as of the 20th

◀ さ ▶

〜先　an objective/destination

取引先　business client

提携(ていけい)先　tie-up partner; affiliate

得意先　customer

去る〜　this past 〜 e.g., 去る5月20日　this past May 20th

(〜する・した)次第だ
such being the case; in brief 〜; upon (doing)〜

(〜し)次第　as soon as 〜

◀ た ▶

(〜に)つきまして・ついて
in regard to 〜; on the subject of 〜

当〜　this; our; my 〜

当方　this/our/my side

当社　this/our/my company

当部　this/our department

(こちら)としては・としましては・といたしましては
for 〜; considering 〜
e.g., for this side; for us

(〜た)ところ　when 〜

〜中　while 〜; during 〜; in (the process of) 〜

ご多用中・ご多忙中　while you are busy

検討中　in (the process of) investigations

(〜の)通り　as 〜; like 〜

◀ な ▶

〜ながら　though 〜; in spite of 〜

お手数ながら　though troublesome 〜

末筆ながら　excuse me for not mentioning this earlier in the letter; last but not least; last of all
略儀ながら　in an informal way
突然ながら　I'm sorry it's so sudden

何らかの～　some ～ or other

～願いたい　want to request ～

◀ は ▶

弊～　our ～

弊社　our company
弊店　our store
弊課　our section

別～　separate ～

別紙　separate sheet
別添　separate enclosure
別途　separately
別便　separate post

～の程　about ～

本～　this ～

本件　this issue
本案　this proposal
本状　this letter

◀ ま ▶

まずは～まで　first of all ～

(○月○日)をもって　on ～ (day, month)

(書状)をもって　through (this letter); by means of (this letter)

3 自分と相手の呼び方の例

Examples of how to refer to yourself and the other party

	自　分	先　方
人	私 小職(管理職以上)　小役(役員の場合)	貴殿　貴兄　貴職　貴役　貴台 ○○様　そちら様　○○課長殿
組　織	弊社　小社　弊店　弊行　弊工場 弊支店　弊課 (「当社」・「当店」など「当～」といったことばも使われるが、それはこちらが対等以上の立場にある時に限られる)	貴社　貴店　貴行　貴工場　貴支店 貴課 (「御社」という表現も使われるが、どちらかというと話しことばで使われる)
書　類	弊信　弊状　書面　手紙　見積もり 請求	貴信　貴書　貴簡　貴状　お手紙 お便り　お見積もり　ご請求
意　見	私見　私案　愚考　愚案	貴意　貴見　ご意見　ご高説
配慮など		ご配慮　ご愛顧　ご高配　ご厚情 ご芳情　ご指導　ご鞭撻　ご尽力 ご了承　ご理解　ご容赦　お許し

4 授受に関係する表現の例

Example phrases related to giving and receiving

自分が	先方にあげる 先方に～してあげる	さしあげる　ご送付いたす・ご送付申しあげる　ご報告いたす・ご報告申しあげる　ご案内いたす・ご案内申しあげる　ご紹介いたす・ご紹介申しあげる　ご説明いたす・ご説明申しあげる
	もらう	いただく　拝受いたす・拝受する　受領いたす・受領する　～いただく・～してもらう　～させていただく(「自分が～する」という意味の、最も一般的な言い方)
先方が	自分にくれる 自分のために～する	くださる　賜る　ご高覧になる・ご高覧くださる(見る)　ご一考になる・ご一考くださる(考える)　ご検討になる・ご検討くださる(検討する)　お調べになる・お調べくださる(調べる)
	受け取る	ご査収になる・ご査収くださる　お受け取りになる・お受け取りくださる　お納めになる・お納めくださる

先方に何かを頼む時によく使われる表現

Phrases often used when requesting something from the other party

(名詞)＋　下さいますよう・賜りますよう、お願い申し上げます。
(名詞)＋　の程、お願い申し上げます。
(名詞)＋　下されば・賜れば、幸いに存じます。
(動詞)＋　いただきたく存じます。
(動詞)＋　ていただけないかとお願いする次第でございます。

5 忌みことば —— 使ってはいけない表現の例

Examples of words and phrases to be avoided

めでたい手紙のとき：不吉な感じのする次のようなことばは避けます。

In letters written for auspicious occasions, avoid using such ominous words as follows.

倒れる／壊れる／流れる／落ちる／焼ける／傾く／離れる／別れる／戻る／古い／浅い／苦しい

お見舞いやお悔やみの手紙とき：繰り返す意味を持つ次のようなことばは避けます。

In get well letters or letters of condolences, avoid using such words that hold a repetitive meaning, like the following.

また／しばしば／次々／たびたび／重ねて／重ね重ね／重々／再度／再三／ますます

6 ビジネス文書でよく用いられる、複数の書き方がある語句・表現
Words and expressions with multiple written forms often used in business letters

次のカタカナの語句・表現は会社によってまた人によって書き方が違い、それぞれ次のようないくつかの書き方があります。

There are a number of ways to write words and phrases often found in a business letter. Depending on the company, or the individual, there are different ways of writing the following *katakana* words and phrases on the left, as you will see from their written form, as follows.

◀ 動詞 ▶

～イタス	～致す／～いたす
(～て)イタダク	(～て)頂く／(～て)いただく
(～て)クダサイ	(～て)下さい／(～て)ください
タマワル	賜わる／賜る／たまわる
チョウダイする	頂戴する／頂だいする／ちょうだいする
ワカル	分る／分かる／わかる

◀ 動詞／名詞 ▶

ウケツケ	受け付け／受付け／受付
ウケトリ	受け取り／受取り／受取
ウチアワセ	打ち合わせ／打ち合せ／打合せ
ウリコミ	売り込み／売込み／売込
オネガイ	御願い／御願／お願い
シハライ	支払い／支払
ツキアイ	付き合い／付合い／つき合い
テツヅキ	手続き／手続
トリアツカイ	取り扱い／取扱い／取扱
トリキメ	取り決め／取決め／取決
トリヒキ	取り引き／取引き／取引
ネビキ	値引き／値引
ハナシアイ	話し合い／話合い／話合
ヒキトリ	引き取り／引取り／引取
フリコミ	振り込み／振込み／振込
ミツモリ	見積もり／見積り／見積
モウシイレ	申し入れ／申入れ／申入
モウシコミ	申し込み／申込み／申込／申しこみ

◀ 形容詞 ▶

ヨイ・イイ	良い／よい／いい

◀ そのほかの表現 ▶

アシカラズ	悪しからず／あしからず
～アテ	～宛／～宛て／～あて
アラタメテ	改めて／あらためて
イロイロ	色々／いろいろ
～したウエ	～した上／～したうえ
オヨビ	及び／および
カナラズ	必ず／かならず
サマザマ	様々／さまざま
サラニ	更に／さらに
シタガッテ	従って／したがって
ジュウブン	十分／充分
スベテ	全て／すべて
タトエバ	例えば／たとえば
～(の)タメ	為／ため
～のトオリ	～の通り／～のとおり
～する・したトキ	～する・した時／～する・したとき
トモニ	共に／ともに
トリアエズ	取り敢えず／取りあえず／とりあえず
トリイソギ	取り急ぎ／取急ぎ
ナド	等／など
ナニトゾ	何卒／何とぞ／なにとぞ

ナニブン	何分／何ぶん
ナラビニ	並びに／ならびに
～のホウ	～の方／～のほう
ホカ	他／ほか
～のホド	～の程／～のほど
マタ	又／また
マタハ	又は／または
マッタク	全く／まったく
ヤムヲエズ	止むを得ず／やむを得ず／やむをえず

文書のインデックス

語句さくいん

各文書の単語リストの語句、および「ビジネス文書の基本」「資料」内の重要語句を、五十音順に並べた。**1-1**、**1-2** 等は文書の番号を、p[25]、p300 等はページ数を表す。

This index includes all the expressions found in the vocabulary list of each letter, as well as important words and phrases appearing in “Basics of Japanese Business Letters” and Appendix. They are listed in the *a-i-u-e-o* order with the number of letters (e.g., **1-1, 1-2**) or pages (e.g., p[25], p300) in which they appear.

◀ か ▶

◀ き ▶

◀ く ▶

◀ け ▶

◀ こ ▶

◀ さ ▶

◀ し ▶

◀ ち ▶

◀ つ ▶

◀ て ▶

◀ と ▶

◀ へ ▶

◀ ほ ▶

◀ ま ▶

◀ み ▶

◀ む ▶

◀ め ▶

あとがき

『Talking Business in Japanese』（ジャパンタイムズ刊）に続くビジネスマン用の教科書も、ようやくこのような形にすることができました。非力な私たちをつき動かして２冊の教科書を書かせたのは、ここ数年の外国人ビジネスマンの驚くほどの質の向上でした。以前は外国人ビジネスマンといっても「お客様」扱いですまされていたのがその実態でしたが、今日の外国人ビジネスマンはあらゆる意味で独立した企業戦力であるといえます。そうした時代の流れは、'90年代初頭のバブルの崩壊と不況を経ても一向に衰えません。そのような有能な外国人ビジネスマンが熱心に学ぶ姿を教室で見るにつけ、何とか彼らが真に求めているものを教材化できないかと悩んだのが、これら２冊の教科書作成の発端でした。

出来上がった２冊の教材を前に高揚と反省とを同時に感ずる私たちですが、これらを使って指導してみた今までの経験から、少なくとも日本語教師とビジネスマンとの共同指導(作成)態勢、その場の課題構造を明らかにするフローチャート分析という手法は、ビジネス日本語の指導においては極めて有効なものだという感触を抱いています。とはいえ、さらに有効な、もっと効果的な形の指導を目指すには、まだまださまざまな課題があるに違いありません。本書ならびに『Talking Business in Japanese』をお使いになった教師・学習者の方々から、そうした観点からの忌憚のないご意見、ご批判をいただければ幸いです。

なお、本書作成にあたったのは、ビジネスマンと日本語教師が一体になって、おもに中級・上級段階のビジネス日本語の指導と教材のあり方を考えようという教師集団「ビジネス日本語フォーラム」の以下のメンバーです。

各課文書及び留意事項など執筆――小沼正博、安井達也

フロー、重要表現、文書のインデックス作成など教材化作業

――井口裕子、桑原和子、土井真美、横須賀柳子

ビジネス文書の基本、各文書の単語リストなど執筆及び編集、総務――丸山敬介

（五十音順）

ほかに、半田稔、有馬祐子、樺沢由美子、山本一男の各氏にもご協力をいただきました。

ジャパンタイムズの斎藤純一氏、関戸千明氏及び翻訳・英文校閲に当たってくださったRuth McCreery氏、Robert Gilhooly氏、Cindy Mullins氏には、大変お世話になりました。この場をお借りして、心からお礼申し上げます。

本書が、そしてこうした共同指導態勢が、外国人ビジネスマンの円滑な業務遂行に少しでも寄与できれば、「ビジネス日本語フォーラム」一同、この上ない喜びです。

1998年12月

ビジネス日本語フォーラム